Praise for *Impossible Owls*

"There is a section in *Impossible Owls* where Brian Phillips writes about tigers, and he notes that what's most astonishing about the animal is not its size or power or beauty, but its capacity to disappear. This is an excellent description of a tiger, but also an excellent description of how Phillips writes. These are big, powerful, beautiful essays—but no matter how personal the content, he just seems to disappear into the paragraphs."

—Chuck Klosterman, author of *But What If We're Wrong?* and *Eating the Dinosaur*

"The journeys that make up *Impossible Owls* lead us to some remarkable, unpredictable places, from the Alaskan wilderness to a supermarket parking lot in southern Japan, from an old movie palace in Moscow to the underground histories of northern Oklahoma. But these far-flung tales all share the same inspirational spark: Brian Phillips's soulful, intrepid spirit, and his masterful ability to turn everyday curiosities into epic quests that you can't stop reading."

—Hua Hsu, author of *A Floating Chinaman: Fantasy and Failure Across the Pacific*

"Brian Phillips's *Impossible Owls* takes the American essay in new directions—these narratives are simultaneously stories of questing and of strandedness. Characters and landscapes become knowable and disorienting. Tigers, royals, mysterious Russian artists, and foreign countries are subjects of Phillips's close, careful journalism, as well as

the glittering, ungraspable things that lie outside us. Witty, pensive, sometimes whimsical, always truthful, *Impossible Owls* is a testament to Phillips's gift for enchantment and his genius for knowing exactly where our alienation from the world meets our sympathy for it."

—Supriya Nair

Brian Phillips
Impossible Owls

Brian Phillips is a former staff writer for *Grantland* and a former senior writer for MTV News. He has written for *The New York Times Magazine*, *The New Yorker*, and *Slate*, among other publications, and his work has appeared in *The Best American Sports Writing* and *The Best American Magazine Writing*. He lives in central Pennsylvania. *Impossible Owls* is his first book.

Impossible Owls

Impossible Owls

ESSAYS

Brian Phillips

FSG Originals

Farrar, Straus and Giroux

New York

FSG Originals
Farrar, Straus and Giroux
175 Varick Street, New York 10014

Some of these essays originally appeared, in somewhat
different form, in *Grantland* ("Out in the Great Alone,"
"Sea of Crises," and "In the Dark") and MTV News
("Lost Highway" and "The Little Gray Wolf Will Come").

Library of Congress Cataloging-in-Publication Data
Names: Phillips, Brian, 1976– author.
Title: Impossible owls : essays / Brian Phillips.
Description: First edition. | New York : Farrar, Straus and Giroux,
   [2018] | Series: FSG originals
Identifiers: LCCN 2017057596 | ISBN 9780374175337 (pbk.)
Subjects: LCSH: Essays.
Classification: LCC PS3616.H4534 A6 2018 | DDC 814/.6—dc23
LC record available at https://lccn.loc.gov/2017057596

Designed by Jonathan D. Lippincott

Our books may be purchased in bulk for promotional, educational, or
business use. Please contact your local bookseller or the Macmillan
Corporate and Premium Sales Department at 1-800-221-7945, extension
5442, or by e-mail at MacmillanSpecialMarkets@macmillan.com.

www.fsgoriginals.com • www.fsgbooks.com
Follow us on Twitter, Facebook, and Instagram at @fsgoriginals

1   3   5   7   9   10   8   6   4   2

For Siobhan

Shut your eyes and you'll burst into flames.
                                        —Margaret Lanterman

Contents

Impossible Owls

Out in the Great Alone

I. SNOW CRASH

In the summer of 1977, a fire swept across the wilderness of interior Alaska, west of Denali, which was then still officially known as Mount McKinley. Tundra burned to rock; 345,000 acres of forest—more than 530 square miles—disappeared in flames. When the smoke cleared, it left behind a weird scar on the map, a vast, charred crater littered with deadfall. In the winter, when temperatures in the interior dive to forty below, the skeletons of burned trees snapped in the cold or were ripped out by powerful winds. Tussocks of tundra grass froze as hard as bowling balls.

Every year in early March, the Iditarod Trail Sled Dog Race sets out from Anchorage, in the south-central part of the state, and runs northwest toward the finish line in Nome, on the coast of the Bering Sea. In its early stages, the trail runs uphill, into the mountains of the Alaska Range, then plunges down, into the interior, where it enters the fire's scorched country.

For the mushers of the Iditarod, the Farewell Burn, as that country became known, was a nightmare. The race had been founded only four years earlier, as a way to commemorate the importance of sled dogs to Alaska. Large expanses of the state had, for much of its history, been unreachable by other forms of transportation. Now dog teams were forced to navigate through blackened stumps and fallen limbs, along a trail that was often impossible to follow. Many years, the Burn accumulated little precipitation. Sleds intended for snow and ice had to be dragged across hardened mud and gravel. Runners broke; tree shards snagged tug lines; speeds dropped to three or four miles per hour.

In 1984, the Alaska Bureau of Land Management cut a swath for a better trail. But even then, a seasoned musher could need twelve hours or more to cross from Rohn to Nikolai, the checkpoints on either side of the Burn—a passage that would frequently be made in darkness, through heavy wind and extreme, subzero cold. The novelist Gary Paulsen, who ran the Iditarod twice in the 1980s, describes the Burn as a place where mushers literally go mad. "It was beyond all reason," Paulsen writes in his Iditarod memoir, *Winterdance*. "I entered a world of mixed reality and dreams, peopled with the most bizarre souls and creatures." At one point, he thinks he's on a beach in California; at another, he pulls out a real ax to fend off an attack from an imaginary moose. When he comes to, his dogs have vanished; he's alone in the landscape. He stumbles across them a hundred yards away. He has built a fire and bedded them down without knowing it.

The Iditarod Trail runs across the Farewell Burn for around thirty-five miles of its total length. The total length of the Iditarod Trail is more than one thousand miles. The Burn is not the most difficult section.

———

In late February 2013, I flew to Alaska with the intention of following the Iditarod all the way from Anchorage to Nome. This was a plan of—I might be quoting my editors on this—dubious sanity, even before you consider the logistical complexity of chasing several dozen sled-dog teams across a subarctic wilderness the size of the Eastern Seaboard. That's not an exaggeration: There's disagreement over how long the Iditarod Trail really is, but the best estimates peg it at just about the distance from Carnegie Hall to Epcot. The fastest mushers take around nine days to reach the finish line, and that's assuming ideal conditions, say fifteen below, with blue skies and hard-packed, ice-slick snow.

I was staring at a week and a half of bone-deep cold, probable-verging-on-inevitable blizzards, baneful travel conditions, and total isolation from the civilized (read: WiFi-having) world. I hated snow, did not play winter sports, kept the thermostat at sixty-five on a good day, and hadn't logged out of Spotify since 2011. I wasn't even a dog person.

I called a pilot.

"Do you have experience in winter-survival-type situations?" he asked.

"Sure," I said. "I survive them by staying indoors. It's a technique that's worked well for me so far."

"Have you spent any time in small aircraft?"

"I've, uh . . . I've watched movies where people spent time in small aircraft."

"How about winter camping, backpacking, anything along those lines?"

"Day hikes," I said miserably.

There was a pause on the other end of the line. "Well," he said, "I'll be straight with you. There are a lot of ways to die in Alaska."

That was in September. Over the next five months, the phrase "please don't die" started cropping up with maybe slightly more frequency than you'd like to see in your work e-mails.

Why was I so keen to do this? To make this trip for which I was patently unprepared? It had something to do with Alaska itself, its sheer hugeness and emptiness—731,449 people spread out over 570,640 square miles, a territory larger than Spain, France, and Germany *combined* holding slightly fewer people than the metro area of Dayton, Ohio. The density stats are a *joke*. The U.S. average is 87.4 inhabitants per square mile. The forty-fifth-most-dense state, New Mexico, thins that down to 17. Alaska has 1.28. And more than 40 percent of Alaskans live in one city! Factor out metropolitan Anchorage and you're looking at about three-quarters of one person per square mile, in a land area ten times the size of Wisconsin.

I don't know how you roll, emotionally, with respect to population-density tables. Personally I find this *haunting*.

I've always been fascinated by the cold places at the end of the world. Back when I used to spend a lot of time in libraries, I wasted hours going through polar-exploration narratives, tracking the adventurers who froze to death, the expeditions that vanished. The generation of Scott and Shackleton was probably the last one to live with the old intuitive belief that the world went on beyond the part of it that their civilization had discovered. That there were meaningful blanks on the map, terra incognita. It's riveting to watch these practical-minded emissaries of high European culture hurl themselves into an unknown that they're not equipped to handle. Robert Falcon Scott, who died in Antarctica in 1912, tried to take ponies to the South Pole because he didn't trust sled dogs. Apsley Cherry-Garrard, who wrote, with no trace of exaggeration, a memoir called *The Worst Journey in the World*, nearly died several unimaginably horrifying early-twentieth-century deaths while trying to retrieve an emperor penguin egg, for Science. I know the genealogies of their ships. HMS *Terror* and *Erebus*, the vessels in which James Clark Ross charted the coast of Antarctica in the 1840s—you'll find a Mount Terror and a Mount Erebus there still, volcanoes on Ross Island—which disappeared, along with Sir John Franklin's entire expedition, in 1845. *Fram*, the ship from which Roald Amundsen set out for the South Pole in 1910, which was first designed for Fridtjof Nansen's mad, brilliant scheme to embed himself in Arctic sea ice.

I'm not saying this is right, but there's something magical to me, something literally entrancing, about a place that can inhale a clutch of Victorian sailing ships and leave behind a handful of brass buttons and a copy of *The Vicar of Wakefield*. Terrifying, but entrancing. That high white vanishing fog—doesn't it call to you, too?

No one's sure what the word "Iditarod" means. The best guess is that it comes from the Ingalik and Holikachuk word *hidedhod*, meaning "faraway place." It's the name of a river; in 1908, a couple of prospectors found gold on one of the tributaries, Otter Creek. A boomtown, named for the river, sprang up. Now it's a ghost city, an empty bank vault and an abandoned brothel. This year's race goes right through it. People who'd been there told me about camping out under the northern lights, watching the green shells of the dogs' eyes come gliding out of the dark.

At some point during all this, I copied down a line from Melville. He's talking about being lost at sea here; it's the same thing.

The intense concentration of self in the middle of such a heartless immensity . . .

"Come a week early," my pilot said, "so you can learn how to fly the airplane."

2. CITY OF DOGS

I landed in Anchorage in the middle of the night. The next morning, I drove an hour north to Wolf Lake Airport, a private airfield near Wasilla. You know those old photo-backdrop screens that little kids in department stores used to have their portraits taken in front of? It was like driving into one of those. National-monument mountains framing a sky that was chemical blue. Highway like a rifle sight. Until you actually get to Alaska, it's hard to prepare yourself for the scale of it, the sheer felt immensity. The numbers barely do it justice. Sixty percent of the nation's parkland is in Alaska. Four of the parks—four—are bigger than Connecticut. If you stood the white peak of Denali next to Mount Everest on level ground, Denali would tower over it, thousands of feet higher; Everest is taller only because it rests on an elevated plateau.

The majority of this extreme vastness can't be reached

by road. Juneau, the state capital, isn't on a highway network. Head north, into the semi-populated reaches, and you'll find nothing connecting the villages at all. Alaskans depend on bush pilots, fliers who take small planes into remote and dangerous places, for transportation, mail—almost every type of contact with the outside world. I had come to watch what might be the least spectator-friendly sporting event on earth: To follow the Iditarod requires not only a bush plane, but a bush plane equipped with skis, capable of landing on frozen rivers and lakes.

Jay Baldwin met me at the hangar. He'd flown F-16s back in the day and put in a couple of decades with Delta and Northwest before moving to Alaska to be a bush pilot. He was retired, in some theoretical sense, but he had a flight school, Alaska's Cub Training Specialists, at Wolf Lake, and from what I saw still knocked out around nineteen high-intensity daily hours running that, tinkering with airplanes, and educating anyone within earshot (children, small animals, whatever stray Iditarod reporters happened to stroll past) about the perils of bush flying. Jay was sixty years old and tall, and he had white hair and a smile so enthusiastic it hinted at actual anarchy.

His best friend was a musher, Linwood Fiedler, who'd been the Iditarod's runner-up in 2001. They'd grown up together in the Lower 48, then lost touch before reconnecting as adults in Alaska, having in the meantime become a bush aviator and a professional dog musher, respectively, because obviously that is life. Every year, Jay led an expedition to follow the Iditarod from the air, partly for the flying and partly as a show of support for Linwood. This was the expedition I'd signed up for.

"You're not a pilot in Alaska," Jay said, fixing me with a blue-eyed and somehow piratical stare, "until you've crashed an airplane. You go up in one of these stinkin' tin cans in the Arctic? Sooner or later you're gonna lose a motor, meet the wrong gust of wind, you name it. And OH BY THE WAY" (leaning in closer, stare magnifying in significance) "that doesn't have to be the last word."

Having lost more friends than he could count to wrecks in the remote Alaskan wilderness, he was obsessed with crash reports, fatality statistics, replaying freak scenarios. One wall of the ACTS hangar was plastered with newspaper clippings from accounts of gruesome accidents: "5 Killed as Small Planes Collide," "Sisters Among Dead in Plane Crash," "Flying to Die." The most unnerving clip was titled simply "Pilots: Grief." I pictured tiny mosquitoes of flame blooming against the side of a mountain, torn hulls rolling in black water. "This is the junk that keeps me up at night," Jay said, smoothing his hair under his ACTS baseball cap. "I've flown just about every dangerous kinda bird you can fly. Why are they gone and I'm still here?" One of his mentors had vanished without a trace while transporting a couple of bear watchers over the Shelikof Strait from Hallo Bay to Homer; the authorities didn't know for sure that the plane had gone down until the body of a passenger washed up in a fishing net ten days later. And yet Jay wholly, truly loved flying, the way some people can love it. I have a brother-in-law who's like that. When he's not in the air, it's like he's seeing fewer colors.

This was the paradox of Jay Baldwin: One of the most infectiously happy human beings I've ever been around, his every waking moment was a kind of prolonged existential debrief. He was never not working on how to outwit the horrific eventualities he was forever expecting to befall him, and he was never not just extremely cheerful about this. Jay was a Vermont kid, raised in a small town, and there was a mordant New England pluck in the way he gazed into the abyss and said, "I see what you're trying to do there, abyss."

The plan was for me to spend a few nights in the apartment connected to the hangar—live with the planes, get the feel of them. I'd read that some Iditarod mushers slept with their dogs, to make themselves one with the pack. I needed flying lessons because the little Piper Super Cubs that would carry us to Nome were two-seaters, one in front, one behind. Jay wanted me prepared in case he had a fatal brain aneurysm (his words), or a heart attack (his words ten seconds later), or keeled over of massive unspecified organ failure ("Hey, I'm gettin' up there—but don't worry!") at twenty-two hundred feet.

Choosing an airplane—that was the first step. Jay had four, and as the first ACTS client to arrive, I got first pick.

They were so small. Airplanes aren't supposed to be so small. How can I tell you what it was like, standing there under the trillion-mile blue of the Alaska sky, ringed in by white mountains, resolving to take to the ether in one of these winged lozenges? Each cockpit was exactly the size of a coffin. A desk fan could have blown the things off course.

"God love 'em," Jay said. "Cubs are slower 'n heck, they'll get beat all to hell by the wind, and there's not much under the hood. But bush pilots adore 'em, because you can mod 'em to death. And OH BY THE WAY . . . put 'em on skis, and come winter, the suckers'll land you anywhere."

Two of the Cubs were painted bright yellow. I took an immediate liking to the one with longer windows in the back. Better visibility, I told myself, nodding. Jay said it had the smallest engine of any of the Cubs in our squadron. Less momentum when I go shearing into the tree line, I told myself, nodding.

The name painted in black on her yellow door read: NUG-GET. She had a single propeller, which sat inquisitively on the tip of her nose, like whiskers. Jay told me—his words came as if from a great distance—that she'd had to be rebuilt not long ago, after being destroyed on a previous trip north. Was I hearing things, or did he say *destroyed by polar bears*?

I patted *Nugget's* side. Her fuselage was made of stretched fabric. It flexed like a beach ball, disconcertingly.

Into the cockpit. Flight helmet strapped, restraints active. Mic check. Then Jay's voice in my headset: "Are you ready!" It wasn't a question.

———

And this, ground dweller, is Alaska from nine hundred feet. White-flecked spruce forest. Snow-smothered lakes. Mountains all around. There's Denali, clear and far away. Right here, in the Mat-Su Valley, the southern part of the state, you can see power lines, the sketch of a highway system. A little farther north and all that will vanish. People here can sound mystical when they talk about the bush pilots, about how they knit Alaska together. From nine hundred feet, it makes sense.

We'd done some practice turns and picked out a lake; now all I had to do was get the plane on it. Jay explained to me about landing on snow, how the scatter of light tends to mask the true height of the ground. You can go kamikaze into the ice, thinking the earth is still thirty feet below you.

To gauge your real altitude against the whiteout, you have to use "references"—sticks poking through the snow, a line of trees on the bank. These supply you with vital cues, like "might want to ease down a touch" or "gracious, I'm about to fireball."

I won't bore you with the details of how to steer a Super Cub—where the stick was (imagine the porniest position possible; now go six inches pornier than that), how to bank, what the rudder pedals felt like. Suffice it to say that in theory it was simple. In practice . . .

"You have the aircraft." Jay's voice in my helmet's earpiece. "Just bring us down in a nice straight line."

I felt the weight in my right hand as Jay released the stick. The lake was straight ahead, maybe three miles off, a white thumbnail in an evergreen-spammed distance. The plane was under my control.

Nugget—there's no other way to put this—began to sashay.

"Just a *niiice* straight line," Jay reminded me. "And OH BY THE WAY . . . your pilot's dead." He slumped over in his seat.

Little lesson I picked up someplace: Once your pilot gives up the ghost, it is not so easy to see where you are headed from the backseat of a Super Cub. I mean at the "what direction is the plane even pointing right now" level. You will find that your deceased pilot, looming up against the windshield, blocks almost your entire forward view. To mitigate this, the savvy backseater will bank the wings one way while stepping on the opposite rudder pedal, causing the plane to twist thirty degrees or so to one side while continuing to travel in a straight line, like a runner sliding into base. That way, said enterprising backseater can see forward through the plane's presumably non-corpse-occluded side window.

Yeah. Well. A thing about me as a pilot is that I do not, ever, want to see forward through the side window. Especially not while plummeting toward a frozen lake. It's like, friend, why create the hurricane. I figured that, as an alternative technique, I would just basically try to guess where we were going.

"How's your speed?" my pilot('s lifeless form) inquired.

The ground seemed to be making an actual screaming noise as it rushed up toward us. *Hmm—maybe a little fast.* I cut the throttle. *Nugget* heaved and started falling at a different angle; more "straight down," as the aeronautics manuals say. We were out over the lake. I had a sense of measureless whiteness lethally spread out below me. Either the landscape was baffled or I was. There were trees on the bank, but we were dropping too fast; I couldn't relate them to anything. My references had gone sideways. At the last moment I pulled back on the stick.

There was a chiropractic *skrrrk* of skis entering snow. There was, simultaneously, a feeling of force transmitting itself upward into the plane. *Nugget* bounced, like a skipped stone, off the ice. We were tossed up and forward, maybe fifteen feet into the air . . .

. . . and came down again, bounced again, came down again, and, unbelievably, slid to a stop.

"Guess what," Jay said, popping up. "You just landed an airplane."

I've never felt all that caught up, personally, in the miracle of air travel. I played a little *Wing Commander* once upon a time, but I was never one of those pre-9/11 kids who used to lurk around open cockpit doors hoping some head-tousling type would kick him a set of plastic wings. Still, there are moments when your adrenal glands just aren't even going to pretend to hold back.

I HAVE CONQUERED THE MYSTERIES OF FLIGHT, I hollered inwardly, across the valleys of my emotions. LET THE AIR ITSELF BOW DOWN BEFORE ME.

"That was *pretty* good," Jay said. "Let's try it again."

EEP, NO, I bellowed to the valleys.

———

Anchorage, Alaska's one real city. Fairbanks is a town, Juneau is an admin building with ideas. Anchorage is Tulsa, only poured into a little hollow in a celestially beautiful mountain range on the outer rim of the world.

When you're there, it truly feels like you're at the end of something. Like a last outpost. You're in a coffee shop, you ordered a green tea, you can see white mountains from the window, and on the other side of the mountains is wilderness that hasn't changed since 1492.

That's an exaggeration, but not as much of one as you might think.

It's Saturday, March 2, the start of the Iditarod. Here's how this works: In the middle of the night, large trucks beep-reverse in and dump snow over an area of downtown. Race volunteers wearing little lanyard-clipped name badges spend the night smoothing snow down over the streets. Early the next morning, mushers and their dog handlers roll into the staging area in pickup trucks, the beds of which have been fitted with multi-compartmented dog carriers.

The compartments on the carriers are arranged in a tic-tac-toe grid with little doors that open to the outside. Your reference here is a wall of PO boxes, only behind each door there's a sled dog lying in a petite bed of straw. Some of the dog carriers have cards hanging from their side clamps with clothespins attached to them. A quick investigation reveals that each clothespin has a dog's name markered on it: Cutter, Lyra, Harp, Sable, Chisel, Bree. Soon the mushers are opening compartment doors and pulling out dogs. The dogs have their toes examined and their lips peeled back so the mushers can check their gums. There's a scholarly air, on the mushers' part, to these inspections. You get the impression that they've checked the dogs out of a library. The dogs shake nonexistent water off their coats and are chained, one by one, to the trailer hitches and free grab handles on their mushers' trucks. Dog handlers drop food in each dog's particular vicinity. The food is in some cases raw meat, which leaves soggy pinkish traces in the snow. Human food is being vended to the growing crowd of spectators via several small pavilions, which bear signs like ALASKA REINDEER SAUSAGE and, impenetrably, REINDEER BRATWURST LOUISIANA. The air smells of hot meat and hay. I spot Jay talking to a woman near Linwood's truck, so I go over to say hello, and it turns out she's Libby Riddles, the famous Iditarod champion from '85. A shivery breeze keeps blowing up Fourth Avenue off Cook Inlet, maybe six blocks to the west, but the day's sunny; it's thirty degrees Fahrenheit. You can see your breath, but it's pleasant. The crowd milling under the giant carved bear that towers above Grizzly's Unique Alaskan Gifts does sport some heavy-fur wearers, but that's a cultural thing; it's celebratory.

All the heavy furs I spot are on men. There's a stout, bearded race official going around in not only a heavy fur coat but also an astounding brutalist apartment block of a fur hat. The hat has a bobcat's entire face on it. The face has teeth. I make a note to check whether it would be possible to gauge the hierarchy of race officials based on the food-chain status of the dead animals whose faces are on their hats, but though this feels like a searing reportorial lead at the moment, the results of my follow-up investigation will prove disappointing.

Bobcat-hat-face is going around doing little knee dips over dog teams that are starting to be hooked up to their sleds' riggings. It's maybe half an hour before the official 10:00 a.m. start of the race. Volunteers circulate with clipboards; near the starting line, the bulge of the crowd is impassable. The Iditarod is a huge deal in Alaska. Sled-dog racing in general is a big deal; the Iditarod is the best-known race, but there are others, like the thousand-mile Yukon Quest, that draw major attention. Among the tiny population of the state, the top mushers are famous. You can walk into a hardware store in Anchorage and go, "Did you hear about DeeDee," or "Just saw the news—Dallas might lose his nose," and no one will answer, "Who, creep-o?"

I've been YouTubing pretty diligently, so I spot some familiar faces. There's Lance Mackey, maybe the greatest long-distance musher of all time: four straight Iditarods from 2007 to 2010; also four titles in the Yukon Quest. Do you know him? He got nominated for a couple of ESPYs a few years back. Won his first Iditarod after beating throat cancer. He's a redneck icon in Alaska, a sort of ratty, scrawny, patchy, permanently beat-down-looking guy, tiny pinched head like the head of a curious tortoise. I heard somebody describe him as "the white Snoop Dogg," which fits. The first time I saw him I took out a notebook and wrote, "My best friend he shoots water rats and feeds them to his geese." He's got crazy star power even though he seems to be physically disintegrating. Near the end of this year's race, he will bite into a piece of fudge and lose one of his three remaining original teeth.

There's Aliy Zirkle, last year's runner-up, a red-cheeked and physically imposing forty-three-year-old who always seems to be laughing. About half the fans I talk to are pulling for her, many of them out of a feeling that a woman is due to win. At race HQ they're selling shirts that read, "Alaska: Where Men Are Men and Women Win the Iditarod," but only two women ever have, and none since 1990. "It's time, you know?" people say. I'm pulling for Aliy because she makes the Iditarod look fun. (Which, Jesus.) Some glimmer in her happy eyes seems to say the whole race is a game. She's married to a musher, Allen Moore, and they trade their best dogs back and forth, depending on the event. He won the Yukon Quest with the majority of the team just three weeks ago and now she's racing them in the Iditarod.

I also spot Mitch Seavey, the 2004 champion, who's fifty-three and wiry, with a bacterial mustache and angry little wisps of stray hair jabbing out around his cap. Something about the prickly briskness of his movements as he tends to his dogs suggests both a high-school chemistry teacher and a bird building a nest. I had read his book, *Lead, Follow, or Get Out of the Way! Unconventional Sled Dog Secrets of an Alaskan Iditarod Champion, Volume One*, and found it fascinating both as a guide to the art of sled-dog training and as a window into the vaguely paranoid self-regard of one M. Seavey. *Lead, Follow* fixates often on the idea that its author's thoughts and stances are offending unspecified "wackos," who wield unspecified powers and who deserve whatever offense they get. You know how some small-town guys like imagining that everything they say is driving people on the other side of the political spectrum, none of whom they personally know, crazy? Mitch scratched in 2011 after nearly severing his index finger with a knife at the Ophir checkpoint. Then he sued the knife maker, which has led to a lot of eye rolling within hard-core dog-mushing circles. He's feuding with at least one Alaska newspaper over its coverage of the lawsuit. Mitch looks like, and is, the kind of guy who holds grudges.

For most of the Iditarod, mushers will run teams of up to sixteen dogs, which they're not allowed to swap out; dogs that get sick or injured can be dropped, but they can't be replaced with new ones. For the start day in Anchorage, however, the mushers can bring only twelve, to minimize downtown chaos. A key detail about the start day in Anchorage is that it's purely for show. It's not timed and doesn't count toward the outcome of the race. The word that gets used is "ceremonial." It's a chance for city folk to clap for the mushers before they enter the genuine wild. The official, timed start will happen the next day, near the small town of Willow.

Still, there are sixty-six teams entered this year. With twelve dogs each, we're looking at nearly eight hundred dogs within about a five-block radius. The dog factor is crazy, tremendous. Dogs are scratching themselves, snarfing down meat, yawning, whining, wrestling, pissing, drum majoring their tails. Iditarod sled dogs are mostly not the Siberian huskies you may be picturing but smaller, faster mixed breeds, engineered for speed rather than hauling power. Downtown is giddy with barking. I note falsetto yaps, screams, howls, baritone woofs. There's something jungle- or apelike about the cacophony. The presence of so many dogs drives all the dogs crazy. When the handlers start pulling out sleds and clipping the teams to their towlines, the collective canine intelligence realizes that—ohmigosh, *ohmigosh*—it's about to go for a run. This is when the dogs truly begin to freak out.

There's a serious case that animal-welfare people make against the Iditarod; namely, that it's long and cold and dangerous and sometimes fatal, and who are we to subject living creatures to those conditions for our own entertainment? A dog will in fact die during this year's race, buried in a snow-drift one night at the Unalakleet checkpoint. What you can't deny, though, is that these animals, having been bred to want to pull sleds, *really* want to pull them. The dogs are hysterical, they're in raptures. I watch one little guy, a black-and-tan with a shaggy belly, hurl himself forward against the re-straint of his own tug line about fifteen times in a row, bark-ing up a storm, as if he's decided to get the sled going all on his own. He stops every now and again to look incredulously at his teammates. *What—is—the—holdup—here—people?* This is happening all over the place. It's like standing inside the mind of a saint right before an out-of-body experience. The dogs' ropes all have to be braced by straining handlers to stop them from just taking off.

Around 9:40 a.m., I make my way to the starting line. My own lanyard-attached media badge gets me through the crowd and into a kind of holding pen adjacent to the starting chute, which itself is just a roped-off area of the street. The Iditarod starting line is a flag-surrounded banner hanging

above Fourth Avenue. Seven flags correspond to the nationalities of this year's sixty-six contestants: the United States
(obviously), Canada, Norway, Russia, New Zealand, Brazil (!),
Jamaica (!!). A PA guy's warm booming baritone is priming
us with factoids about the race. Every year, the first person
through the chute is an honorary musher chosen for his/her
contributions to the Iditarod. This year's honorary musher
is the late Jan Newton, who died in August. She was a volunteer who helped run the checkpoint at the tiny village of
Takotna. She was known as the Queen of Takotna, the Official 2013 Race Guide says, and she was famous for her
pies. That's how big a deal the race is in Alaska: You can be
famous for baking Iditarod-associated pies. "Her contributions to the race are remarkable and have elevated her to a
position of legendary prominence" is the Official 2013 Race
Guide's line on this. Her sled will be driven by this year's
Junior Iditarod champion, Noah Pereira.

After the honorary musher, the starting order is determined by an elaborate lottery-style number draw at a pre-race
banquet. The numbers are drawn from a sealskin Eskimo
mukluk. I was at this banquet; it ran for five hours. Every
single musher made a speech. That's more than sixty speeches.
It was brutal. The only speech I liked was the one by Scott
Janssen, a funeral-home director by trade who's known as
the "Mushin' Mortician." He introduced himself by saying,
"Hi! I'm Scott Janssen, the Mushin' Mortician."

Once the honorary musher's sled goes skritting out of
sight, it's time for the real race to (ceremonially) start. Bib
No. 2, to the excitement of Iditarod fans everywhere, has
fallen to Martin Buser, a Swiss-born four-time champion
(1992, 1994, 1997, 2002) and race icon who not only named

both his sons after Iditarod checkpoints but was sworn in as an American citizen under the burled arch that serves as the finish line in Nome. He's fifty-four and maybe not quite a top-shelf contender any longer; Norman Vaughan, who went to Antarctica with Admiral Byrd in 1928, completed the Iditarod at the age of eighty-four, but only one musher over fifty has ever won it (Jeff King in 2006). But Buser's known among mushers for his shrewdness, and the fashionable intelligence can't help but speculate about the implications of such a seasoned veteran leaving first.

Bobcat-hat-face, who's emerged as some sort of super-important race marshal with the job of importantly standing in the starting chute, consulting with mushers, and pointing at things that want pointing at, is doing a little waist bend over Buser's sled while Buser goes from dog to dog down the line, patting cheeks and communing. The ex-champ is ceremonially stuffed into so many layers of Arctic gear that all you can really see of him is his clear-eyed handsome Swiss face.

"One minute," the PA guy says.

Buser gets in a few more canine cheek pats.

"Thirty seconds," the PA guy says.

Buser shaking hands, receiving hugs from loved ones. Bobcat-hat-face steps back out of the way.

"Ten seconds," the PA guy says.

Buser on his sled.

"3 . . . 2 . . . 1 . . . GO!"

Profound roar from the crowd. The dog handlers let go of the restraining ropes. The pandemonium in which the dog team was immersed one second ago disappears, replaced by a sense of sudden, efficient shared purpose. The dogs take off;

the towline snaps taut; the sl
back rails, slides out beyon
quiet, running. They buil
more or less sliding on its
down Fourth Avenue;

The next musher's

And we are off.

made out of se
would be 9
Cubs wo
upside-
(singl
sca

3. FLIGHT 985–WHISKEY

We were a squadron of four Super Cubs, assembled by ACTS for Jay's Iditarod expedition. The deal was, if you were a small-plane pilot looking to get some serious Alaska bush-flying experience, you could pay ACTS a fee of approximately a thousand dollars per day to fly along with the race. ACTS provided the planes. Also rural Alaska accommodations, Arctic-survival know-how, and (speaking only about the rear cabin of *Nugget*, here, but) trail mix. Good stuff, possibly homemade. It had the little M&M's in it.

I was the only non-pilot Jay had ever approved for the Iditarod. I don't know why he let me come. He told me a story, early on, about taking along an Israeli fighter ace one year, a guy with jet-combat experience, "multiple unrecorded kills," and asking him what was the most dangerous flying he'd ever done. "This," the fighter pilot said. I thought of that guy often, mostly while calculating whether my empty trail-mix bag could double as an airsickness container.

There were seven of us, including Jay and me, at that first preflight briefing in the ACTS hangar on Monday. We were spread out on a couple of couches. One of the couches was ats from a 737, I think? Some jumbo jet. *Nugget* 5-Whiskey's lead plane, Jay declared; the other ld fly behind, in echelon formation (the familiar own V). Or in rare cases we might switch to trail file) or line abreast (a horizontal line, useful when ning for wildlife). "985-Whiskey" was *Nugget*'s personal call sign and would double as our flight name for the expedition.

Bernard and Christophe, French pilots who'd flown in for the trip, loitered behind the couches, watching Jay point out locations on a huge map. Bernard was sixty-seven, a retired Air France captain, regal of bearing; short, but imperially short, like a famous surgeon. His favorite pastime on the trip was to declare that France was (*fart sound*) and then laboriously list reasons why France was (*fart sound*), in tangled English. His actual favorite off-aircraft pastime, I mean back home, was freestyle skiing. He keenly wished for his wife to spend time freestyle skiing with him; she wouldn't; his marriage was a little bit (*fart sound*). Christophe, his friend and former student, was younger, maybe in his late forties, and cool in a louche French way, with a weird personal ostrich of uncombed gray hair; he was cigarette thin and spent the whole trip with his neck elaborately engulfed in a camouflage-print silk scarf. He had this way of leaning on things. The heir to a rock-quarry fortune, he'd worked as a photographer but retired young to a life of intensively having cheekbones. "So I sink to myself, I 'ave zis job," he would say with a shrug. "I should give it to one who needs it." According to Jay, they were two of the best pilots in Europe. They knew how to land, apparently, on these glaciers in the Alps that you could land on. (Bernard complained about the paperwork associated with this.)

At the briefing, Jay gave us some basic squadron vocabulary—"tallyho" if you're able to spot whatever another flight member points out over the radio, "no joy" if you're not—then showed us where the Iditarod Trail climbed over the Alaska Range, at Rainy Pass. That was where we'd be crossing the mountains into the interior. "Be prepared," Jay said. "It's kind of a maze up there, that stinkin' pass. You take a wrong turn between those mountains, you wind up at a dead end, no room to turn around, and at that point it's pretty much uh-oh time. Just watch your visibility, and if anybody doesn't like what they see, give a shout on the radio and we'll put 'em down till you feel comfortable."

"Guys, my dad's not kidding," Steve said. Steve was Jay's son, on leave from Afghanistan and flying with us in *Sunshine*, *Nugget*'s yellow twin. He told us that the mountains were littered with sheet metal from old wrecks. "Nobody ever cleans up old wrecks in Alaska."

Flying through the pass was awesome. I mean in the sense of inspiring genuine awe. You are a dot moving among white clouds. White cliffs break through the clouds and you fly beside them. You're not high up by mountain standards, twenty-five hundred feet, maybe a little more. But it feels like you're in the sun's own kingdom. For much of the crossing, the snow makes it impossible to tell where the ground is, and then when you spot it, it's crazy, striations of ice and rock like the inside of a marble. It doesn't seem to exist in any measurable relation to where you are. (Even crazier: the occasional glimpse of mushers and dog teams moving against this background, lowercase *i*'s crossing a sheet of crumpled paper.) Little canyon-like channels go wriggling off the main path. It's like passing into another world.

We touched down at the Rainy Pass checkpoint, a smooth plain below a small wooden lodge. White with purple shadows. It was cold, and the snow was knee-deep where it hadn't been packed down by volunteers' snow machines. We watched the dogs sleeping in piles of straw. We flew over Dalzell Gorge, the steep, twisty run where the trail descends toward the interior, dropping hundreds of feet in just a couple of miles. We flew over the freaky bleakness of the Burn. We flew over a herd of wild buffalo, then landed on an icy lake, just for a pause, moments before a musher, who knows which one, came bursting out of the trees on the far side. I got out my phone and snapped pictures.

We flew north, ahead of the race. Airplanes—even Super Cubs, which would be pressed hard in a race against a riding lawn mower—go faster than sled dogs, so "following" the Iditarod means traveling out in front of it, stopping, and waiting for the mushers to come to you. Then you do it again, and so on till the finish line. Our first stop was the village of Takotna, where there was a lodge and a race checkpoint from which we could watch the mushers glide through.

When we landed for fuel at McGrath, we heard that a Cessna 182 carrying three people had crashed after taking a wrong turn in the mountains. The pilot and both passengers were killed. They were following the Iditarod and bound for the same village where we planned to spend the night.

———

It turned out that Martin Buser, the musher whom I'd watched start the race, had come up with a strategy that was blowing people's minds. He wasn't stopping. Conventional Iditarod tactics call for frequent voluntary rest periods in addition to the two eight-hour breaks and one twenty-four-hour break mandated by the rules. Iditarod sled dogs are bred for stamina, but they need food and sleep. Mushers, who will be almost unimaginably sleep deprived by the time they reach Nome, need at least token periods of semi-unconsciousness.

Buser, though? He ran from Willow to the Yentna checkpoint and stopped for just twenty-one minutes. Then he ran to Skwentna and stopped for half an hour. He ran to Finger Lake, in the snow country just before the mountains, and stopped for twenty-six minutes. Then he ran practically all the way over the Alaska Range on no rest. Through Rainy Pass on no rest. When he reached Rohn, just before ten o'clock on the morning of Monday, March 4, he'd driven his dogs nearly two hundred miles in less than twenty hours, and he hadn't stopped for longer than it took to have a vet eyeball them at the checkpoints. It was demented, was the feeling on the trail. What the pound-sign-percent-asterisk-dollar-sign was the guy thinking?

Then at Rohn, way earlier than most top mushers would even consider doing this, he declared that he was taking his twenty-four. And this move, which he later told reporters he'd spent eight months plotting out (I pictured the lonely candle in the window, Buser bent over the table with graph paper and a set of miniature pewter dogs)—this move, I think it's fair to say, baffled Iditarod experts for the whole first two-thirds of the race. The Iditerati were confounded. Because while Buser was sleeping in Rohn, everybody else passed him, and passed him by a lot, by hours. But everybody else, and this was the rub, *still had to take their twenty-fours*. When they did, Buser would end up hours ahead of *them*. He'd have a huge lead, because of all the rest he'd skipped at the beginning. But could he cover the last nine hundred miles of the race without a significant break? Could his dogs handle it? The volunteers were shaking their heads at the checkpoints.

Late Tuesday afternoon we landed at Takotna, in the Kuskokwim Mountains, about 170 miles northwest of Rainy Pass. There was fresh snow, deep snow, on the river, and two of the Cubs got stuck, their skis sunk too far to slide. A couple of villagers had to come down with snow machines to drive Jay and me back to where Steve and the Frenchmen were waiting with the stranded planes. The villager who drove me was Frankie. While we drove along the river she told me that she and her husband had a gold mine and that was how they made their living. They mined at Takotna in the summer and spent the winters in Homer. Every March, Frankie came back to Takotna to help with the Iditarod.

But then everyone helped with the Iditarod in Takotna. According to the printout of a report about the village by the Alaska Department of Fish and Game that I stole from the dormitory where we spent the night, there were thirty-three households in the village and fifty-two people, evenly split between whites and Athabascan Indians, though Takotnans I talked to said that the number of full-time residents was really closer to thirty. Takotna could be a thousand times bigger and still be a pretty small town. But as an Iditarod checkpoint, it's legendary. This year, thirty of the sixty-six mushers opted to take their twenty-fours here, and that's only partly because it's an ideal strategic resting spot, a little over a quarter of the way to Nome and safely past the rigors of the Alaska Range. It's also due to the hospitality of the villagers, which is truly above and beyond. Every musher gets his or her choice of meal, and if that doesn't sound impressive, please mull over the logistics of supplying and staffing a temporary restaurant kitchen in a remote Alaskan village of thirty-odd people that isn't reachable by road. It's a point of pride, even of identity, for the villagers. Kids get off school. Everyone works in twelve-hour shifts. When we arrived, none of the mushers had come in yet and here and there volunteers were counting the blue plastic bags that held the teams' hay bales and making tiny checkmarks on their clipboards.

There was a dining hall set up in the community center, and because Jay had made a donation to the village we were allowed to have dinner there, in a crowded warm room with long tables. Green-and-white plastic gingham tablecloths. I ate roast moose. *Comprehensive Subsistence Harvests of Takotna*, a report compiled by subsistence resource specialist Seth Wilson, a printout of which was just lying around in the dormitory where I'd already dumped my duffel bag, estimates that moose accounts for 77 percent, pound-wise, of wildlife harvested for subsistence purposes in the area, putting it well ahead of spruce grouse (4 percent), black bear (4 percent), and beaver (3 percent), and in easy lapping distance of pretenders like wild rhubarb, chinook salmon, and blueberry (1 percent each). You could fill a tiny plastic cup with Kool-Aid or Tang from the dispensers in one corner. I drank Kool-Aid and talked to Colin, the downy-bearded young guy who ran the local medical clinic. He could patch up bumps and bruises, he said. If anything serious happened, they'd have to fly you out.

Colin had a fascinatingly odd way of maintaining intense eye contact while simultaneously all but squirming with agony over the fact that he was being noticed—the way, say, your fifteen-year-old goth cousin might do. This was something I noticed time and again in the inhabitants of remote Alaska, this total, helpless acuteness in the presence of a stranger. It was as if isolation had kept them from numbing themselves to the fact of other people. You walk down the sidewalk in Manhattan and maybe you know on some level that every single person you pass is a constellation of memory and perception as huge and unique as whatever's inside you, but there's no way to really *appreciate* that on a case-by-case basis; you'd lose your mind. You get anesthetized, living among crowds, to the implications of faces. The terra incognita of every gaze, Saul Bellow calls it. Whereas if you walk up to a remote Alaskan, I mean just buying a bag of chips in the village store, a lot of the time the response you get is this sort of HELLO, VAST AND TERRIFYING COSMOS OF PERSONHOOD. The apertures are wide open.

I took a walk through the village. Couple of roads twisting down a couple of hills, some pretty rough-looking houses. Moose antlers over the doorways. Things happen to the color blue during an Alaska twilight that I've never seen anywhere else. Imagine that the regular, daytime blue sky spends all its time floating on the night sky, the way you'd float on the surface of a pool. Now it's submerging itself. You could see it vanishing upward. The cars looked derelict, half-buried in snow. Snowdrifts rammed up doorknob high against the houses. Every now and again a snow machine would go screaming by; the drivers always waved. Snow three and four feet high on the roofs.

But it was such a warm place. I mean, fine, we're all jaded here, but you could feel it: this fragile human warmth surrounded by almost unmanageable sadness. Outside the checkpoint building, the Takotnans had set up a row of burled tree stumps beside the flagpoles, and now two guys with chain saws were carving long crosscuts in the stumps. Each night during the Iditarod they'd pour diesel into one stump's cuts and then light it, making a torch as wide as two people embracing that would burn for hours and hours. Mushers coming down the river toward the checkpoint would see the torches from—I don't know about miles, but a long way off. Eight or nine villagers, along with a few volunteers, stood around the fire. Jay was there, talking about airplanes with Bernard—you could tell from the way he'd bank his hand at the wrist and slide it through the air. Christophe went around taking pictures. A little gang of kids played king of the hill on a snowdrift. The night just dwarfed all this. I mean a sadness that's unmanageable in the sense that you can be in the middle of an outwardly happy scene and suddenly feel yourself ringed by it, feel it closing in, to the point that you have to excuse yourself for a while and go back to the dormitory where you've dropped off your duffel and regroup by reading whatever Seth Wilson–penned subsistence-harvest reports happen to be lying around in color-ink-jet printout form on the table.

The first mushers started arriving around nine that night. You'd see dogs' eyes shining green down the trail with the reflected light from the fire, then their bodies would emerge around them. Finally the musher would come sliding up.

The mushers looked haggard, frost-rimmed. I hadn't seen them up close for 180 miles, and the distance told. I kept thinking about a story Linwood told me at the Baldwins' house, about how he'd arrived at a checkpoint one year at fifty below and one of his ears had turned black from frostbite. He hadn't even noticed. The volunteers had to break the news. Volunteer pilots rushed him back to Anchorage so the hospital could save the ear. This year had been warm by Iditarod standards, teens and twenties, and when the dogs came to a stop they'd turn their heads upside down and flip over and shimmy in the snow to cool off. The mushers signed the checkers' clipboard and then bang, they were off their sleds, putting down straw and scattering food for the team. Not wasting time. The volunteer vets came out in huge parkas and knelt by particular dogs. There were hasty conferences. "Is it a shoulder?" "A bicep." "A bicep!" "He looks okay; I just want to get his breathing slowed."

Aliy Zirkle rolled in at 9:35, smiling; scowling Mitch Seavey followed ten minutes later. They both declared their twenty-fours. The crowd was thinning out. I stayed outside and watched Lance Mackey tend to his dogs. He was being shadowed on the trail by a personal camera crew, because Canada Goose, his primary sponsor, had decided to finance a documentary, tentatively titled *Lance!*, about his run through this year's race. He started bedding down the team, looking bleary as hell, eyes kohled with red, beyond exhausted, unclipping harnesses and shucking out handfuls of straw, and here are two guys in shiny Canada Goose jackets orbiting him with a video camera and a boom mic, ten inches from his face, bright light on the camera, surreal. Hardly anybody was still out. A wonder-struck volunteer

named Cindy watched him with her hands sort of romanti-
cally clasped, and he kept half eyeing her while he rubbed
ointment into one of his dogs' chests. "How's the show so
far?" he asked.

"Well . . . you're my first . . . this is my first Iditarod,
so . . . pretty wonderful."

"Oh, is that right?"

"Your dogs are beautiful."

"Thank you."

"It's . . . it's wonderful to see the magic of what you do."

"Stupid-ass harness, anyway," he murmured to the dog,
in sympathy.

"You must be tired," Cindy said.

"I could use a little nap," he said. "Actually fell asleep
on the sled. Went out for about ten minutes back on the
trail."

"Oh, goodness. Good thing your dogs know where to go."

"Ha! You'd think so. You wasn't watchin' 'em back at
McGrath. Ran me right off the trail. Tried to give 'em a
command and I might as well've spoke Japanese for all they
was listenin' to me. They were not. Listenin'. For *shit*."

Cindy made empathetic noises. Lance got up and strode
into the checkpoint building. It was starting to fill up with
mushers—standing in line for food, chatting with each other
about dogs. Lance ordered a cheeseburger and talked to Aliy
while he ate it. He took off his shoes and socks.

I met Dick Newton. Jan's husband. Remember the Queen
of Takotna, with her pies? He introduced himself to me in
the dining hall. "Introduced" is a strong word. He walked
up to me and said, "Well, who are you?" Not in an un-
friendly way. Just in a way that said he was eighty-two and

still handled deep Alaska wilderness on a daily basis and
maybe shouldn't have to smile extra just because he met
some kid who knew how to order pizza with an app. We
started talking. He had weepy pale eyes and a grizzled John
Brown beard and unkempt hair and liver spots. He wore a
camouflage button-neck sweater with red suspenders. By
trade he was a fur trapper. He could sell a marten pelt for
two hundred dollars and a wolf pelt for three hundred. But
martens were one hell of a lot easier to skin and haul around.
He'd come to Alaska forty-plus years ago to work oil but gave
it up because it meant spending months away from "her,"
not specifying who that was. My heart felt like a helium balloon when he said that. Just reporting. Everyone in Takotna
called him "my uncle." He'd made the trip from the village
to Nome via snow machine for twenty-one straight years,
and he was going again this year, with a buddy. "Call ourselves Team Viagra," he said. The distance from Takotna to
Nome is way more than six hundred miles. Actually, his
buddy hated the name Team Viagra. "But that's how it is."

He'd known frenzied living in his time. In the sixties he
did detective work in Sacramento, but he couldn't make ends
meet kicking down motel doors. "I gave it up for my health,"
he growled. "I was starvin' to death." He kept finding himself on the wrong side of the law, without quite knowing how
it happened. He described police chases, remembered hiding out in bars. Alaska had loomed for him as a possibility
of freedom, a life of not being interfered with. In the nineteenth century, he'd have lit out for the Territory.

"I kept seein' the inside of them jail cells in California,"
he told me. "But up here, a fella can do just about anything
he's big enough to do."

He let me take his picture. "I don't care," he said. He wouldn't smile or look at the camera. I got him to laugh by asking about books. He read a lot, he told me, but he never remembered anything he read, so he only had a few books in his cabin. They were good ones. He kept cycling through them again and again, always encountering them as if he were reading them for the first time.

That night a storm blew in and didn't let up. The whole next day is kind of a blur. We were stranded till the weather cleared. I remember Jay hopping behind the food counter at the checkpoint building, grilling bacon for the mushers. Linwood slid up to the checkpoint late in the morning, looking five years older and vacant; he gave Jay a hug, then me one. "I know now that this run is a celebration," he said. "I'm not racing to win, I'm racing to *be here*."

Everyone was asking when Martin Buser would arrive. He pulled in a little after one o'clock and stopped for just eight minutes. His rivals were sleeping in the village; it was time for his big passing move. By the time Mitch and Aliy left town, they were nine hours behind him. Still no one could say whether his strategy made any sense.

I remember standing on the riverbank, looking down at our planes on the river. It was still snowing. A small airplane emerged from the clouds overhead, and Dick the fur trapper, who was tottering past, squinted up at it and said, without changing his expression, "Ol' Blackie. Come after all. Blackie, you crazy bastard."

There were dogs everywhere; of course there were. Sleeping in every hollow. They seemed different here than they'd been in Anchorage, calmer, more noble somehow. They'd watch you watching them, snow on their foreheads, faces shagged with ice. In the late afternoon, they started waking up in large numbers. There was no barking. Dog teams when they're contented do these controlled, sustained group howls. A pack thing, I guess. They did that now, till Takotna rang with it. The sound prickled the hair on the back of my neck. That was how I spent the afternoon—walking through the village while the air filled up with the sound of the dog teams singing.

4. THE DARK PYRAMID

"Okay, uh . . . 985–Whiskey Flight, radio check."

"Two."

"Four."

"Okay, uh . . . three? Do we have three?"

(*Conspicuous silence.*)

"Bernard, you there?"

(*Sustained, heavy silence.*)

"Okay, Steve, is he still on one-two-two-niner, you want to jump over and check?"

"Two . . . Yeah, Dad, I'm not getting him."

"Okay, uh . . . push to common. Repeat: 985-Whiskey, push to common, that's one-two-three-four-seven-five. Bernard?"

(*Silence so profound it seems almost passive-aggressive.*)

"Well, puke."

I don't know what it was about the Frenchmen and their planes. Actually, I know exactly what it was; it was that their planes broke down every time Bernard and Christophe so much as glanced at them. *Nugget* never gave us a peep of trouble, as Jay put it; Bernard could be sitting at dinner *visualizing* a button in his Cub and it would pong off in a spume of fire. I don't know what caused it. You could trace this subtle tension throughout 985-Whiskey's whole existence. The Alaskans thought the French guys were careless about maintenance, that in France "the pilot just shows up and 'Oh, here's a cup of coffee, sir' and some other poor scrub does all the work." The French guys—well, Christophe was pretty chill on the whole, but I know Bernard thought he'd been handed inferior equipment. As he saw it, this whole expedition was at least 30 percent (*fart sound*).

One problem in particular we couldn't shake. The radio in Bernard's Cub cut out every time Bernard—but only Bernard—tried to use it. Steve would test it and it worked great, tallyho; then Bernard would take charge, we'd get airborne, and within a couple of minutes we'd be looking down the long cold barrel of a no-joy situation. We lost hours to this. Mechanics at tiny nowhere airstrips would say they'd locked down a problem with the electrical system. Then the next day the glitch would migrate somewhere else. I didn't follow it all, but apparently the logic was Gordian. We started making jokes that the flight was haunted, talking about "the ghost." Did the ghost bring his luggage. Was the ghost angry today. Had the ghost been eating my trail mix.

Things got weird after Takotna. We flew into a blizzard, for one. The world just disappeared. It was Thursday afternoon. We'd been trying to find a route through the Nulato Hills, west of the Yukon River, on our way to Unalakleet, an Inupiaq village on the coast of Norton Sound. We'd planned to spend a few nights in a bear-hunting cabin about eight miles from the village. We'd be well ahead of the dog teams, and we could use the cabin as a base, flying out on day trips to track the mushers as they made their way north to the sea. But we couldn't get to Unalakleet. Up in the hills every pass we flew into would dead-end in this huge gray wall. Then the wall was all around us. Thanks to the ghost, we had no radio contact with Bernard's plane; if we got separated in the hills, we'd have no way to find each other again.

Jay scanned for a place to land. We were over the Anvik, one of a snarl of small rivers running down from the hills to the Yukon. He'd glimpse a stretch of seemingly unobstructed river and we'd dive-bomb it, no fooling around now, doing urgent arcs, and we'd get to within six feet of touching down and only then be able to see the up-thrust broken ice that would rip the planes' skis off. Finally we found a spot. To pack down the snow, we had to go into trail formation and do multiple passes where we'd touch down at full speed and instantly take off again, veering off at crazy angles to come back around as quickly as possible. Somehow Bernard knew to follow. I was not in peak shape, stomachwise. I'd like to say I was grateful for the nausea because it kept me from being terrified, but the thing about nausea is that it sucks and you hate it. I did little breathey-county exercises while Jay focused on the less immediately urgent work of keeping the plane from crashing.

We tumbled out of the cockpit onto the river. The air stung. Huge wet flying flakes of snow. If you stepped carefully you'd sink up to your shin before the snow compressed enough to hold you; if you stepped a little harder you'd break through up to your thigh. Along the riverbank there were these spindly collections of upraised sticks. They looked like scrawny bushes but were in fact the tops of trees.

I felt oddly light. I congratulated myself for not having thrown up, and also for, as I thought, not freaking out, for keeping a cool head in the crisis. I had it together, I thought, as I slipped out my iPhone, in the middle of the blizzard, to check what was happening on Twitter. I could tell weather jokes, maybe post a picture. I was disappointed—saddened— to see the "No Service" message here, untold miles from the nearest human infrastructure, but I wasn't exactly surprised. I was far too collected to be surprised. Verizon wasn't as together as I was, that was all.

We put on snowshoes and took the shovels out of our planes' belly pods. Getting out of the wind was the first priority. We dug a sort of recessed shelter in the snow and made a bivouac out of one of *Nugget*'s wing covers. Jay pegged the temperature at -15°F. Wind at 35 knots. I had no idea what a knot was. I ate trail mix.

At first we thought we might be able to make a quick escape, that the storm was bound to blow over. But an hour went past, and if anything the snowfall intensified.

Here was a problem: 985-Whiskey wasn't equipped to fly after dark. We had about a three-hour window to get out before we'd be forced to dig a snow cave and spend the night.

On the map Jay pointed out the peak of a hill a mile off, with a higher peak a mile or so behind it. It'd be safe to take off when we could see both peaks. We kept getting these fleeting, torn-curtain glimpses of the first; the second might as well not have been there. Another hour and we started scouting downriver for a place to dig the cave.

We would have been fine. Uncomfortable, but we'd have survived. We had plenty of food and water, and we'd brought Arctic-grade sleeping bags. We'd have spent a claustrophobic night and left the next day when the storm passed. Fully alive, one big memory. But about twenty minutes before our takeoff window closed, Steve jumped up. "I see the far hill! Dad! Dad, look!"

So we made it out. But my lasting memory of that time on the river is not the crazy, elated scramble to strip the blankets off the planes and take off. It's from about an hour earlier, when Jay, I guess to keep our morale up, suddenly started talking about poetry.

"You guys ever hear of a writer called Robert Service?" he asked.

I said sure, but I didn't know his work well, and Jay went on: "To my mind—in my opinion—Robert Service is *by some measure* the greatest poet who's ever graced the English language. Why, compared to Bob Service, Shakespeare is a piker. And OH BY THE WAY . . . it's beautiful how he captured the soul of the Arctic."

And he broke into "The Ballad of Blasphemous Bill." "Recited" is too flimsy a word; he *performed* it, in a wild sea-captain brogue, eyes bulging under the beaver hat with the dangling earflaps. In the blowing snow in the middle of the Anvik River, waving his arms all around. Here's how it goes. Bill MacKie (rhymes with "die") is a gold-rush type who's scared he'll meet his end in the Klondike with no one to bury him. So he slips this other gold-rush guy some money in exchange for the promise that when the time comes, the other guy will find his body and put it in the ground. Well, sure enough, Bill dies, and when word reaches the burial guy (who's narrating the poem), B.G. bundles himself up and sets out to look for the remote hut where the body is waiting. And Jay goes,

> You know what it's like in the Yukon wild when it's
>   sixty-nine below;
> When the ice-worms wriggle their purple heads
>   through the crust of the pale blue snow;
> When the pine-trees crack like little guns in the
>   silence of the wood,
> And the icicles hang down like tusks under the
>   parka hood;
> When the stove-pipe smoke breaks sudden off, and
>   the sky is weirdly lit,
> And the careless feel of a bit of steel burns like a
>   red-hot spit;
> When the mercury is a frozen ball, and the frost-
>   fiend stalks to kill—
> Well, it was just like that that day when I set out to
>   look for Bill.

He finds the hut. Bill's corpse is there. Mission accomplished, except for one problem: Bill's frozen solid. And he's managed to die "with his arms and legs outspread," so he won't fit into the coffin that our by this point extremely cold and downcast speaker has hauled here for him.

> Have you ever stood in an Arctic hut in the shadow
>   of the Pole,
> With a little coffin six by three and a grief you can't
>   control?

> Have you ever sat by a frozen corpse that looks at
>   you with a grin,
> And that seems to say: "You may try all day, but
>   you'll never jam me in"?

Well, he's not a quitter, our B.G., so he takes the obvious
next step. He builds a fire and tries to thaw Bill out. But
after days by the stove, Bill's still a star-shaped icicle. So B.G.
does the only thing he can think of. He takes out a saw,
hacks Bill into pieces, and lays the pieces in the coffin.
Boom, contract fulfilled. In his later and more contempla-
tive years, B.G. tells us, his mind sometimes drifts backs to
that day:

> And as I sit and the parson talks, expounding of the
>   Law,
> I often think of poor old Bill—*and how hard he was
>   to saw.*

Jay—what an endlessly surprising person. We were laughing and clapping on the ice. I asked him if he knew Rudyard Kipling's poems—I think I described Kipling as "pretty
much the Robert Service of British India," which isn't going
to win me tenure at Berkeley, but it was cold out—and he
said, oh, sure, he'd read Kipling. Actually grew up in Vermont near the house where Kipling lived for a while, where
he wrote *The Jungle Book*. Got hired one summer to clean
the first floor. He had spent a day of his childhood vacuum-
ing Rudyard Kipling's carpets.

———

We learned later, from the radio, that Martin Buser had taken the lead that same day, at Iditarod, and extended it as the mushers started their grueling two-hundred-mile run up the Yukon River. Conditions on the trail were getting worse; dogs were struggling through mashed-potato snow, falling into overflow holes where fresh water had broken through a solid surface of ice. Freezing water slopped over into the sleds. Ice gnarled the mustaches of the men pulling in to checkpoints.

My old friend the Mushin' Mortician had been the first to scratch, at Rainy Pass on the second day of the race. Now more started calling it quits. Lance Mackey, who'd made a push around Takotna, stayed in, but he fell off the pace.

It rained on the Yukon, in heavy slashing lines. The trail there runs down the middle of the river, which is perfectly flat, half a mile wide in places, leaving the mushers no cover from the wind. The cold and the unchanging blank land-scape make it one of the most brutal stretches of the race, a place where sleep-deprived mushers regularly hallucinate. "While I had taken thirty, even forty below and some wind," Gary Paulsen writes in *Winterdance*, "and had even become something close to cocksure about my ability to handle winter, I had absolutely no goddamn idea what was about to hit me. The Yukon River defines that which is cold."

Slowly, the teams fought their way forward. Buser's dogs, forced to break trail for the chasing pack, and with their daylong rest a memory, finally wore out. They needed nine hours to get from Grayling to Eagle Island; Buser's five-hour lead shrank to three. And this was where the strategy he'd spent eight months perfecting, began to come unraveled. "Felt like I was going backwards," he told reporters. "No trail. Lots of wind. No bottom. Lots of water." Then his dogs got diarrhea from slurping groundwater, a constant problem in long-distance mushing. They lost weight. They went slower.

On Saturday, Aliy and Mitch passed him around Kaltag, as did a handful of others. He never led again.

Slowly up the river, days and nights of rain. At the cabin near Unalakleet, where we'd finally landed safely after our close call on the Anvik, heavy snow kept us grounded for two days. We sat around the radio, listening for updates every hour as the mushers made their way toward us. Finally, Jay and I managed a solo flight down the Yukon, to Grayling and Eagle Island. We saw mushers on the river, words in a font too small to read. Miles separated them. We spotted a team we thought might be Linwood's, so Jay—it's a signal they have—rocked *Nugget*'s yellow wings back and forth. Whoever was down there waved back like someone hailing help from the deck of a sinking ship.

On our second day at the cabin I walked in to find a woman covered in blood.

The cabin was wood paneled and lined with hunting photos, dozens of them, frame after frame of kneeling tourists grinning with their rifles. The owner was a bear-hunting guide named Vance, a big friendly fist of a guy who normally used the cabin as a staging area. The hide of a huge grizzly (face attached) sprawled across one wall, next to the head of a big bull musk ox. No running water; instead, there was a pot for melting snow on top of the cast-iron woodstove.

Vance's daughter Andri was the one holding the knife. Actually it was only her hands that were bloody; she'd looked bloodier at first because of the soupy bowlful of dark-red organs on the coffee table in front of her.

She was dismembering the ptarmigan, fifteen of them, that she and Steve had shot that afternoon.

"Bro," Steve said. "It was incredible. These birds are so dumb! I missed one from twenty feet and it reacted by *walking toward me*."

Since the snow was keeping me from following the race, and Jay was busy taking the Frenchmen's Cub apart to try to chase down the ghost, I'd decided earlier that day to hike into Unalakleet, eight miles down the Iditarod Trail, hoping thereby to experience something of the isolation amid mind-annihilating beauty that the mushers encountered every day. But Bernard and Christophe came with me, which sort of defeated the purpose. Christophe hung back half a mile or so to take pictures, but Bernard, after days of being marginalized in fast-paced English conversations, most of which barely even *touched* on French tax policy, was delighted to have a captive listener. He went nonstop the whole way, his chest thrust out like the chest of a singing bird.

No one wanted to work—that was the problem with French society. Now, did they want money? They did. But they wanted it given to them. Given by the government, just for being born. And taxes. Oh la la. Taxes in France were a (*fart sound*)–level absurdity. (Here on the river the Iditarod Trail was a snow-machine track. Teepee-shaped wooden markers stood beside the track, spaced every two or three hundred yards.) People thought the Revolution had been fought so they could have a paid vacation every August. Bernard had worked hard, flying a big, big jet from Paris to

Tahiti, and now he was retired, but still the government wanted more. The blacks and the Arabs—don't get him started on the blacks and the Arabs. (Seriously, don't.) Give Bernard the Corsicans any day. (Every now and then at a particularly long bend in the river the trail would run up onto the bank and cut across the forest. After a few miles the forest stopped, and then the trail would cut across tundra.) A special people, the Corsicans. Ancient. He could introduce you to one Corsican innkeeper, Pierre—eighty years old, and was he taking it easy? Never. Ridiculous. (The sun glinted off the snow.) But the French government made it harder and harder to work. France had its cathedrals and nothing else. Europe was, how do you say, destructing.

Where the little pools had frozen, there were flats of turquoise ice. Old-god hills in the distance.

"A lot of people who come to Alaska say they come here to feel free," I ventured.

"Ah, *oui*," he breathed, taking in the landscape with a gesture. "Fweedom! Alaska is fweedom."

We were standing in the open. All of a sudden I felt . . . but I don't want to overstate it; it wasn't despair or anything, just melancholy, just a rush of forlornness. A strange kind of loneliness for history. Alaska has its own past: the murderous flaming wreck of the Russian colonies, the gold madness, the deep-time traditions of the indigenous peoples. But it doesn't saturate the landscape. In the Lower 48, you carry around a sense that the human environment has been molded by people who went before—this battle on this hill and so on. There's a texture that you, too, are part of, even when it's bloody or frightening, a texture within which your life can assume some kind of meaning. You have references.

And that, of course, can be its own nightmare, but in remote Alaska the nightmare is *It's not there*. There are no prewritten meanings. A fella can do just about anything he's big enough to do. One strong gust of wind could blow the whole edifice of human habitation away.

So we reached Unalakleet. Pastel siding, jumble of metal roofs. Boats buried in snow on the coast of a frozen sea.

———

I had a long talk with Andri after she'd finished gutting the ptarmigan. It turned out that she was a graphic designer who'd earned an MFA in San Francisco. She had declined a coveted spot at the Rhode Island School of Design and come back to Unalakleet, where—the bear guide's daughter— she kept a shotgun in her car in case she happened to run across dinner. Recently she'd won a small-business grant to make *uluit*, a type of traditional knife, and sell them online. She was obsessed with the occult mysteries of Alaska. Late one night she'd been out with a friend when an unexplained semicircle of light appeared on the horizon. It started out small and expanded for several minutes, holding the same proportions, a mathematically perfect half circle or half spheroid of soft white light, until it covered half the sky. Then it faded away. *X-Files* stuff, nothing like the northern lights. She'd sent the pictures she took to a physicist and an astronomer at the university in Anchorage. They'd confirmed that it wasn't a celestial or known phenomenon. It looked like the pulse of a futuristic weapon. But it had been absolutely silent. I saw her pictures. Did you know that there are military installations hidden all over Alaska? Relics of the Cold War, abandoned. Underground bunkers. Empty Quonset huts. White Alice sites, some of them are called. Ruins of a once-sophisticated communications relay. The phrase "White Alice" made me shiver. Folks who snuck in came back talking about unexplained voices. About visions. There were stories about ghosts.

Andri didn't believe in ghosts herself, but she'd heard the stories. Her own philosophy was, don't rule anything out until you've looked into it. She had a friend who with her own eyes had seen the *ircenrraat*, the little people of Alaska, sinister gnomelike creatures who inhabit the deep tundra. And not a friend who goes in for those kinds of legends, Andri said; a responsible friend. Around Nome, where alien abductions were reported with unusual frequency, those who reported them told eerily similar stories, often involving the number 333 and the appearance of a strange white owl. They'd wake, late at night, from a dream of the owl and find the clock flashing 3:33. Each year five out of every thousand Alaskans go missing. People vanish without a trace at twice the rate of Outside. Start reading about why the disappearances happen, Andri said, and you'll encounter rumors of a dark or underground pyramid, a huge structure, bigger than the Great Pyramid at Giza, buried beneath the ice west of Denali. There were anomalies in the aerial photographs, men in black uniforms, hints on Google Earth. There was a little-understood link between the pyramid and the abandoned airport inside the Farewell Burn. Some speculation held that the pyramid was a covered-up nuclear site; further speculation countered that the nuclear-site rumors were themselves a cover-up meant to divert attention away from the pyramid's true identity as an ancient power source of unknown origin. Andri was an expert, had in fact corresponded with the leading amateur researcher into the pyramid's presumed existence until his e-mails suddenly ceased, a cessation that was itself troublingly mysterious. Some people said that the pyramid would be capable of powering half of North America. It made sense, didn't it, because if the government had discovered an energy source of that magnitude, it'd do everything it could to keep it secret. So the lack of evidence became a kind of evidence. Sitting by the fire in the hunting cabin, a million miles from everywhere, I could believe it was down there, darkly pulsing.

The first mushers passed us the next morning, on the river just below the cabin's porch. They were close enough to talk to. Mitch had moved into the lead. "How far ahead is he?" a couple of the guys who went by next called out to us.

"Shoot, you can practically see him," Jay called back.

How had the trail been? we called. "Slow," they said. "Awful night. Awful. So slow."

In eight miles they'd stop at Unalakleet, at the checkpoint. Then they'd start the final phase of the Iditarod: the long sprint up the coast of Norton Sound, two hundred miles on the sea ice.

5. ENDS OF THE EARTH

We flew to Russia. It was the Frenchmen's idea. For two days in the cabin, Christophe had spent all his free time studying this giant map of western Alaska, folded up to show one square of the Bering Sea coast; he kept making little marks with a mechanical pencil and frowning. Then he and

Bernard huddled over the map together, murmuring in French. Finally they went to Jay.

"Ah, *oui*," Christophe said. "I inquire. Is it possible . . . we go to Diomède?"

"The Diomede Islands?" Jay said. His lips stretched in an exaggerated grimace. "It's . . . *possible*. I've never done it, but it's possible. Let me hop on the radio."

Christophe had circled two tiny islands in the middle of the Bering Strait, the stretch of water, just fifty-three miles across, that separates Alaska from the eastern coast of Russia. The islands couldn't have been more than a couple of miles apart. The border, as well as the international date line, ran right between them. Big Diomede was on the Russian side, Little Diomede on the American.

"Okay," Jay said the next day. "What I'm hearing is, during the winter, they carve an airstrip on the sea ice right plum in the middle of the islands. Weather's only clear for a Cub to land about two percent of the time. Partner, it is rough stuff out there. But we can darn sure give it a crack."

On Monday we set out for the Diomedes. It meant flying on past Nome, past the Iditarod's finish line, and losing touch with the race for a day. But when you're on an Arctic expedition and fate beckons you to a frozen sea on the edge of Chukotka, how can you say no?

Once you leave behind the spruce forests, and leave behind the tundra, and go out over the sea ice, Alaska becomes a different thing, even huger, almost unbearably bright. The sheets of ice crack and collide and form fault lines, spaces of open sea called leads, so that the world becomes a field of snow that's crazed in places with zigzags of black water.

It's the other side of the mist. Beluga whales swam up into the leads and you would see these little divots in the water where their foreheads poked through. White forms streaming down beneath the divots. We surprised a small herd of musk ox near some sort of deserted military compound on the coast and flew low over them while they formed their protective circle. We chased a herd of caribou. I saw three seals lying on the edges of three adjacent leads.

Steve chimed in over the radio: "Dad, we might want to go to line abreast. We've got bear tracks *everywhere* down there." And there were. Heavy dashed lines across the snow, like blue stitches around the edges of the leads. Jay had gone searching for polar bears every year on the Iditarod expedition and never found one. (He'd gotten up close and personal with the bears that destroyed *Nugget*, but that was farther north, way up in the Arctic Circle. "Only time I see those little pukes," he told me, "they're chomping on my airplane.") We circled for ten minutes, fifteen minutes without luck. The flight to the Diomedes was already going to stretch our fuel reserves to the limit; we'd have to break off in another couple of minutes. "They hide from me!" Jay moaned. "They always hide."

Then I saw her.

She was almost invisible: a tiny yellow-white spot against the rim of the water, a slight imperfection in the snow. I screamed something that might as well have been in Japanese and Jay banked the plane hard and dove while I whipped my head around trying to keep the polar bear in view. I couldn't keep my o'clocks straight. "Polar bear at three o'clock! Twelve forty-five! Eight seventeen! No! Eight seventeen*ish*!" Then Jay saw her, too.

The nine seconds of video I managed to shoot during the first pass we made over the bear shows a tiny lumbering ivory *something*, the size of a fly on a kitchen floor, galloping across the ice shelf under *Nugget*'s yellow right wingtip. We made a second pass and got close enough to see her haunches shuddering, but by that point I'd dropped the camera.

Everybody pretty jaded here? Fantastic.

I couldn't feel my spine, she was so beautiful.

———

In the summer, I guess they look like islands, but in the winter, when the sea freezes, the Diomedes just look like cliffs, dusty white rocks towering up out of the snow. The runway between the islands was a thin plowed line, too rough to land on; we touched down beside it, on the sea ice. The day was bright and clear. Apparently we'd picked a moment that fell within the lucky 2 percent. On the American island, a tiny village was bunched in one corner at the base of the cliff—home, we'd read, to about a hundred Inupiat. There had once been a sister village on the Russian island, but it was forcibly disbanded by the Soviets, to prevent ideological contamination. (Communism, unaccountably, fell anyway.) Now the Russian side held only a border guard headquarters and a weather station.

We were only supposed to look. That was the deal. We'd hop out of our planes, eat a sandwich, and take a picture of Russia. Then we'd head home. Anything more would be illegal. But I was so giddy from the flight and the polar bear (we all were, we were grinning like idiots) that as soon as I'd finished throwing an engine blanket on *Nugget* I turned to the villager who took care of the airstrip—Henry, his

name was, he'd come out on a snow machine to greet us—
and asked how far to the border.

"Oh, about four hundred yards over yonder," Henry said.

And I took off. I didn't ask permission. Looking back, I
can see that I was undergoing pretty intense mood swings as
a result of the PTSD from all the amazing experiences I'd
been having. But I was free, wasn't I, in Alaska? It was slow
going, because I was too free to bother with snowshoes and
thus had to churn through thirty inches of snow.

I headed across the frozen strait, toward the jagged white
rock of Big Diomede.

This was it—the actual end of America. Sure, we had
borders with other countries. We had nothing close to this.

Every way you could think of that sentence was true.

How far I'd come! Hundreds and hundreds of miles to
reach this place. You couldn't fathom how huge Alaska was
until you'd seen it from a Super Cub, one horizon crawling
into the next, day after day after day. And the white rock in
front of me was the end. Somewhere behind it lay the
beginning of Siberia.

When I estimated I'd gone five or six hundred yards, I
went up on tiptoe and waved like mad to the Russian side.
I thought I saw something flash, like light striking a mirror, off
a tower whose top could just be made out over the rock.
But that was the only thing that happened.

A few minutes later, Steve and the Frenchmen caught
up with me. When I'd bolted for the border, they'd taken it
as an excuse to follow. I'd built a lead because they put on
snowshoes first. Jay, who was an adult, had stayed behind
with the airplanes.

A few minutes after that, a border-patrol agent came

from the American side and called out that if we didn't come back the Russians would start firing warning shots.

On the way back I noticed that my face felt curiously sandblasted. Jay came forward to meet me. "We need to get these stinkers out of this cold, ASAP. If the engines freeze, we'll never get out of here. Are you okay? Your face is as red as a beet."

Oh, right—it was cold! I'd had too much adrenaline to notice. Now I realized that the wind was roaring down the channel between the islands. I'd staggered through it without even realizing. Thirty knots, Jay said, whatever that meant. And we were looking at probably thirty-five below. Still, it was hard to move quickly. We ate our sandwiches and took pictures. The villagers who came out from Little Diomede told us ours were the first planes, not counting the helicopter that brought the mail, to land at the island all winter. More and more people kept coming out, just to look at us.

Someone should have noticed that the Frenchmen had neglected to put a blanket on their plane. Afterward, there was disagreement about what had happened. Jay insisted that they'd asked him and he'd told them not to bother, which makes so little sense that I'm sure he was being diplomatic. Regardless, I am an idiot non-pilot who never even flew the Tahiti route for Air France, and I was out of my head with excitement, and I threw the blanket on *Nugget* without being told. It's just something you do. And Steve described for me, in dark tones, the time Bernard had taken after we landed to retrieve and then put on his finespun red wool face mask, how carefully he'd straightened out the mouth. We wound up writing it off with a shrug as the final revenge of the ghost. Whatever happened, by the time we'd finished taking snapshots and meeting villagers, by the time we'd gotten our helmets strapped on and our windows latched, it was too late. Jay climbed out of *Nugget* and tried to manually start the Frenchmen's propeller with a two-handed spin, the way you see in old movies. It was no use. Their engine was as dead as the island rock. It was as dead as a gun-shot ptarmigan. It was as dead as the alien civilization that had built the dark pyramid, probably.

We were stranded out there for three hours. It was the first time I ever understood why freezing to death is sometimes described as "peaceful" or "soothing" or "just like falling asleep," descriptions that had always seemed to hint at some unfathomable mind transformation within the freezing person, some power extreme cold had to enchant the brain's basic mechanisms of homeostasis. It didn't feel violent, that was the thing. Even with the wind ripping past you. Certain parts of your body accrued this strange hush. Like you were disappearing piece by piece. I thought I'd be warmer outside and walking around than inside *Nugget*, so I would sort of exaggeratedly move one limb at a time, my left arm or whatever, and while I was concentrating on my left arm, my right leg would start to be erased.

More than affecting my sense perceptions, though, the cold seemed to affect the way I thought about my sense perceptions. I'd take my glove off to adjust a zipper and lose feeling in my hand, and instead of thinking *Holy no I need to get my glove back on right this second*, I'd sort of pause and go, *My, how interesting that my hand feels physically translucent*. Then my brain's inbox would gently ding. PLEASE DON'T DIE.

Jay had it the worst. He was out there the whole time,

crouched under the plane, trying to get the engine heated. Villagers from Little Diomede kept forming little peering semicircles a few feet away from him. Finally he walked back to *Nugget*.

"We're taking off," he said. It was the least cheerful I'd ever seen him. He almost looked mildly put out. Bernard and Christophe would stay in the village; the teachers had agreed to put them up at the school.

The last I saw of our two French pilots, they were being carted away on snow machines, half-bewildered, waving back at us.

———

Nome, a northern Alaskan metropolis of 3,731 souls, may be the most steampunk city in the world. Imagine a Wild West mining town, the sort with free-swinging saloon doors and a jailhouse with a rocking chair on the porch—call it Buzzard Gulch—then transport it away from cacti and outcroppings to a snowy waste on the shore of a frozen bay. Modernize it some, give it electricity. Now litter it, and be enthusiastic, with twisted hulks of sheet metal, headless fuselages, giant noseless propellers, detritus of air travel that no one has the resources or motive to clean up. Picture *McCabe & Mrs. Miller*, only if the climactic battle involved two blimp armadas. Sink, at weird angles in the snow outside town, locomotives not used since the gold rush. Freeze eerie derelict mining ships into the ice. Now draw back. Look over your work. And: Nome.

There's a story that it was named by accident, through a misreading. Before anyone had thought what to call it, they penciled in "Name?" on the map. Some nearsighted cartographer mistook the writing and handed the wrong vowel to history.

Front Street is where they'd have gunfights, if they had gunfights. It's a skinny thoroughfare with its back to the sound; the drunks lurch-strutting to the next bar, of whom at any moment there are several, get glimpses of the sea between the buildings. The town's put up Christmas lights to celebrate the end of the Iditarod. Big zigzagging strings of them. The snow-packed road terminates in a chute exactly like the one at the starting line in Anchorage. Above the chute there's a wooden arch, and above the arch there's a banner that reads FINISH.

This is Tuesday, March 12. The end of the Iditarod, for the winners, anyway. Here's how this works. It's night. A small crowd turns out, maybe three hundred people, under the Christmas lights. I'm here alone, because Jay and Steve have flown back to Little Diomede on a mission to rescue the Frenchmen. There's a screen the size of a king-sized bed hanging from the second story of one of the storefronts across the street. It's playing "Idita-Rock n' Roll," a kid-friendly Iditarod-themed music video from the 1990s. The spectacle is largely financed by Anchorage Chrysler Dodge, one of the Iditarod's major sponsors, whose owner, Rod Udd, is known as Idita-Rod due to his obsessive love of the race. The storefronts—Nome Liquor Store, Gold Buyers of Alaska, the Bering Sea Bar and Grill, Arctic Trading Post Gift Emporium, the Nugget Inn—are doing slow but respectable trade, almost none of which seems Iditarod related. The night is a very deep blue. It's -2°F. The church next to the "Idita-Rock n' Roll" screen has a banner in front advertising Icy 100.3 FM.

This year's race has come down to a straight fight between Mitch and Aliy. Unsurprisingly, given the times and distances involved, Iditarod finishes are rarely close, but this one's going to be. Leaving the White Mountain checkpoint, seventy-five miles from the finish line, Aliy's only thirteen minutes behind. In 1978, Lance Mackey's father, Dick, won the Iditarod by just one second; certain reckless members of the crowd speculate within my hearing that we could be fixing to see that all over again. Certainly the guy who seemed to be in charge at the media briefing an hour earlier said to expect both dog teams to be in the chute at once, something that hadn't happened in his previous twenty-plus years of seeming to be in charge at Iditarod media briefings. Every single person I talk to wants Aliy to win, and so do I. There's a feeling, when the crowd first assembles, that she has a slim but real chance.

You find out early, though. Barring an actual photo finish, there's almost no scenario in which the end of an Iditarod can be surprising. The mushers are half-mad and starved and frozen and the dogs have run a thousand miles in a week; the sleds are going maybe seven miles an hour; no one's making up much ground under those circumstances. When the PA guy, after we've been standing around for an hour, says, "Mitch is three miles out," it means Mitch has won, only you end up waiting another half an hour for him to finally arrive. In the end, Mitch pulls in at 10:40 p.m. and Aliy's twenty-three minutes behind. It's head-twistingly close by Iditarod standards, but Mitch has plenty of time to sob and embrace loved ones and commune with dogs and have camera lights pointed in his haggard frost-mustached face and shake hands for official photos and still clear out of the chute a good while before Aliy arrives.

He's the oldest winner in the history of the Iditarod, Mitch, at fifty-three. Last year, his son Dallas became the youngest champion when he won at twenty-four. Now they're bookending all the other winners, age-wise, a fact that will lead most of the newspaper coverage tomorrow.

There's such goodwill at the press conference. Mitch and Aliy eat cheeseburgers and crack jokes. There's no sense that one of them just suffered an agonizing defeat; instead, there's an air of conspiratorial wonder, like, *Oh wow, can you believe we made it?* As the sporting event that most closely mimics the experience of sustained brutal catastrophe, the Iditarod is maybe uniquely designed to amplify sport's natural euphoria-making power with basic human relief. Relief is one of the most thrilling things there is, if you think about it. Imagine if Game 7 were played on inflatable rafts in a shark tank; afterward LeBron would be all, *That happened! I survived!*

Everyone in the room gets this: fans, volunteers, media. It's a close-knit world; people know each other. So when Mitch says, "The brain kind of stops working somewhere along the Yukon. I offered Aliy a cough drop this morning, and she decided it was too complicated to unwrap it," the laugh that rolls through the room is not the brittle pre-deadline laugh of reporters being fed good copy but a delighted and leisurely laugh of people who've been there, or know someone who's been there, and who just want to share in the moment.

What are you going to do tomorrow? someone asks.

"Probably hang out with my dogs and my family," Aliy says.

"I'm going to sleep and eat," Mitch says. "My family can hang out with my dogs."

They'd both had hallucinations. Near the end, kind of beautifully, each had visions of the other. Aliy thought she saw Mitch's yellow sled floating somewhere ahead of her. Whenever Mitch looked behind him, the world kept turning into Aliy. "I saw the raven Aliy. I saw the fuel-tank Aliy. And the upside-down-boat Aliy," he says. The way he says it, it's like something from a myth. They share a look, like, hello, vast and terrifying cosmos.

At around midnight, as I'm on my way out, this happens at race HQ: I see Uncle Dick. From Takotna, remember? He made it, all seven hundred miles on his snow machine. He's sitting at a folding table with six or seven other race fans, drinking coffee. Team Viagra kept the streak alive.

There are taxis in Nome. In fact there are whole taxi companies. Somehow this makes economic sense in a town of thirty-seven hundred people just below the Arctic Circle. Small fleets of battered gray minivans, 800 numbers on their sliding doors spackled with winter curb silt. Mr. Kab, Checker Cab, E-Z Transportation. I called one in the middle of the night. My driver's name was Roxy. She was a young Native woman, maybe twenty-seven, with a round laughing face and sparkly star-shaped glasses. I remember them as sunglasses, which can't possibly be right. I remember that the reflections of the Christmas lights shone out of them. I was thinking about this city, Nome, which felt like something someone had generated by accident during a first try at a video game, and how it was crisscrossed by all these nonsensical taxis—this arbitrary pattern of routes, so many origins and destinations, dots appearing and disappearing on a map. I asked Roxy how she'd gotten into cab driving.

She seemed kind of taken aback. "Oh," she said at length. "I'm only doing this for a while, you know? My family, we're more into subsistence stuff. Fishing, gathering berries." She reached into the van's ashtray, where there was a loose ball of rubber bands, and rolled the rubber bands between her fingers. She spoke so slowly I wasn't sure she'd go on. "We practice those skills, my family, because who knows, we say. Who knows what'll still be here tomorrow?"

I thought of Jay, who'd flown with me for eleven hundred miles, who'd kept me alive, and who'd given me a copy of his book, *Survival Flying: Bush Flying Tales and Techniques as Flown and Taught in Alaska*, by "The Piper Poet" C. Jay Baldwin. He'd inscribed it, "Read and heed!" It was a textbook, but it opened with a poem about bush pilots, a poem Jay had written himself:

Here's to the brave souls that aviate,
Across that vast Alaskan state . . .

The poem was dedicated to the memory of Jay's friend and mentor Bert, the one who'd disappeared in the waters of the Shelikof Strait.

Who knew what would be there tomorrow? And it hit me that that was exactly the point of the Iditarod, why it was so important to Alaska. When everything can vanish, you make a sport out of not vanishing. You submit yourself to the forces that could erase you from the earth, and then you turn up at the end, not erased. I'd had it wrong before, when

I'd seen the dog teams as saints on the cusp of a religious vision. It was the opposite. Visionaries are trying to escape into something larger. Mushers are heading into something larger that they have to escape. They're going into the vision to show that they can come out of it again. The vision will be beautiful, and it will try to kill you. And (oh by the way) that doesn't have to be the last word. That's why you go to the end of the world—to lose yourself. And not to.

Sea of Crises

I

When he comes into the ring, Hakuho, the greatest *sumo-tori* in the world, perhaps the greatest in the history of the world, dances like a tropical bird, like a bird of paradise. Flanked by two attendants—his *tachimochi*, who carries his sword, and his *tsuyuharai*, or dew sweeper, who keeps the way clear for him—and wearing his embroidered apron, the *kesho-mawashi*, with its braided cords and intricate loops of rope, Hakuho climbs onto the trapezoidal block of clay, two feet high and nearly twenty-two feet across, where he will be fighting. Here, marked off by rice-straw bales, is the circle, the *dohyo*, which he has been trained to imagine as the top of a skyscraper: One step over the line and he is dead. A Shinto priest purified the *dohyo* before the tournament. Above, a six-ton canopy suspended from the arena's ceiling, a kind of floating temple roof, marks it as a sacred space. Colored tassels hang from the canopy's corners, representing the Four Divine Beasts of the Chinese constellations: the azure dragon of the east, the vermilion sparrow of the south, the white tiger of the west, the black tortoise of the north.

Over the canopy, lit with spotlights, shines the white-and-red flag of Japan.

Hakuho bends into a deep squat. He claps twice, then rubs his hands together. He turns his palms slowly upward. He is bare-chested, six feet four and 350 pounds. His hair is pulled up in a topknot. His smooth stomach strains against the coiled belt at his waist, the literal referent of his rank: *yokozuna*, horizontal rope. He lifts his right arm diagonally, palm turned down to show he is unarmed. He repeats the gesture with his left. He lifts his right leg high into the air, tipping his torso like a watering can, then slams his foot down onto the clay. When it strikes, the crowd of thirteen thousand men, women, and children inside the Ryogoku Kokugikan, Japan's national sumo stadium, shouts in unison: "Yoisho!"—*Come on! Do it!* He slams down his other foot: "Yoisho!" It's as if the force of his weight is striking the crowd in the stomach. He squats again, arms held winglike at his sides, and bends forward at the waist until his back is almost parallel with the floor. With weird, sliding thrusts of his feet, he inches forward, gliding across the ring's sand, raising and lowering his head in a way that's vaguely serpentine while slowly straightening his back. By the time he's upright again, the crowd is roaring.

———

In 265 years, only sixty-eight sumo wrestlers have reached the rank of *yokozuna*. Two other *yokozuna* are recognized as having practiced before 1749, but it's only with the ascension that year of Maruyama Gondazaemon, the third holder of the title, that we reach a point where we can be reasonably sure about names and dates and whether wrestlers existed outside folklore. Only the holders of sumo's highest rank are allowed to make entrances like Hakuho's. Officially, the purpose of the elaborate *dohyo-iri* is to chase away demons, and this is something you should register about sumo, a sport with TV contracts and millions in revenue and fan blogs and athletes in yogurt commercials—that it's simultaneously a sport in which demon frightening can be something's official purpose. But the ceremony is territorial on a human level, too. It's a message delivered to adversaries, a way of saying, *This ring is mine*; a way of saying, *Be prepared for what happens if you're crazy enough to enter it.*

Hakuho is not Hakuho's real name. Sumo wrestlers fight under ring names called *shikona*, formal pseudonyms governed, like everything else in the sport, by elaborate traditions and rules. Hakuho was born Mönkhbatyn Davaajargal in Ulaanbaatar, Mongolia, in 1985; he's the fourth non-Japanese wrestler, and second Mongolian, to attain *yokozuna* status. Until the mid-1970s or so, foreigners were rare in the upper ranks of sumo in Japan. But some countries have their own sumo customs, brought over by immigrants, and some others have sports that are very like sumo. Thomas Edison filmed sumo matches in Hawaii as early as 1903. Mongolian wrestling involves many of the same skills and concepts. In recent years, wrestlers brought up in places like these have found their way to Japan in greater numbers and have largely supplanted Japanese wrestlers at the top of the sumo rankings. At the time of my arrival in Tokyo, January 2014, there has been no active Japanese *yokozuna* since the last, Takanohana, retired in 2003. This is a source of intense anxiety to many in the tradition-minded world of Japanese sumo.

As a child, the story goes, Davaajargal was skinny. His father had been a dominant force in Mongolian wrestling in the 1960s and 1970s, winning a silver medal at the 1968 Olympics and rising to the rank of Undefeatable Giant. Somehow this titan produced a scrawny son. Davaajargal was captivated by wrestling, and he had learned a great deal from his father, but to his bitter frustration he was too small to stand a chance at higher levels. When he went to Tokyo to seek sumo training, in October 2000, he was fifteen years old. He weighed 137 pounds. Sumo apprentices live in training stables called *heya*. No stable master wanted to take him in. All agreed that he had a stellar brain for wrestling, but he was much too small, they said; too small, too old, and too unfamiliar with the culture. Finally, on the last day of his stay in Japan, an older Mongolian wrestler persuaded the master of the Miyagino *heya* to give him a chance. The gamble paid off. After a few years of training and a late growth spurt, Davaajargal emerged as the most gifted young *rikishi* (wrestler) in Japan. He was given the name Hakuho, which means "white Peng"; a Peng is a giant bird in Chinese mythology.

Hakuho's early career was marked by a bad-tempered rivalry with an older wrestler, a fellow Mongolian called Asashoryu (morning blue dragon), who became a *yokozuna* in 2003. Asashoryu embodied everything some Japanese feared about foreign *rikishi*. He was hotheaded, unpredictable, and indifferent to the traditions of a sport that's been part of Japanese national consciousness for as long as there's been a Japan.

This is something else you should register about sumo: It is very, very old. Not old like black-and-white movies; old like the mists of time. Sumo was already ancient in the mid-eighteenth century, when the current ranking system came into being. The artistry of the *banzuke*, the traditional ranking sheet, has given rise to an entire school of calligraphy. Outside the few seconds of furious action that make up a match, nothing in sumo is spontaneous; each gesture is prescribed, each moment decorously choreographed. Yet Asashoryu brawled with other wrestlers in the communal baths. He barked at referees. He pulled another wrestler's hair, a breach that made him the first *yokozuna* ever disqualified from a match. *Rikishi* are expected to wear kimonos and sandals in public; Asashoryu would show up in a business suit. He would show up drunk. He would accept his prize money with the wrong hand.

The six-hundred-pound Hawaiian *sumotori* Konishiki launched a rap career after retiring from the sport ("Built to last like the Energizer Bunny / Pushin' seven hundred, and still makin' money"); another Hawaiian, Akebono, the first foreign *yokozuna*, became a professional wrestler. That was bad enough. But Asashoryu flouted the dignity of the sumo association while still an active *rikishi*. He withdrew from a summer tour claiming an injury, then popped up on Mongolian TV playing in a charity soccer match. In 2007, a tabloid magazine reported that Asashoryu had paid his opponents ten thousand dollars per match to let him win one tournament. Asashoryu won a settlement against the magazine, but even that victory carried a whiff of scandal: He became the first *yokozuna* ever to appear in court. "Everyone talks about dignity," Asashoryu complained when he retired, "but when I went into the ring, I felt fierce like a devil." Once, after an especially contentious bout, he reportedly stormed off to the parking lot and attacked his adversary's car.

The problem, from the perspective of the traditionalists who control Japanese sumo, was that Asashoryu also won. He won relentlessly. He laid waste to the sport. Until Hakuho came along, he was, by an enormous margin, the best wrestler in the world. The sumo calendar revolves around six grand tournaments—*honbasho*—held every two months throughout the year. In 2004, Asashoryu won five of them, two with perfect 15–0 records. In 2005, he became the first wrestler to win all six *honbasho* in a single year. He would lift four-hundred-pound *rikishi* off their feet and hurl them to the clay. He would bludgeon them with hands toughened by hours spent striking the *teppo*, a wooden training shaft as thick as a telephone pole. He won his twenty-fifth tournament, then good for third on the all-time list, before his thirtieth birthday.

Hakuho began to make waves around the peak of Asashoryu's reign. Five years younger than his rival, Hakuho was temperamentally his opposite: solemn, silent, difficult to read. Asashoryu made sumo look wild and furious; Hakuho was fathomlessly calm. He had an instinct for angles and counterweights. How to slide an inch to the side at the least expected moment. How a fractional shift of his hips could annihilate his enemy's balance. In concept, winning a sumo bout is simple: either make your opponent step outside the ring or make him touch the ground with any part of his body besides the soles of his feet. When Hakuho won, how he'd done it was sometimes a mystery. The other wrestler would go staggering out of what looked like an even grapple. When Hakuho needed to, he could be overpowering. He didn't often need to.

The flaming circus of Asashoryu's career was good for TV ratings. But Hakuho offered a way forward for a scandal-riddled sport. He was a foreign *rikishi* with deep feeling for Japanese tradition, a figure who could unite the past and the future. At first, he lost to Asashoryu more than he won, but their contests always ran hot. In 2008, almost exactly a year after the Yokozuna Deliberation Council recommended Hakuho for promotion to the top rank, Asashoryu gave him an extra shove after hurling him down in a tournament. The two momentarily squared off. In the video, you can see the older man grinning and shaking his head while Hakuho glares at him with an air of outraged grace. Over time, Hakuho's fearsome technique and Asashoryu's endless struggles with injury and controversy turned the rivalry in the younger wrestler's favor. When Asashoryu retired unexpectedly in 2010, allegedly after breaking a man's nose outside a nightclub, Hakuho had won their last seven regulation matches and notched a 14–13 lifetime record against his formerly invincible adversary.

With no Asashoryu to contend with, Hakuho proceeded to go 15–0 in his next four tournaments. He began a period of dominance that not even Asashoryu could have matched. In 2010, he compiled the second-longest winning streak in sumo history, sixty-three straight wins, which tied a mark set in the 1780s. He has won, so far, a record ten tournaments without dropping a single match. At the start of 2014, Hakuho has twenty-seven championships, two more than Asashoryu's career total. The record for championships is thirty-two. It is considered a foregone conclusion that Hakuho will break it. He is in his prime, and since winning his first *basho* in May 2006, he has won more than half of all the grand tournaments held in Japan.

—

So this is where we are. It is time for Hakuho's first match of the *hatsu basho*, the first grand tournament of the year. *Rikishi* in sumo's top division wrestle once per day during the fifteen-day derby; whoever has the best record at the end of the final day wins the Emperor's Cup. Hakuho opens against Tochiozan, a Japanese *komusubi*—the fourth-highest rank, three tiers below *yokozuna*. Tochiozan is known for outmuscling his opponents by gripping their loincloth, the *mawashi*. The wrestlers squat at their marks. The referee stands between them in shining purple robes, holding his war fan up. The crowd calls Hakuho's name. Spectators roar as the fighters lunge for each other. Nothing Hakuho does looks difficult. He spins slightly out of the way as Tochiozan grabs, unsuccessfully, for his *mawashi*. Then he uses his rotation as a windup to smash the other wrestler in the chest. Tochiozan staggers back, and Hakuho presses the advantage—one shove, two, three, and now Tochiozan is over the barrier, the referee pointing his fan toward Hakuho's side to indicate victory. The match lasted four seconds.

He doesn't celebrate. He returns to his mark, bows to Tochiozan, and squats as the referee again points to him with the fan. Win or lose, sumo wrestlers are forbidden to betray emotion. That was the sin Asashoryu used to commit; he'd raise a fist after winning or snarl a happy snarl.

Hakuho is not so careless. There are many crimes a *sumo-tori* can commit. The worst is revealing too much.

2

Some Japanese stories end violently. Others never end at all, but only cut away, at the moment of extreme crisis, to a butterfly, or the wind, or the moon.

This is true of stories everywhere, of course: Their endings can be abrupt or oblique. But in Japan, where an awareness of evanescence is the traditional mode of aesthetics, it seems truer than in other places.

For instance: the concept of *mono no aware*, which means something like "a pleasing sadness at the transience of beautiful things." The literary scholar Motoori Norinaga described this idea in the mid-eighteenth century while discussing *The Tale of Genji*, the thousand-year-old novel at the center of the Japanese canon. *Genji*'s author, Murasaki Shikibu, left her work unfinished, perhaps deliberately. When the protagonist dies late in the book, his death is never mentioned directly; instead, it's marked by a blank chapter called "Vanished into the Clouds."

For instance: my second-favorite Japanese novel, *Snow Country*, by the twentieth-century writer Yasunari Kawabata. Its last pages chronicle a fire. A cocoon warehouse where a film has been playing burns down. We watch one of the characters fall from a fiery balcony. The protagonist runs toward her, but he trips in the crowd. As he's jostled, his head falls back, and he sees the Milky Way in the night sky. The book ends there, with no resolution. It's left to the reader to discover how the pieces fit together, why Kawabata thought he had said everything he needed to say. Why he decided not to give away more than this.

The first time you read a story like this, maybe, you feel cheated, because you read stories to find out what happens, not to be dismissed on the cusp of finding out. Later, however, you might find that the silence itself comes to mean something. You might realize, for example, that you had placed your emphasis on the wrong set of expectations. That the real ending lies in the manner of the story's turning away from itself. That the seeming evasion in fact conceals a finality, a sudden reordering of things.

For instance: In January I flew to Tokyo, to spend two weeks watching sumo wrestling. Tokyo, the city where my parents were married. My father was stationed there. I remember gazing up at their Japanese wedding certificate on the wall and wondering what the characters meant. Tokyo, the biggest city in the world, the biggest city in the history of the world, a galaxy reflected in its own glass. It was a fishing village four hundred years ago, and now: thirty-five million people, a human concourse so vast it can't be said to *end*, only to fade indeterminately around the edges. Thirty-five million, almost the population of California. Smells mauling you from doorways: stale beer, steaming broth, char-broiled eel. Intersections where a thousand people cross each time the light changes, under J-pop videos ten stories tall. Crowds of schoolgirls in blue blazers and plaid skirts. Boys with frosted tips and oversized headphones, camouflage jackets and cashmere scarves. Throngs of black-suited businessmen. Twelve hundred miles of railway, a thousand train stations, endless alleys, houses without addresses, streets without names. Immense, unnavigable, and yet: clean, safe, quiet, somehow weightless, a place whose order seems sustained (if you are not from there, as I was not from there) by the logic of a dream.

It's a dream city, Tokyo. At least it was for me. I was a tourist there, half-knowledgeable only about books and movies, clueless about real life, and I moved through the city with something like the blurred openness of sleep. The tunnel between subway stops might become a dance club, with a shaking floor and flashing lights; or the turnoff from a teeming street might lead to a deserted graveyard, soundless but for the clacking of *sotoba* sticks; or the window in the high tower might look out across the reason-defying extent of the city, windows and David Beckham billboards and aerial expressways floating lightly downward, toward the Ferris wheel on the edge of the sea. Nothing was amazing, nothing was startling; each seeming non sequitur was only another pivot in the dream.

All that winter I had been forgetful. Things kept slipping my mind: appointments, commitments, errands. My parents' phone number. Sometimes, and for minutes at a time, what city I was in. Have you ever opened a browser window and realized that in the second between clicking the icon and seeing your cursor flash in the address bar, you've lost all sense of what you opened it for? I felt that way looking out of real windows.

What was wrong with me? In fact nothing was wrong; I was merely in crisis. I was in crisis and I was evading it. I was in trouble and instead of confronting the trouble I was pulling the curtains closed on the part of my mind that wanted to name it out loud. To name anything out loud seemed unbearable to me that winter. To name anything out loud meant having to make choices, to be definite; I found it easier to trail off in the middle of any sentence that seemed likely to reach a point. Easier to stay within the margins of a safe semi-oblivion, around whose edges things kept erasing themselves.

I drifted through the city like a sleepwalker, with no sense of what I was doing or why. Professionally, I managed to keep up a facade of minimum competence. I met with photographers. I arrived on time for the first bell at the Kokugikan. I took notes. (I have: "arena French fry cartons made of yellow cardboard with picture of sumo wrestler printed on it." I have: "bottle openers attached to railings with string, so fans can open beer." I have: "seat cushions resting on elevated platforms, so fans can slide their shoes underneath.") One cold morning I stood in a narrow side street between a bike rack and a pile of garbage bags, spying on a sumo practice through windows steamed over from the heat of the bodies within. Occasionally a wrestler, sweat slick and naked but for his brown *mawashi*, would come out and stand in the doorway, to let the winter air wash over him.

I wandered through Ryogoku, the neighborhood of the Kokugikan, past run-down *chanko* joints where you could buy the high-calorie protein stew that *rikishi* guzzle to gain weight. I followed wrestlers running errands: soft kimonos and wooden sandals, working their iPhone touch screens with round thumbs. Bopping their heads to whatever was playing in their earbuds. One afternoon I spied on a young *rikishi* who was sitting alone on a park bench. He was watching some tiny kids play soccer. He sat on the left side of the bench,

375 pounds if he was an ounce, and he was very careful not to let his kimono spread onto the right side, as if he were conscious of the imposition his bulk might represent. Every once in a while a mother would approach and give him her child to hold, and he would shake the little baby, very gently.

Most of the time, though, I was lost in Tokyo, and if I wound up anywhere I was supposed to be, it felt like a fortuitous accident. The slight but critical unfocus I had experienced all winter latched onto the city and found a home in it, like one of the silent water buses—glass beetles from a science-fiction film—that glide up the Sumida River.

Part of this had to do with another Japanese story, one I found myself increasingly preoccupied by, even though it had nothing to do with the wrestling culture I'd come to Japan to observe. This story fit into mine—or maybe the reverse—like the nesting sumo dolls I saw one afternoon in a *chanko*-shop window, the smaller fighters enclosed in the larger, tortoises in a strange shell. The story was a distraction. But unlike almost everything else during those weeks, I couldn't get it out of my mind.

———

On the flight to Tokyo, I brought a novel by Yukio Mishima. *Runaway Horses*, published in 1969, is the second book in his *Sea of Fertility* tetralogy, which was the last work he completed before his spectacular suicide in 1970. What happened was that he sat down on the floor and ran a dagger through his abdomen, spilling twenty inches of intestine in front of the general whom he had kidnapped, bound, and gagged. He had taken the general hostage in the general's own office at the headquarters of the Japan Self-Defense Forces. He had done so in a failed attempt to overthrow the government of Japan. If you tour the building today, you can see the gouges his sword left in the doorframe when he fought off the general's aides.

Mishima was a contradiction. Handsome, rich, a perennial contender for the Nobel Prize, he was at forty-five a national icon, one of the most famous men in the country. He was also possessed by an increasingly charismatic and death-obsessed vision of Japanese culture. After its defeat in World War II, Japan had turned away from martial values, accepting severe limits on its military; Mishima not only rejected these changes but found them impossible to bear. As a child, he had been sickly and sheltered. Now he worshiped samurai and scorned the idea of peace. He fantasized about dying for the emperor, dying violently: He posed for a photographer as the martyred Saint Sebastian, his arms bound to a tree, arrows protruding from his sides.

In 1968, appalled by the scale of left-wing protests in Tokyo, Mishima founded his own private army, the Tatenokai. He advertised for soldiers in right-wing student newspapers. He then fell in love with the officer he recruited to be his second-in-command, a young man called Masakatsu Morita. He began to imagine a coup attempt that would double as a kind of erotic transfiguration, an all-consuming climax of the sort that sometimes falls at the end of kabuki melodramas.

And so in 1970 Mishima made an appointment to visit the headquarters of the Self-Defense Forces. He went accompanied by four young Tatenokai officers, including Morita. He wore his brown Tatenokai uniform. His sword, a seventeenth-century weapon forged by the Seki no Magoroku line of swordsmiths, was in a scabbard on his belt. An orange tassel hung from the hilt. When the general asked to see the blade, the writer requested a handkerchief to clean it. This was the signal for the four Tatenokai officers to seize the general and barricade the door.

Mishima stepped onto the general's balcony and delivered a fiery speech to the thousand soldiers below. He urged the members of the SDF to take their place as a true national army, as warriors devoted to the emperor—a move that, had it succeeded, would have shattered the social structure of postwar Japan. The soldiers jeered him. There is broad consensus among scholars that Mishima never expected the coup to succeed, that his only aim was to die in dramatic fashion. But he had planned to speak for half an hour, and he gave up after seven minutes. "I don't think they even heard me," he said as he climbed in through the window. Back in the general's office, he unbuttoned his uniform jacket. The young officers could hear helicopters circling outside, police sirens wailing. Mishima sat down. He screamed. Then he drove the dagger with both hands into his stomach.

None of the Tatenokai officers in the room with Mishima were older than twenty-five. On the way to his house that morning, they had stopped to wash their car. Later, on the drive to SDF headquarters, Mishima had joked about the music that might play in a *yakuza* movie at that moment. He began to sing a song from the gangster flick *A Lion Amid Peonies*; the younger men tentatively joined in. Now Mishima lay bleeding on the floor. The young men were suddenly in charge of the situation.

"Please," Mishima gasped, "do not leave me in agony too long." He was speaking to his lover, Morita, the student leader of the Tatenokai, whose role in the ritual was to cut off Mishima's head. In a formal seppuku, the *kaishakunin* decapitates the dying man, sparing him the prolonged anguish of death by evisceration. Morita hacked at Mishima's neck but missed, slicing into his shoulder. He tried again and left a wound across his back. A third stroke cut into the neck, but not deeply enough. Finally another Tatenokai officer, a law student named Hiroyasu Koga, took the sword from Morita—the writer's sword, the sword with the orange tassel—and beheaded Mishima in one blow.

Morita, as planned, then knelt and tried to commit seppuku. He couldn't do it. At his signal, Koga beheaded him, too.

In the confusion afterward, as Koga and the other officers surrendered, as reporters struggled to piece together the sequence of events, Mishima's sword was taken into custody by police. Some time later, it went missing.

I thought about Hiroyasu Koga. What had it been like, I wondered, to have followed Mishima into that place and then, unexpectedly, been called on to end his life? To have lived the rest of his own life with that memory? To have drifted out of the center of the story, drifted into obscurity, carrying those moments with him? Koga, too, had been prepared to commit seppuku—all the young men had— but Mishima ordered them to live and explain his actions to the world. At the trial, where he was sentenced to four years in prison for (among other things) "murder by agreement," Koga said that to live as a Japanese is to live the history of Japan. What a history he must have conceived, I thought, to have said that, having done what he had.

On my third day in Tokyo I discovered that he was alive.

3

Watch the slow, sad figure of the *yobidashi* with his broom, endlessly sweeping the edges of the ring. For the long minutes between bouts, while the wrestlers move through their preparations, this slight man circles gravely and patiently, smoothing sand, erasing footprints. No mark can be allowed beyond the line at the start of a bout, because the judges must be able to tell, from a glance, whether a toe has landed outside the *dohyo*, whether a heel has slipped.

The wrestlers face off at their marks, not once but twice, three times, squatting and flexing, glaring intimidation at each other. Then they break and walk to their corners, where they scoop salt out of a bowl and dash it across the clay—another Shinto purification ritual. The *yobidashi* sweeps the salt, mixing it into the sand. Tall silk banners, representing sponsors' bonus prizes—extra money reserved for the winner of the bout—are carried around the ring on poles. The *yobidashi* sweeps around the banners. The wrestlers slap their bellies, slap their thighs, signaling massiveness to their enemies. The spectators, old men in tan jackets, young families, groups of slouching school friends, chat lightly, snap pictures, reach out to receive bags of snacks from the tea-shop waiters who wander through the aisles. At the center of the ring, the referee poses and flits his fan, a luminary in silks; the hilt of his knife, which he wears as a reminder of the days when one wrong decision meant his immediate seppuku, peeks out from the sash at his waist. Through all this, the *yobidashi* sweeps.

Then the atmosphere changes. The crowd grows quiet. The *rikishi* toss one last handful of salt and stamp back to their marks, taut bulk shining. The referee's fan hangs in the air between them. And in the last split second before the combatants launch at each other, the *yobidashi*, who has never changed his pace, who has never at any point moved without perfect deliberation and slow, sad care, lifts his broom and steps down from the *dohyo*.

And here is something else you should register about sumo: how intensely hierarchical it is. It is not only the *rikishi* who are ranked. Referees are ranked, too. So are *yobidashi*.

Hakuho glides through his first five matches. On day 2, he lets a diminutive root vegetable named toyonoshima— five feet six inches tall and maybe five eight from rump to navel—push him almost to the edge of the ring, only then, when Toyonoshima lurches forward with what looks like the winning shove, Hakuho isn't there; Toyonoshima does an arms-flailing slapstick belly flop over the line. On day 3, Hakuho gets a grip on the *mawashi* of Okinoumi, a wrestler known for his movie-star looks. Okinoumi outweighs Hakuho by twenty pounds, but the *yokozuna* lifts him half off the clay and guides him out of the ring; it's like watching someone move an end table. On day 4, against Chiyotairyu, a wrestler whose leg he once snapped in a match, Hakuho slams his adversary with the first charge, then skips aside; Chiyotairyu drops; the bout lasts one second. On day 5, he grapples with Ikioi, a physically strong wrestler known for controlling his opponent's *mawashi*. Hakuho ducks out of Ikioi's grasp, plants a hand on the back of his neck, and thrusts him to the floor. It takes a sumo novice perhaps ten seconds of match action to see that among the top-class *rikishi*, Hakuho occupies a category of his own. What the others are doing in the ring is fighting. Hakuho is composing little poems of battle.

There is a feeling of trepidation in the stadium over these first five days, because the Yokozuna Deliberation Council has come in person to observe Kisenosato, a wrestler of the second rank, *ozeki*, who is being considered for promotion to *yokozuna*. This is a rare event. Unlike a *sumotori* of any other rank, a *yokozuna* can never be demoted, only pressured to retire, so the council must make its recommendation with great care. It has fifteen members, all sumo outsiders, professors and playwrights, dark-suited dignitaries from various backgrounds. For five days they tilt their heads back and scrutinize the action. Their lips are shriveled, their gazes cold. The crowd is anxious because Kisenosato is Japanese, his country's best hope for a native-born *yokozuna*, and he has already failed in one promotion attempt. The council has recently announced that if Kisenosato wins thirteen matches here, he could be promoted even if he does not win the tournament. In fact, Kisenosato has never won a tournament, and the number of *yokozuna* of whom that could be said at the time of their promotion is small.

The hope of Japan is sour-faced and prim, a six-foot-two, 344-pound maiden aunt in a crimson loincloth. His stomach protrudes inflexibly straight in front of him; his soft breasts hang to either side. When he enters the *dohyo*, his posture is erect. When he swings his arms before the fight, he does so with a strange, balletic slowness. On the first day, with the council looking on, he wrestles Toyonoshima, the root vegetable. The crowd is afraid because Kisenosato is thought to be weak under pressure. The smack as the fighters' bellies collide is kettledrum-like. Toyonoshima drives his stubby legs into the clay, trying to force Kisenosato backward. Kisenosato gets a right-handed grip on Toyonoshima's *mawashi*, but he fails to lift Toyonoshima, his hand slips off, and his fallback attempt to throw his opponent also fails. Now he is in trouble. Toyonoshima is a little locomotive, churning forward. The wrestlers' guts grind together. Muscles leap in their thighs. With a huge effort, Kisenosato grunts his way back to the center of the *dohyo*. Toyonoshima twists his torso hard to divert the larger man's momentum, and the throw works; Kisenosato's knee folds, and he tumbles over onto his back, then rolls over the edge of the clay platform and into the photographers' trench. He rests on his hands and knees, defeated, surrounded by flashbulbs.

On the fifth day, Kisenosato goes over the edge again, this time battered out by the frenzied shoves of Aoiyama, a gigantic Bulgarian. The frowns of the Yokozuna Deliberation Council go right to the pit of your stomach. There is talk later that Kisenosato has suffered a toe injury. Regardless, he will lose more than he wins at the *hatsu basho*, finishing 7–8, falling to Hakuho on day 13, and there will be, for now, no Japanese *yokozuna* in the sport that most embodies the history of Japan.

———

I thought about Hiroyasu Koga.

The drummer in the tower outside the Kokugikan started pounding his *taiko* at eight o'clock each morning of the grand tournament, but the elite wrestlers, like most of the crowd, didn't arrive till late afternoon, when the *makuuchi* division made its formal ring entrance. For a day or two

I enjoyed watching the skinny teenagers and mid-level hopefuls who wrestled first. But if I spent all day in the stadium, I started to feel as if the wrestlers were slamming together in my brain rather than on the *dohyo*.

So I wandered, lost, around Tokyo. I found the shrine of Nomi no Sukune, the legendary father of sumo, who (if he lived at all) died two thousand years ago. I thought I should look for the past, for the origins of sumo, so early one morning I rode a bullet train to Kyoto. I climbed the stone path of the Fushimi Inari shrine, up the mountain under ten thousand blazing orange gates. I visited the Temple of the Golden Pavilion, rebuilt in 1955 after a mad monk burned it to the ground (Mishima wrote a novel about this). I visited the Temple of the Silver Pavilion, weirder and more mysterious because it is not actually covered in silver but was only intended to be. I spent a hundred yen on a vending-machine fortune that told me to be "patient with time."

As of 2005, Wikipedia told me, Koga was a practicing Shinto priest on Shikoku, the smallest of Japan's main islands. I pictured him in white robes, standing in a cemetery behind a dark gate.

Back in Tokyo, I thought the city was a river, the urban element somehow changed to liquid form. War, earthquakes, fire, and human ingenuity have annihilated it over and over again, for centuries; the city never stops building because it never stops rebuilding. Change comes like a crash, like a wave, the crowd parting and then re-forming around whatever new reality has fallen from the sky. The way you remember things in a dream is not precisely like remembering, yet anything you've experienced can come back to you in a dream. Under the shoguns, sumo wrestlers often appeared in ukiyo-e—"pictures of the floating world"—woodblock prints from the pleasure districts whose other great subjects were courtesans and kabuki actors, musicians and demons and ghosts. I went to an ukiyo-e exhibit and noted the wrestlers intermixed among the geisha, among the snarling samurai. Their bellies were rendered with one or two curved brushstrokes.

And I thought about Koga. I'm not sure why. I didn't know how I'd find him. I didn't know how I'd speak to him. But I priced tickets to Shikoku. I looked at the sumo schedule to figure out when I could get away. To be honest, Mishima's suicide had always struck me as absurd—in bad taste, at the very least. But I thought: *It is a small island. If I start from the train station, I can walk to the shrine, and I will find him there.*

Then I looked at a map of Shikoku. "The smallest of Japan's main islands" covers seventy-three hundred square miles, is home to 4.1 million people, and contains dozens of Shinto shrines. I gave up.

And yet whenever I stepped onto a subway train, whenever I rode an escalator up into the light, the idea came back, and I thought, *If I can track down the shrine, I will find him there.* I tried to locate a directory of Shinto sites on Shikoku— but how to make contact with one, how to ask for him?

Hello, yes, are you familiar with this celebrated author? Wonderful. Now, did one of your priests by any chance decapitate him in the early 1970s using a four-hundred-year-old samurai sword that has since vanished?

It was an impossible question to imagine putting in English, much less Japanese. And I spoke no Japanese.

I pictured the look on the face of whomever I asked to be my interpreter.

One thing struck me, though: The only source for the "Shinto priest in 2005" line on Wikipedia was a *Sunday Times* article that mentioned Koga only in passing. Even that article was hard to find online. What if it was misinformation? Perhaps Koga was no longer in Shikoku. Perhaps he had never gone there at all. Perhaps he was a priest someplace else.

Finally I wrote an e-mail to my friend Alex, a college professor who studies Japanese literature and film. "WEIRD JAPAN QUESTION" was the subject line. I asked if he had any thoughts about how I could track down Mishima's *kaishakunin*. I hit Send. And I wandered through the city, waiting for an answer. I listened to jazz in blue doorways. I pulled my coat a little tighter. I watched the setting sun float in pale glass.

4

In the Kokugikan there are stories of ghosts, stories of sounds with no sources, invisible hands that seize you from behind. Security guards are reluctant to enter a certain hallway at night. A reporter from the *Asahi Shimbun* recalls being shoved in the back by something large and round, "like a volleyball," only to turn and find that "no one was there." A clerk is pulled from behind while using a urinal. The clatter of sumo practice comes from an empty dressing room. Somewhere under the stadium, it is said, or at least somewhere near it, lies a mass grave containing victims of the great fire of 1657, which razed two-thirds of Tokyo. A hundred thousand died. The shogun built a temple to commemorate the dead; the temple became the site of sumo matches whose popularity led to the construction of the first national arena in 1909.

Hakuho is frictionless, devastating. He wins his next eight matches. On day 13, he wrestles Kisenosato, the Japanese *rikishi* who has flubbed his chance to be promoted to *yokozuna* and is fighting only for pride. The match is furious, Hakuho thrusting his open hand repeatedly into Kisenosato's neck; neither man can get a grip on the other's *mawashi*, so they simply bash each other, tactically berserk. They release little violent nasal exhalations, which sound like a spray bottle's trigger being squeezed. Finally, with his foot braced on the edge of the rice-bale circle, Kisenosato twists to throw Hakuho and fails. The *yokozuna* loses his balance and lurches forward but Kisenosato stumbles backward in the same movement. They fall together. Kisenosato's foot touches out of bounds a fraction of a second before Hakuho's hand; Hakuho wins. The *yobidashi* sweeps up the marks.

On day 14, Hakuho wrestles Kotoshogiku, an *ozeki* from Fukuoka who specializes in bodying his opponents with his torso. Kotoshogiku seems to have grappled Hakuho to a standstill. The two men are bent at the hips, clinging to each other in the middle of the *dohyo*, counterpoised in a massive stalemate. Then Hakuho slaps his left hand against Kotoshogiku's knee. Kotoshogiku crumples. The move is so unexpected—no one saw the opening except Hakuho, no one could have anticipated the reaction except Hakuho—that it flummoxes expert analysis. Hakuho shows no emotion.

On the second-to-last day of the tournament he is 14–0 and one win away from another perfect championship.

His body is strange, Hakuho's. It's smooth, almost un-formed, neither muscled like a boxer's nor bloated like many *rikishi*'s. Gagamaru, the Georgian wrestler who is currently the largest man in top-division sumo—440 pounds and a little over six feet tall—looks like a canyon seen from the air, all crevasses and folds. Hakuho, by contrast, is a single large stone, an owl quickly sketched by Miyazaki. His face is vague. Once in a while he will glance to one side with what looks like critical intelligence. Then he blurs again. The sources of his strength, whether physical or psychological, are almost totally hidden from view.

Another Mongolian, the *ozeki* Kakuryu, has fought his way to a 13–1 record, making him the only *rikishi* with a chance to tie Hakuho and force a play-off. Kakuryu is the son of a university professor who, unlike Hakuho's father, had no background in Mongolian wrestling. With the cham-pionship at stake, Hakuho is scheduled to face him on the tournament's final day.

———

"Re: WEIRD JAPAN QUESTION" dinged into my inbox in the middle of the night. "Sounds like a cool piece," Alex wrote. He had looked into the Koga question, and as far as he could tell, Shikoku was a red herring. Koga had never lived there. Nor was he a Shinto priest. He had indeed joined a religious group, but it was Seicho-no-Ie, "the House of Growth," a spiritual movement founded in the 1930s with the aim of fusing Christianity with Buddhism and Shintoism.

After prison, Koga became the head of its branch in Hokkaido, the snowy island in northern Japan where he had been born and raised. He married the daughter of the group's leader and changed his name to reflect his adoption into her family. His new name was Hiroyasu Arechi. "Arechi" was an unusual Japanese name, formed from characters that meant "wild land" or "barren ground." "If you want to get really literary," Alex told me, "Arechi" was also a Japanese translation of the title of "The Waste Land." But that was only a coincidence.

Seicho-no-Ie struck a chord, so I looked it up in one of the Mishima biographies. There it was: Mishima's grandmother had been a member. When Koga said at his trial that to live as a Japanese is to live the history of Japan, he was quoting one of the group's teachings.

Then Alex sent me a link that made me cover my mouth with my hand. The link led to a streaming video from the website of an apartment complex in the city of Kumamoto, on the southern island of Kyushu. In the video, a sixty-five-year-old man named Hiroyasu Arechi answers questions about being a new resident of the complex. He mentions at the beginning that he is from Hokkaido. He wears a black V-neck sweater over a red-and-white gingham sport shirt. His features match those of the young Koga in a photograph I'd seen, in which he stood posed with his fellow Tateno-kai conspirators, in their absurd fake-military uniforms. It seemed that Koga/Arechi had retired in 2012 and moved from Hokkaido to the other end of Japan.

The older man in the video has warm, appraising eyes. As he speaks, we see a bit of his apartment in the background. Flowers hanging on a light-flooded balcony. A cream-colored curtain, tied back. An inset picture on the website shows a console table lined with framed photographs of children and grandchildren. A couple holding hands in front of a landscape. Young people at a wedding. Someone in a parka, smiling, surrounded by snow.

He does not mention decapitation, or suicide, or Mishima. He says that the bus is very convenient to the building. The sales representatives are compassionate and polite. The park nearby is a good place to take walks. There is a MaxValu store across the street, open twenty-four hours, a handy place to shop. There is a roof garden. He has a balcony. There are beautiful views at night.

———

At the Kabuki-za Theater, there were pictures on the curtains. Herons in a stream. Mount Fuji. A hummingbird breaking out of a tangle of cherry blossoms. The curtains kept changing, and each time they changed their reflected light tinted the auditorium a different shade. Tiny old women in surgical masks changed colors faintly with the curtains; packs of theater kids in leather jackets and fishnet tights turned from gold to green to violet. An old man (blue, then pink) slept in his seat with both hands balanced on his cane. The kabuki play I had come to see was about sumo, or involved sumo, I was not entirely sure. The English-language audio guide I had rented for seven hundred yen left certain details indistinct, probably by necessity. The play's story was fantastically complex and was itself only a tiny peripheral fragment of a larger story, a legend about two brothers seeking revenge for the murder of their father. The plot spanned decades and flowed inexorably from an equally long backstory. The story when the curtain opened was simple, though. It was a story about love.

A beautiful young woman was adored by two men. She herself loved the handsome youth with the impossibly sad white face, but the burly cross-eyed villain with the orange-red face was determined to win her hand. The villain (I learned from the voice in my ear) had never lost a sumo-wrestling match. So the youth with the sad white face and the villain with the orange-red face wrestled to decide whom the woman would marry. They danced this, spinning slowly and not quite touching their hands. At last the youth with the sad white face won the match. But the cross-eyed villain explained in an evil aside to the audience that he would yet betray the lovers. Spotting a pair of mandarin ducks in the lake, he threw his dagger and killed the male. A little wooden duck turned upside down, like a prop in a parking-lot carnival. The villain told the audience that if he could trick the youth into drinking the duck's blood, the youth would go mad. And he did so.

But the mandarin duck is a symbol of marriage, of fidelity, and now, in some magical way, the two young lovers began to swirl. They swirled and became the ducks. They became, by magic, the souls of the ducks. The guide did not have to explain this. They took to the air on bright wings. They had become transcendent, timeless. On the same ground where the sumo match was fought, the duck-souls attacked the villain. They danced this, darting and bending their backs. The ducks drove the cross-eyed villain to the ground, making him even more cross-eyed. Then the lovers' costumes turned inside out, revealing brilliant plumage, plumage like an illustration in a children's book, feathers as vivid as fire. Then they all froze in place and the curtain dropped.

5

Yukio Mishima's novel *Runaway Horses* tells, in part, the story of a samurai rebellion. In 1868, the reign of the shoguns ended and power reverted back to the emperor of Japan, or (because nothing is ever as simple as the official story) to a group of elites acting in his name. One of the consequences of this event, which is called the Meiji Restoration, was that the large samurai class that had governed Japan for hundreds of years was stripped of its power and dissolved. Imperial edicts compelled members of the former warrior caste to stop styling their hair in topknots, to stop carrying swords.

In 1876, a group of two hundred ex-samurai called the League of the Divine Wind launched a surprise nighttime attack on Kumamoto Castle. The league's aim was to eradicate all traces of Westernization and return Japan to its feudal past. As the barracks burned, they drove back the conscript soldiers of the Imperial Army, wounding hundreds and killing the wounded. Fires broke out everywhere. "Even his garments, drenched in enemy blood, glowed crimson in the flames," Mishima writes of one samurai. At last the imperial soldiers regrouped and reached their guns and ammunition. The league had chosen to fight with swords alone. The samurai were slaughtered. The leader of the attack, gravely wounded, called on a follower to cut off his head. Most of the survivors committed seppuku.

Old buildings in Japan are seldom really old. A country that builds with wood instead of stone runs the constant risk of losing its monuments to fire. Ancient shrines are copies of ancient shrines. The Imperial Palace in Kyoto has been rebuilt eight times, and its current layout would be unfamiliar to any emperor who had lived there. The main keep of Kumamoto Castle, which burned to the ground during another samurai uprising, in 1877, was reconstructed from concrete in 1960.

His building is there. Koga's, I mean. In Kumamoto, just down the hill from the castle. I found him a few hundred yards from the scene of the battle in the book that made me think of him in the first place.

To get to Kumamoto from Tokyo you ride the Shinkansen train south to Kyushu, changing in Osaka. The trip takes six hours. The train passes just below Mount Fuji at the start of the journey and stops near the end at Hiroshima, where the windows look out on the baseball stadium. As you hurtle south, you pass into a misty country. Blue hills lean in the mist. If it's raining when you get out at Kumamoto Station, you can buy a clear plastic umbrella for 350 yen from a bucket in the station shop. If you have time and don't mind getting wet, you can walk into town along the river, the Shirakawa, which lies in a wide, ugly basin.

The castle is on a hill in the center of the city. There is a tiny parking lot at the base of the hill with a vending machine that sells hot coffee. The castle's fortifications merge with the hillside just behind the parking lot, a tortoiseshell of large, dark stones too steep to climb. Behind the castle keep, green mountains disappear into the clouds.

His building is down the hill. A five-minute walk, if that.

Come around the slope and you will see the complex, a series of squat, identical gray blocks, each around eleven stories tall. Cars speed by on a busy street. A security guard in a gray jacket and white motorcycle helmet stands beside the gate, near some orange traffic cones.

There is a bus stop very convenient to the building. There is a MaxValu just across the street.

———

So this is where I am. I am standing in the parking lot of the MaxValu. I'm thinking about endurance. The day is drizzly and cool. The cars that turn in to the lot are blunt, compact hatchbacks, little modern microvans in gold and turquoise and white. They are shaped like sumo wrestlers, I think, and I think, not for the first time, that sumo is essentially a sport of refusing to die, refusing to pass into history, refusing to accept the insolidity of the dream. It was a street entertainment, really, until the early twentieth century. Then the samurai tradition burned down and had to be rebuilt.

And soon I will think about this while I watch Hakuho wrestle Kakuryu on the TV in my hotel room, on what is supposed to be the last match of the last day of the tournament. Hakuho will miss his chance to seize Kakuryu's *mawashi* just as Kakuryu wins a two-handed grip on his. Kakuryu will leap forward with spasmodic sliding jumps, backing the *yokozuna* to the edge of the rice-bale circle, where Hakuho's knees and then his ankles will flex frantically, until he goes toppling, the greatest *sumotori* in the world, off the edge of the clay, twisting onto his stomach as he falls.

When he gets to his feet, Hakuho will offer no reaction. In the play-off match a few minutes later he will grapple

Kakuryu in the middle of the ring and then drop his hips and lift Kakuryu halfway off the sand and force him backward, and they will both fall out of the ring at the same moment, but Kakuryu's foot will touch first, giving Hakuho the Emperor's Cup and his twenty-eighth tournament championship. The *yobidashi* will sweep the marks away. Hakuho will smile slightly, not a smile that is meant to be read.

But that will happen later. Now I am leaning on a railing in the parking lot of the MaxValu, thinking about endurance at four o'clock in the afternoon. I am looking across a busy street at the apartment complex of the man who beheaded Yukio Mishima and then lived a whole life afterward, lived another forty years. Had children and hung flowers on his balcony. I think: He is in there. I think: It is time to decide what to do.

I get up and move toward the crosswalk. The wind is damp. It's January, so I don't see any butterflies. It is a cloudy day, so I do not see the moon.

Lost Highway

Life could be a dream.
—The Chords, "Sh-Boom"

From the air, I did the inevitable thing, the thing anyone who flies into Roswell, New Mexico, must do: I imagined I was looking down from a flying saucer. The outline of the town had surely changed, but the pale gray desert where it's set would have looked more or less the same on July 4, 1947, the approximate date when, depending on whom you believe, either a military surveillance balloon listening for Soviet atomic activity or a spacecraft of extraplanetary origin went down in a violent storm, fireballing to the ground at a ranch thirty miles north of the city. Depending, again, on which source you trust, this mysterious silvery object either did or did not leave a five-hundred-foot scar in its wake, and the resulting twisted wreckage either did or did not contain a number of alien corpses, the number itself being intensely disputed, which might or might not have been taken to the nearby Roswell Army Air Field, flown to

Washington, D.C., to be viewed by General Dwight D. Ei-
senhower, and/or transported, along with the remains of the
craft and its potentially recoverable advanced extraplanetary technology, to the secret military installation known as
Area 51, in Nevada, where they were autopsied, or not,
and/or redeployed in military applications whose potential
significance and near-certain danger to humanity absolutely
boggle the mind, or else are total bunk.

This, then, was the alien's-eye view. A small, whitish
cluster—the town—resting on the gray seafloor of the desert,
a short distance to the west of the Pecos River. Framed in
the airplane window, the image looked timeless, the old
American nowhere in its parcel of dust. Easy to imagine
that long-ago Fourth of July. Easy to imagine that you, too,
were sailing down from the dark side of the moon.

Just then the spider that lives in my brain twanged a
thread, and I remembered a theory I'd read somewhere, in-
sane but unforgettable, which held that the Roswell aliens
weren't extraterrestrials at all but surgically altered human
children. After World War II, the story went, Stalin tracked
down Josef Mengele, the Nazi doctor-sadist infamous for his
experiments on live human subjects at Auschwitz. This
would have been in 1946 or so, when Mengele was still living in hiding in Germany. Stalin offered Mengele asylum
in the Soviet Union if he'd engineer a crew of mutant child-
pilots, eyes hideously enlarged, adult crania grafted onto
their skulls. The idea was that they'd land an aircraft in the
United States, where they'd be mistaken for Martians, sow-
ing panic. Evidently, Stalin had been boning up on his Orson
Welles. But the vessel crashed near Roswell, Stalin went

back on his promise, and Mengele fled ahead of Nazi hunters to South America, where he died in 1979, at the age of
sixty-seven, while swimming.

We touched down. Roswell's civilian airport occupies
the same spot as the former military airfield. Flying into
the city, you land at the very spot where the alien bodies
were taken, if there were bodies, if the bodies were moved.
Now, however, the only space creatures you see are the
tourist-friendly Little Green Men that peep out from every
signboard, every folded sweatshirt, every postcard on the
rack. There's one on the welcome banner over the terminal.
He's holding up, with his green cartoon hand, a Native
American sun symbol, which sheds its beams onto the town
seal; the town seal is itself flying saucer shaped.

That's how central the UFO crash is to the identity of
this place. It's the radioactive core of the wildest conspiracy
theory in American history; in Roswell, they put it on the
government letterhead.

———

At the rental counter, the agent looked me up.

"And you're dropping off in . . . oh, hon, lucky you. Las
Vegas!"

"Well, sort of," I said. "I'm dropping the car off in Vegas,
but first I'm driving to Area 51."

I figured people must say this sort of thing all the time in
Roswell—*oh, sure, just casually road-tripping out to America's
most sinister top secret black site*—but she looked taken aback.
"Area 51," she said, "that's . . ."

"Yes," I said.

"You know it's not . . ."

"It's a thousand miles away," I said. "That's why I'm dropping the car off in Vegas."

"Okay, because sometimes people come here and they think—you know—they think it's right next to Roswell, because they hear about them together and whatnot. But Roswell, we're like a tourist attraction, and that's . . ."

"I know," I said.

"That's not," she finished. She handed back my ID. Then she sighed, as if committing herself to doing what little she could for me, in my foolishness. "Well, we've got you in a Nissan Sentra."

"I'm driving on Route 66," I told her. "Not the whole way, because you can't, but as much as I can."

"Okay," she said. "Well! We've got you in a Nissan Sentra."

I declined insurance. She slid over the gargantuan clove of key fobs.

"Hon, before you go. Can I ask . . . do you mind if I ask why you're doing that?"

———

An hour or so later I was driving through downtown Roswell when, to my surprise, I found Jesus Christ.

He was walking down Main Street, trailed by a small group of disciples. The disciples wore long robes and biblical head scarves. They were holding up signs. JESUS LOVES YOU, the signs said. JESUS DIED FOR YOU. JESUS SAVES. They were walking south, toward the UFO Museum, and walking slowly, because Jesus was stooped under the weight of the true cross, which he carried over one shoulder,

Passion-style. One of the disciples, a woman in her late twenties, didn't have robes. She was wearing a sweat suit.

Slowly I remembered that today was the day before Easter.

It was twilight. There were alien eyes on the frosted glass orbs of the streetlamps. The street was lined with floating alien heads. Everywhere you looked there were inflatable aliens, alien window displays, alien marquees. Alien bumper stickers: I WANT TO BELIEVE on an RV docked across three parking spaces. Alien murals: wasp-waisted aliens flourishing matador capes on the wall outside the Mexican restaurant.

As I rolled by in the Sentra I saw that Jesus was wearing a crown of thorns. Red blood stained his white garment, though not, as far as I could make out, his gray athletic sneakers. The procession reached an intersection as I passed. In the rearview mirror, I watched Jesus look both ways before crossing the street.

———

Late that night, I lay on my bed at the Holiday Inn, sipping Diet Coke with ice from the machine. The TV was on mute, tuned to some news channel: Hillary Clinton's face looked out over ominous chyrons. Weeks before, in March, the news had broken about her private e-mail server, and the shows were roiling with conspiracy theories, dark innuendos about the Benghazi attack, hints of secret corruption at the invisible heart of things. Donald Trump, who'd risen to new heights of prominence peddling what half the country saw as patriotic concern about Barack Obama's birth certificate, had just launched a presidential exploratory committee. The air seethed with suspicion. What passed for the national discourse had become a sealed maze of internal data points. Everything tended toward a final conclusion that was somehow both terrifying and indefinite, unspeakable— the total minus, the apocalyptic blank.

That night I wasn't paying much attention. I'd made a playlist for the trip, a days-long Spotify mix of 1950s singles, and when I got sick of watching the news on mute I'd put on headphones and listen to the Platters or the Flamingos with my eyes closed, blue swerve into an alternate dimension.

Only you can make this world seem right,
Only you can make the darkness bright.

Those had been the years, that first weird decade after the war, when the UFO narrative was codified in America. Not that UFOs were exclusively American; they were a transnational concern, even a transhistorical one if you tilted your perspective the right way. (The pyramids, heard of them?) The so-called foo fighters, mysterious balls of darting-eye light that appeared to pilots on both sides during World War II, belonged to Europe. In 1954, a town in France, Châteauneuf-du-Pape, had passed a law banning flying saucers, in the interest of protecting the grapes. But it was in this country that unexplained aerial lights were first widely correlated with the idea of extraterrestrial ships.

I fished my iPad out of my bag. On the plane, I'd been browsing through a book, a work of sensationalist mid-century journalism that played a role in charting the outlines of the narrative, pre–Close Encounters version. The book was called The Flying Saucers Are Real. Forgotten today outside hard-core UFO circles, but a mainstream bestseller in 1950. Its author, an ex-marine pilot and pulp fiction writer named Donald Keyhoe, had started with a series of articles for *True* magazine (*True: The Man's Magazine*), then expanded them into the book. I'd dug up a PDF online. Keyhoe's work is a fascinating tour through a bygone paranoia matrix. Its tone is hard-boiled, way more Smoking Man than Mulder; James M. Cain could have written it. We're in that early Cold War moment when something sour starts creeping into the mood of national triumph. The war is over, blue skies ahead, and yet already many people sense that something is wrong, something hard to explain or define, a bad secret fizzing under the atmosphere. Waiting for a myth to inhabit.

Keyhoe begins by collating data. A tower reports a flyover at an impossible rate of speed, by a craft it can't identify. A fighter pilot crashes while chasing a gigantic *something*—but surely the description he called in doesn't make sense? Once Keyhoe picks up the trail of what he suspects is a government cover-up, he shifts into flinty-eyed investigative mode. Just about every scene in *The Flying Saucers Are Real* depicts him marching into some scientist's lab or federal office, overcoat flapping at his ankles, and *listen here, buster*-ing whoever's inside. *I want the truth, see? The truth!* The New Age dimension of alien contact hadn't emerged yet, and neither had the idea of a government conspiracy whose depths made it functionally magical. What you have, instead, is the suppressed hysteria of a generation that had seen the atom split, had lived through the war's devastation, had seen humanity's idea of itself transfigured more than once, in a few short years, and in progressively more disturbing ways. By telling the story of the alien cover-up, Keyhoe is registering an early flutter of the needle in what became the slow collapse of democratic faith. But he's also preserving the fantasy that the truth is still attainable, that a strong man's moral outrage would be enough to tear down the lies and bring the people the facts. Nothing ever seems more naive, I thought, watching the faces flickering across the television, than the paranoia of the dead.

It's fascinating, from this temporal distance, that the hypothesis Keyhoe offers to explain the alien presence actually coincides with what's sociologically the likeliest reason for the atmospheric anxiety he detects. That is, he thinks the aliens are here because of the bomb. Because America has the bomb. The old order is a memory; what can come from the sky puts everyone at risk. Why *wouldn't* aliens show up?

I don't want to set the world on fire
I just want to start a flame in your heart.

———

At the UFO Museum, in downtown Roswell, a group of six-foot-tall animatronic aliens occupies the prime Instagram real estate at the center of the main hall, and a thing happens every few minutes where the flying saucer behind them starts blooping and spinning and flashing laserish lights, and a little space-fart of white steam escapes from the base of the saucer, and a sci-fi musical score slide-whistles cosmically, and the aliens start talking to the crowd. What they say is—I'm paraphrasing—"*bzzzzrrg bzzzzoom ppozz bzrg pzow.*" Imagine Donald Duck trying to mimic a dial-up modem; it's like that.

I wandered near a pair of startlingly beautiful bikers, a man and a woman in black leather jackets with diagonal zips. They wore eye black smeared across their cheeks, which made no practical sense to me, a man who had recently taken possession of a rented Nissan Sentra, but they were striking. Neither one possibly more than twenty-five. They looked like leather cultists from the future after the fall. Only the most aristocratic genes would endure in the cliff fortresses.

When the aliens' light show buzzed on, they both turned and made a face.

"Fuckin' Yodas," the male biker said, chuckling.

———

This isn't much remembered now, or much talked about, but during World War II there were POW camps throughout the United States, holding hundreds of thousands of prisoners. There'd been one outside Roswell. Five thousand German soldiers. Most captured from among Rommel's forces in North Africa. They were put to work on local ranches and farms—and try to picture that, if you can, thousands of troops from the Nazi Afrika Korps picking cotton in the New Mexico desert.

In 1943, a small detachment from this group, fifty or so men, was assigned to pave a section of the Spring River, which runs through town. They were told to line the sides of the channel with large stones. Working in secret, the prisoners managed to construct a mosaic, which they embedded in the riverbank. It's a crude but unmistakable depiction of the Iron Cross.

When the townspeople discovered what the soldiers had

done, they were furious. The second-most-recognizable symbol of the Wehrmacht right there in the middle of Roswell—unthinkable. They buried it under concrete. Over the years, though, the river washed the concrete away. Now the town had a dilemma. On the one hand, the mosaic was history, a remnant from a time that deserved to be remembered. On the other hand, Nazi symbolism, even of the ad hoc and vaguely pitiful sort that Roswell found on its riverbank, is tricky to memorialize. Do it wrong and you're inviting alt-right photo pilgrims in by the subreddit-load.

Roswell's solution was to build a park. The park is dedicated to the world's prisoners of war and soldiers missing in action. It's across the river from the Germans' mosaic, which you can see from a special viewing platform. There's a historic marker, telling the story of the POW camp. There's a piece of the Berlin Wall in a display case. There's a little basketball court, which looks out at the Iron Cross.

I stood on the platform and looked across the river. It was late morning. There was the cross, at the center of a ring of pale stones. It was hard to connect it to the things I was trying to connect it to. Whatever meaning it had once held, whatever concentration of hatred or nationalism or even defiance, had gone out of it. It was a shape on a riverbed. One more thing that hadn't disappeared.

———

Out of town now, driving through the desert, I found myself remembering Robert Goddard, the rocket scientist. Did you know he'd lived in Roswell? He did some of his important experiments there, the ones that paved the way for human spaceflight. Also for long-range missiles. He was there before the war, an intense, tubercular obsessive firing projectiles into the wasteland. Without him, there'd be no moon landing, no ICBMs, no Cold War as we know it. No rovers on Mars. Goddard thought we could use rockets to reach the far cosmos, spoke of sending messages to alien civilizations inscribed on metal plates. To me, the circularity felt eerie. This was where we'd started the trip to space, and it was where space, or the idea of space, came crashing back down to us.

———

It was dusk when I found Route 66. Or when I found the ruins of it. It's mostly ruins now because Route 66, probably the most important and certainly the most celebrated segment in the history of the American highway system, the road that stitched together Chicago and Los Angeles, making the southwestern desert traversable by car, a road that could plausibly be said to represent the final critical attainment of American westward expansion, the culmination of something that started with Lewis and Clark—Route 66 was decommissioned in 1985, a casualty of the modern interstate. From an infrastructural perspective, this was sensible. Overdue, even. A skinny, two-lane string wound around mountains and ridges and stretched along canyon rims, 66 was in some ways outmoded before it was even finished. It hadn't been fully paved until 1938, and please pause here to consider the lateness of that date—how, far into the twentieth century, well within the lifetimes of many living people, you could not drive across the Southwest without venturing onto gravel. Onto dirt. Stretches of 66 were so lethally twisty and hairpin crazed that drivers crossing, say, the Black Mountains in Arizona would hire locals to guide them, like explorers from earlier centuries.

The demise of Route 66, though, also meant the slow bleeding away of the roadside culture that flourished along its edges, a weird medley of mid-century tourist kitsch and car worship (the first fast food was here, the first McDonald's) and a very pure expression of the American genius for deranged carnivalesque. It was slow moving; that was the key. The roadside attractions were right on the side of the road. You just pulled over. There were rattle-snake farms and custard stands, sideshow tents, cases of dinosaur bones. You could see Jesse James's cave hideout and take your picture on the back of a giant jackrabbit. You could stop and tour Meteor Crater, where a meteorite nearly one mile across crashed in the desert fifty thousand years ago.

Visually, this was all bound together in Route 66's cosmic drive-in aesthetic, which is still instantly recognizable today. Maybe you caught *Cars*, for instance, the Pixar movie, which borrows major elements of both its plot and its look from the history of Route 66. Or a million indie flicks where a guy in a bowling shirt gets murdered, and they bury him under a cactus, and there's a motel across the road, and the lurid light from the motel sign keeps blinking on the one shoe they left aboveground. Seen a filling station with an icebox on one side, a chrome-plated handle on the icebox, a car with big fins under the over-hang, and in the background, purple desert? Seen the center line tick past in lonely headlights, cliffs in the distance, a monotony broken only by tumbleweeds? That's Route 66.

It was gone now, or mostly gone. But there were traces, stretches of the old road that were either incorporated into I-40 or accessible via detours, and those were what I wanted to see.

It's extraordinary. I mean, sure, in this day and age we live with our fingertips fused to an archive that holds everything that's ever happened, and one mistyped web search takes you to a streaming clip of the actual assassination of Julius Caesar. Still. Ruins are not so common in America that encountering one is ever a familiar experience. Even Native American ruins aren't exactly (for obvious reasons) around every corner. As for our late-breaking U.S. culture itself, you sometimes have the sense that we're rolling up the historical carpet behind us as we go, that when we finally vanish, we'll leave behind nothing but garbage dumps and videos whose codecs won't play.

"Ruins" may not be the right word, at least not for all of it. There are places along the way where you stand knee-deep in weeds on what used to be the concourse of a gas station, the burned-out retro-sci-fi sign above you slashed with whiskers of rust, nothing else in sight but foggy ridges and, in the far distance, one tiny, moving train: That is a ruin. Elsewhere, the old shrines are still at least semi-inhabited, still eking out some sort of existence. A giant jackrabbit, for instance, can still be ridden, and the curio shop next to it still visited, in Arizona. Across the blacktop lot, there's an ancient yellow billboard, famous in its day, that shows a black rabbit and the words HERE IT IS in giant red letters. Surrounding it now: miles of desert, of nothing.

Is that a ruin? No, obviously, because people work there, stop there; when I visited, I found a cash register on the counter and a Mustang parked outside. But somehow the lingering trace of human activity made it seem more lost, not less. The faintness of what was present made what was absent feel so vast.

I'd been streaming my playlist on the Sentra's speakers. As I pulled in to Albuquerque, "Sleep Walk," by Santo & Johnny, came on. The unnerving quaver of that steel guitar, which keeps bending back on itself, like a snake swimming. It sounds beautiful until you pay attention, and then it sounds unbearably sad and strange.

The sun was setting over Albuquerque. Cathedral-ceiling clouds. The light reflecting on the city was like disintegrating violet. Central Avenue here is one of the best-preserved stretches of urban Route 66, and there it was, the famous antique neon, the row of historic motels. The Crossroads. The Nob Hill Court. The Monterey, which advertises "luxury rooms" and "European hospitality" for nonsmokers. The Westward Ho!, whose sign is a neon cactus. The Premiere, whose sign is the word "motel" on blue and orange circles, each letter on its own circle, arranged top to bottom: MOTEL.

I checked into my room and went upstairs for a drink.

———

On the hotel roof, looking out at the nighttime city. Headlights glimmering between banks of motel neon. Sense of mountains somewhere out there, stars. I was drinking gin and lost in my own thoughts (was it too late, had I already ruined everything) and I remembered the question the rental-car clerk had put to me. The one who'd seemed so skeptical about my recent life choices, not that she'd been wrong.

Why was I going to Area 51? It wasn't as if you could show up and take a tour. Area 51 was no longer secret—that is, its existence wasn't, having been formally acknowledged by the CIA in 2013; before that, it was officially a non-place, occupied but unconfessed, somehow real but also not. But even after that formal admission, whatever went on there, alien related or otherwise, was hidden in top secret midnight. To find out, you'd need a level of security clearance it took security clearance even to know about.

And it wasn't as if the site itself was accessible. Geographically, Area 51 is part of the Nellis Air Force Base Complex, the New England state–sized military training and testing Xanadu in the desert northwest of Las Vegas. But it operates on its own, via protocols of impenetrable ghostliness. The Internet told of unmarked backcountry roads, of navigation via baleful-sounding landmarks ("the black mailbox"). Of unmarked white pickup trucks that sat on high hills, watching. The front gate, near the minuscule town of Rachel, Nevada, wasn't even a gate, I mean it didn't close, was what I'd heard—there was just a sign telling you to turn back in the middle of what was otherwise fathomless emptiness.

Your wisest course of action, the Internet felt, was to listen to the sign.

"Area 51" was probably not even Area 51's real name. We don't know where the term came from. It first shows up in a declassified CIA document from 1967, where three "Oxcart" planes—a code name for the Lockheed A-12 high-altitude reconnaissance aircraft—are said to be deploying "from

Area 51 to Kadena" for surveillance of North Vietnam. Beyond that, the name's origin disappears into a tangle of competing hypotheses. The base has been a locus for UFO sightings since the 1950s, when Project Aquatone, the U-2 spy plane program, started sending very high-altitude aircraft over the Nevada desert under conditions of extreme secrecy. For civilians on the ground, those were UFOs in the technical sense, unidentified objects that flew. But Area 51 only became mainstream famous in 1989, when a man named Bob Lazar gave an interview on Las Vegas TV.

Lazar claimed to have worked at the site, reverse engineering alien spacecraft. Said he'd encountered elements not on the periodic table. He talked about alien entanglements in human history going back ten thousand years. Lazar's claims were torn to shreds by critics; it turned out he'd possibly lied about his education (MIT) and background, and there were plenty of reasons to think he was making the whole thing up, but other details checked out. He knew things he shouldn't have known, and some of those claims could be verified. When the National Lab at Los Alamos said he'd never worked there, for instance, he produced a W-2 showing otherwise. So there was a controversy, which put Area 51 on the map and, in the same motion, took it off it.

I'd seen Lazar in person that winter, at the International UFO Congress near Scottsdale, where, after a show of reluctance, he'd agreed to give a Q&A. Before that he'd been in what he portrayed as a self-protective withdrawal from the UFO community, which he blamed for ruining his life. He'd been busted in 1990 for his involvement in a prostitution ring. Some people thought that discredited him. Others thought the opposite—that he'd been set up because he was telling the truth.

I thought he seemed weary more than anything. Weary from problems of his own making or because the government really had tried to ruin him, who knows. He'd slumped in his chair onstage, a hangdog guy with a thin face and a toothy '80s-nerd quality—the Bill Gates who lost.

Lazar didn't call the place where he said he'd worked "Area 51," though; he called it "S4." The CIA was known to use the term "Groom Lake," but that was merely the name of the nearby salt flats. People who worked at the facility were said to call it "Dreamland."

But none of those names told you anything. It was as if the jigsaw puzzle of the American West had had a piece pulled out, and the resulting blank space, a nowhere bounded within somewheres, became Area 51.

What overwhelms is not the meaninglessness of the universe but the coexistence of an apparent meaninglessness with the astonishing interconnectedness of everything.

The fascination Area 51 exerted, as the vanishing center of every rumored cover-up and labyrinthine conspiracy theory, was essentially the fascination of a vacancy.

———

I drove west, streaming oldies. Albuquerque toward Flagstaff. *I guess I'll never see the light, I get the blues most every night.* There are plateaus in central New Mexico that look like lavender shadows from a distance, like something in a Chinese ink painting. Then you get close and see the rusts and bronzes in the rock, reddish-brown blotches like liver

spots. *Guardian angels up above, take care of the one I love.*
I stopped at the mining museum in Grants, once known as
the uranium capital of the world, and rode the elevator down
to the mine floor. The atom bomb was created in New
Mexico in 1945, and then—but only afterward, in 1950—a
Navajo shepherd named Paddy Martinez discovered the
first of what would turn out to be massive concentrations of
uranium there. *Time goes by so slowly.* Across the street
from the museum stood one of the classic surviving Route
66 signs, an unlit wreck of green neon: Uranium Cafe.
And time can do so much.

That night a former chief of the Defense Intelligence
Agency, General Michael Flynn, was a featured guest on Fox
News, where he told Megyn Kelly that Hillary Clinton's
e-mails had "likely" been hacked by the Russians. "The
Russians, the Chinese . . . they're good at it," he said. Blue
light sinking into the hotel TV before I fell asleep.

———

Other absences suggested themselves. In a hippie diner, the
painting of a UFO over blue mountains stood angled on a
shelf next to a Navajo medicine bag and a painting of a Native American warrior. Native American imagery, mythology,
traditions, locations, have a way of popping up in UFO stories. Accounts of the Brown Mountain abductions in North
Carolina, for instance, often mention a great battle between
the Cherokee and the Catawba that happened there nine
hundred years ago. The November/December 2011 issue of
Atlantis Rising magazine includes a movingly preposterous
study, attributed to "Arlan Andrews, Sr., Sc.D., P.E.," of

possible extraterrestrial encounters in Cherokee mythology, which is full of scenes like this:

> The Cherokee hunting party may have indeed come upon alien creatures with reptilian heads (or with hard, head-covering helmets that could look similar to a tortoise's), dressed in pressurized suits of a shiny, reflective or radiant material that crinkled as the creatures moved or the wind blew.

There is a strong aesthetic appeal, for some people, in the idea that aliens and shamans open the same doors of consciousness, or that aliens are what's behind the doors the shamans open. Months earlier, at the UFO Congress, I'd listened to a self-described former Texas Ranger explain from the lectern that if you had "the blood of colonized peoples" in you, you were especially "attractive" to what he called "the alien." I think it had something to do with proteins? The speaker's name was Derrel, a big square-built guy in a black sport coat, Stetson, and bolo tie. Claimed proficiency in multiple martial arts. He showed us pictures of his pet Bengal tiger, Christina, then told us Christina had perished in a "tragic flood." Not the easiest analysis to follow. The point is that he thought Indians, along with "gypsies" and the Irish, shared some sympathetic vibration to which extraplanetary life-forms were unusually attuned. Variations on this idea were common in UFO talk.

On Route 66, too, Native American imagery was everywhere. There were genres and subgenres of it; in the old photos, it's haunting. Cabins in the shape of wigwams. Neon headdresses looming over motels. Arrowheads for sale. Tomahawk-brandishing "chiefs" on billboards for roadside "trading posts." Anything that could be used to sell a pack of cigarettes to a 1950s driver. Any form of cultural iconography that could be pumped full of local-color neon.

What was missing from these scenes? Correct: anything resembling actual Native American culture. Also anything resembling actual Native Americans.

That's less true in real life, of course, than in old photos. West of Seligman, Arizona, Route 66 passes through the Hualapai Indian reservation; there are casino hotels here and there along the way. Still, there's a feeling of erasure here that's different from what you find in, say, Massachusetts. This may be because the landscape itself holds such emptiness. There are fewer protective layers between you and American history. That is: You know that a history of invasion, displacement, and (let's use the word) genocide permeates almost every place you go in this country. But most of the time, you are encouraged toward distraction and repression by everything around you, all the noise and glitter of contemporary culture—here's Dunkin' Donuts; there's the Guggenheim Museum; is that corgi in a muumuu? Here, none of that operates. On Route 66, you are even subtly coaxed into thinking about the destruction of ancient cultures, of culture itself, by the general Ozymandias fading away of the Americana through which you're passing.

This started to affect the way I thought about the UFO phenomenon. I started to see it as less a problem of individual experience than one of cultural psychology. For a reference point here, think about the peculiar valence the word "alien" has in the Southwest—about what other group, besides extraplanetary visitors, it's often applied to. Notice anything sinister there? Is it so crazy to imagine the UFO narrative as a kind of disguised psychic reckoning with the guilt-terror of white xenophobia? The kind of thing that you—millions of you; of us—can't talk about, so you remake it as a myth? All those people, all those histories, erased; where do they go? What happens to your consciousness of them, when almost every feature of your lived reality tells you not to be conscious of them? Maybe, I thought, what happens is that you bring them back as dreams, as nightmares, surreal figures of punishment and transformation. As beings who come for you in the dark.

———

Which says nothing about what individual people experience.

———

I met a man who said owls forecast his destiny. Not in person—we spoke on the phone. People who've lived through what are called "high strange" paranormal events, including alien abduction, are often reluctant to get close to writers and reporters, whom they've learned to regard with wariness. Say you've experienced an abduction event; here's what will happen. First, the media will approach you with an outward show of understanding. Your amazing story! We want to treat it with sensitivity, with taste. Then, once you've signed the release forms, the media will paint you as a raving crackpot. Tell me, sir, were you probed?

Mike wasn't shy, though. He's a people person, a wilderness guide in the mountains, where he lives. Balding, with a warm smile and salt-and-pepper beard. He talks at the speed of thought, down a proliferating idea tree of tangents: He'll bring up Jung's theory of synchronicity and then describe his "mission in life" and then talk about "vocabulary words," as in "I don't have the right vocabulary word for what happened next."

There's a beauty to his stories, though, most of which are about how, when something truly inexplicable happens, owls tend to turn up around the edges of the event. You'll see a dozen of them on a telephone wire, and then, around the next corner, the spacecraft. Owls appear with unnerving frequency in what those who believe they've been abducted call screen memories, artificial recollections implanted by aliens to mask what really took place. Mike's written a book, collecting accounts of owls in paranormal events. He thinks they might be psychic projections of extraterrestrial beings. As in cloaks that aliens wear to hide from us. The more real an owl appears, perhaps, the less likely it is to be what it seems. Perhaps many of the things that seem most vividly real to us seem so because they overlap a world of dreams. Mike described lying in the woods, looking up, feeling the silent passage of owls' wings.

He'd encountered so much strangeness. Not just the owls, although owls haunted his memories, but also floating orbs, glowing beings, missing time, coincidences for which the only possible explanations flirted with magic. He'd been brought onto alien ships. He'd woken in the night to find himself floating in the air. There are videos on the Internet of Mike speaking to UFO groups, something he does a fair amount of, and you have to pay close attention because he jumps so fast from one thing to the next. Now we're having a vision of a terrifying face, now we're in a sweat lodge with a shaman.

He's not crazy, that's the thing. Much of what he says is beyond incredible, but you never doubt that there's a reliable, if slightly high-key, consciousness on the other end. You'd trust him to get you back out of the forest. The same held for most of the UFO experiencers I met in the months before I flew to Roswell. Yes, some of them seemed nuts, and some of them were lying, and some of them were probably both, but the bulk of them? The bulk of them seemed sane. Fragile and shy and scared of attention, some of them, sure, just as you might be if you'd lived through something that ripped open your sense of reality. And the same could be said for the ones with an exaggerated sense of self-importance, of grand mission—you might think you were important, too, if you were bringing news of cosmic significance. But neither timidity nor grandiosity mean you aren't telling the truth.

And they weren't being consciously untruthful. I mean, I'm speaking only about my own reactions here. Maybe I'm easily misled. Regardless, my inner sirens, most of the time, did not start wailing. There are psychological studies that bear this out. People who say they've been abducted by aliens tend to show PTSD-like symptoms when they're pressed on the topic of alien abduction; otherwise, they're not appreciably mentally ill, or not more so than the rest of us. They pay taxes and watch Hulu and decide which toothpaste to use, and then just happen to live with this one deep sinkhole of terror. (Or of wonder; I don't know the ratios here, but there's at least a noticeable minority of experiencers who feel they've been chosen, not singled out for torment.) But not trusting their honesty because they seem "strange" makes no sense, because being lifted into the sky by extraplanetary beings would of course have that effect on "normal" people. This is one of the logical switchbacks you have to navigate around UFO culture. It's like saying, "Jake seems really on edge—he must be lying about the horrors he saw in the war."

What I'm saying is that there's a legitimate mystery here, which is: Why do so many people say, and apparently believe, that they have had experiences that cannot, according to any plausible reading of reality, have happened? Stats are hard to come by for obvious reasons, but the number of people who say they've been abducted runs at least to many thousands. And yet no indisputable photographic evidence, in an era when nearly everyone carries a camera? No multiple-eyewitness accounts that aren't at least somewhat slippery? Nothing undismissable picked up by, say, news satellites, by Google Earth? At a moment when it sometimes seems the planet is encased in a shell of surveillance? In a sense, the conspiracy-theory aspect of the UFO phenomenon, the *but that's just what they'd want you to think!* side of it, was inevitable, because something had to reconcile the certainty of experiencers with the lack of ironclad evidence. The only way to do that was to suggest that the *real* evidence had been suppressed—that it was too important, too civilization upending, for the government not to hush it up. That way the lack of evidence could become its own kind of negative proof.

———

Here UFO believers will stop me to insist that there *is* evidence, mountains of it, and they're right. There are countless reports of lights materializing over cities, of group-abductees who forgot the event, then underwent hypnosis and recovered identical memories. There are countless photographs, of varying degrees of graininess. Project Blue Book, the 1950s and '60s U.S. Air Force study of UFO activity, really did happen; the government really did take flying saucers seriously at one time, and this is not because postwar American intelligence was so silly but because once you are tasked with mapping the line that separates folklore from reality, you discover that the line is maddeningly blurred. But all this evidence has an odd sort of vanishing-around-the-edges quality. So much of it is (even if just barely) explicable by other means. So much of it is confirming to people who are already inclined to believe and unpersuasive to people who aren't. So much of it is on the order of "children in a small town all started drawing the same picture of a gray man with big, dark eyes" (this has happened). Which is compelling, haunting, but not quite the same as "an ocean liner appeared in the sky over Times Square."

———

The problem this creates is analogous to the problem of religious experience; it's fascinating and disturbing in the same way. What do you do when someone whose word you have no reason to doubt claims to have seen God? When you yourself haven't? Either your sense of reality expands around that possibility or it doesn't. A big difference between religious faith and the belief that aliens walk among us, of course, is that God is often thought to occupy what we might crudely call a higher order of reality, while aliens presumably exist within ours. (Another difference is that the experience of religious visitation leaves most people *overjoyed*; you don't get a lot of PTSD from it, although it blows your perceptions wide open.) Still, the abduction narrative has many features in common with, say, the writings of mystic saints—the blinding light overhead, the sense of telepathic communion, the slow floating upward. You don't have to look hard for theories that the "angels" described by ancient writers were actually beings from space—or, on the other hand, that the aliens described by experiencers are the atomic-age equivalent of fairies.

Paranoia is skepticism taken to the point where it becomes faith. In the same way, the UFO narrative takes twentieth-century scientism to the point where it becomes mystical. I mean that in all transparency: It takes the aesthetic paraphernalia of mid-century science (advanced aircraft, faster-than-light travel, gleaming labs, silvery fabrics, shiny implements) and uses them to clothe a story whose whole underlying structure is religious (superior beings watching from above, secret truths revealed only to a few, problems of faith and proof, and so on). Which, again, says nothing about whether people have actually experienced it. Remember how I said that Area 51 was both there and not there at the same time? Spend enough time with these questions and you end up feeling like Augustine, who wrote of God and heavenly creatures that "they neither are nor are not in existence."

Or almost. Looking back at the *Confessions*, I realize I have that Augustine line backward. It's *God*, in Augustine's formulation, who is entirely in existence. (Of course it is.)

It's what *isn't* God—our world, our rooms, our memories, our faces—that is both there and also not. It's real, because it comes from God, and not real, because it isn't God. What's real and also not? A dream, right? Augustine isn't saying that God is like a dream we're having. He's saying the opposite. He's saying we're the dream.

———

In western New Mexico, on the edge of the Zuni Mountains, there's a place called Inscription Rock. It's a pale sandstone cliff rising out of the desert. Bleached-looking bluffs. A kind of rough-hewn natural fortress, towering two hundred feet over low tangles of juniper and ponderosa pine. The conquistadors called it El Morro: "the promontory." (Or else: "the nose.") Walk around the base and you find a fold in the cliff that makes a small, shaded grotto where rainwater gathers in a pool.

Just rainwater—there's no underground spring or anything like that. But for hundreds of years, if you wanted to cross this desert and survive, the pool was your best hope. Going back to the Spanish, even before. Even a long time before. The little rain basin at El Morro was the vital link for generation upon generation of travelers.

The oldest carvings on the rock are ancient petroglyphs, made by Native Puebloans around a thousand years ago. Pale handprints. Bighorn sheep. Human forms with box-shaped torsos. Over the centuries, as the land was colonized by successive waves of explorers and then missionaries and soldiers and settlers, a sort of ad hoc traveler's custom arose whereby those who passed through would etch their names into the stone. Not like a formal tradition. Just, one person did it, then the next person saw that inscription and copied it. Many of them wrote a little bit about their journeys. The first message from a European was carved in 1605. That's fifteen years before the *Mayflower* landed.

There are two thousand carvings. Some are crudely scraped, some chiseled with a finesse that's nearly calligraphic. After the petroglyphs, the oldest belong to Spaniards, whose messages are small windows onto the moment when breast-plated and shiny-helmeted conquistadors ventured into this unimaginable (to them) desert vastness. *Paso por aqi el adelantado Don Ju de Oñate del descubrimyento de la mar del sur a 16 de Abril de 1605.* Governor Don Juan de Oñate passed through here after the discovery of the Sea of the South on the 16th of April of 1605. The Sea of the South—that's the Pacific Ocean. Oñate didn't discover it for Spain (Balboa had done that); he was looking for an outlet. They knew it was there, but not how to find it. This was the era of lost cities of gold, of Terra Australis. The map of the world was still full of blanks. To survive on the way back to New Mexico, Oñate's men had to eat their horses.

So right away, as you stroll the path beside the cliff's base, you're looking back in time. At crueler histories, too: Oñate's brutality to the Native Americans he encountered was so extreme that he was eventually put on trial for it, not an easy achievement for a colonial governor in Nuevo México. He "dealt harshly" with "rebellious" Indians, is how old history books put it. Newer ones say he cut off the feet of captives from tribes he wanted to subdue. (In the eyes of the king, his real crime was probably running out of money.) Another inscription, from 1632, tells of the passing of a group of soldiers on their way to "avenge the death of Father

Letrado," a missionary who'd been killed and scalped by the Zuni. In 1680, the Pueblo rose up against Spanish oppression and drove out the colonists; twelve years later, Diego de Vargas arrived with a military force and reconquered Santa Fe. "Here was the General Don Diego de Vargas, who conquered for our Holy Faith and for the Royal Crown all of New Mexico at his own expense, year of 1692," his carved inscription reads. At his own expense—what a glimpse of character in that one tiny flourish.

The Indian Wars are written all over this place. Cavalrymen sent by the U.S. government to secure the Southwest passed through before the first Southern state seceded. When he was secretary of war for the United States, Jefferson Davis had formed an experimental camel corps, had sent American troops with dozens of camels into the desert; one of these contingents passed through here in 1857. P. Gilmer Breckinridge, who oversaw twenty-five camels, signed his name on the rock. The next year saw settlers bound for California. One member of the group who carved her name was twelve-year-old Sallie Fox, traveling west with her family. After they moved on from El Morro, their wagon train was attacked by Mojave Indians. Sallie was shot through the rib cage with an arrow. She endured the long desert trek, mostly on foot and with a high fever, back to Albuquerque with the survivors from her party. The dress she was wearing is now in the historical museum in Vacaville, California. There's a little rent in the right side of the chest, where the arrow went through.

Among the inscriptions, there are countless hidden stories, countless mysteries. That Oñate message, for instance— did he carve it over a petroglyph, expressing contempt for the Indians? Or did the Pueblo carve the image, a human figure, over his words, expressing defiance against a sadistic enemy? It would be fascinating to know, but we never will, because it's difficult to date the glyphs, and also because the inscriptions themselves are vanishing. The sandstone is so soft. That's what made the carvings possible in the first place; it also means that every day, the wind lifts away a little more. Already many of the inscriptions are hard to read. The National Park Service is trying to preserve them; at best, the disappearance can be slowed.

———

A park ranger warned me that it was "breezy," but I wanted to see the top, so I followed the thin track up along the promontory's side and then stepped out onto the rock. The wind was cold. Erosion had left weird, cowboy-dimension shapes in the summit's profile. Shattered-looking steeples. Long protuberances that called to mind fierce masks. The gusts were hard enough at times that I had to hunch down to keep my balance. To my left, the cliff's edge fell away, and the view spread out for miles. At the horizon, a low ridge lay along the sky like a sea monster's surfacing back.

Make your way far enough out onto the bluff and you come to a ruin. There was a village here, established more than seven hundred years ago by Ancestral Puebloans. Most scholars no longer refer to them by the pejorative term the Navajo used, *Anasazi*, meaning "ancient enemies" or "ancient strangers." Little is known about them. They were responsible for many of the petroglyphs; the Zuni who found the site much later called it Atsinna, "place of writings on the rock." Little of the village remains: a small grid of recessed stone walls, a larger room that might have been used for religious ceremonies.

The civilization of the people who built this place leaves a baffling trail in the historic record. If you look at the evidence from a certain angle, they seem, all of a sudden, to disappear. This would have happened centuries before even the Spanish arrived. For many years, what became of them was one of the great unanswered questions in American archaeology. It's now generally accepted that they migrated to the southwest, to areas with more reliable sources of water, where they merged with other Puebloan cultures. Which makes sense. Still, there's an air of mystery around them, and standing on the rock by the ruins of their pueblo, I couldn't help remembering a theory I'd heard repeatedly from UFO aficionados. The theory said that they vanished because they were taken away by aliens, or else because they were aliens—ancient strangers, traveling some long-forgotten road back to the stars.

———

I drove for two more days. *If I could take you up in paradise up above.* West through Arizona, then north, into Nevada. The Black Canyon looked like nothing I'd seen in this world. If you had to dream up a lost kingdom for a fantasy novel, that's the sort of landscape you might invent. I spent a night in a Navajo casino. The next night I spent in Las Vegas, where I walked around for hours, lost in my own head (when would I stop lying to everyone, when would I stop lying to myself?), until the colors started to carousel.

Donald Trump's face flashing across the Bellagio TVs. *Life could be a dream, sweetheart.*

———

To get to Area 51 from Las Vegas, you take U.S. 93 north for ninety or so miles, then exit onto Nevada State Route 375, the so-called Extraterrestrial Highway—the state renamed it in 1996, during promotion for *Independence Day*—and follow that for an hour into increasingly remote desert. You're driving along the northern edge of Nellis Air Force Base, part of that vast reserve of military land, but there's no indication of that, no signage, hardly any other traffic. Eventually, you come to Rachel, population approximately fifty, where there's an alien-themed motel (the Little A'Le'Inn) and not much else. I had lunch at the motel restaurant, a greasy spoon full of alien-themed bric-a-brac. No one else was in the place except a couple of Australians, one of whom was bellowingly drunk and wearing a tinfoil Viking helmet. He'd obviously crafted it himself, from his lunch wrappings. He kept shouting about how "radical" everything here was. The woman behind the counter sighed as she pressed my burger patty down on the griddle.

The roads get smaller as you close in. First you're on a highway, then you're on gravel. Then dirt. The desert here is riddled with Joshua trees. Have you seen them? Twisted, long-limbed evergreens that put Mormon settlers in mind of the prophet Joshua, arms flung up in prayer. This is, incongruously, free-range cattle country—everyone rushed to warn me about that, local people I mean, when I said I was going to Area 51; nothing at all about men in black, but be careful, the bulls will charge your car—and every few hundred yards there'd be a little clutch of them, lying in the brush under the Joshua trees. As if they'd built nests.

The song that came on, as I drove among the cow nests and the contorted trees, was "Maybe" by the Chantels. So I drove for a while and listened to that. *Maybe if I pray every night, you'll come back to me.* I passed the skeleton of a horse, lying on its side in the dust. *Maybe if I hold your hand, you will understand.* I don't think I've ever felt, in the continental United States, so far away from everything.

Then "Maybe" ended, and "Papa Loves Mambo" came on. I wish, for the sake of atmosphere, that I could report otherwise, but it was "Papa Loves Mambo" that was playing as I came into view of Area 51.

There were tourists at the gate. A minivan full of them. In retrospect, that seems inevitable, but at the time I think it was the most surprising thing I could possibly have seen. They'd gotten out and were snapping away with their phones. I stopped the Sentra thirty yards or so behind them, so taken aback that it took me a minute to realize that what I'd read on the Internet was true. Some way back from the gate, there was a sort of rise in the landscape, not quite a hill, but an undulation high enough to give a view of the immediate surroundings. A white truck was parked up there. It didn't move, didn't offer an inkling of life. Just sat there, looking sinister. *Mama loves mambo.*

I keep saying "gate," but there wasn't a gate. Just two warning signs, one on either side of the road, nothing to keep you from driving right past them. Except that the signs say, basically, Abandon hope, all ye who enter here. They say it in crisp military English, *Entry is unlawful without written permission from etc.* The tourists went right up to the signs to take selfies but did not, I noticed, step beyond them.

The whole thing seemed vaguely ridiculous. But then, dreams often are. Here I was, on the threshold of Dreamland. Anyway, what could I do? I'd come here. Now I was here. The minivan drove away and I pulled forward. Beyond the signs, there was nothing. More desert. I walked up to the line and looked over. After days of strange profusion, it was almost a relief to see something so inaccessible to knowledge, such a complete refusal to be anything but an absence. The thought I had was that I had finally reached the frontier, that when we ran out of west in America we locked the idea of it away in places like this, blanks on the map that could never be charted, behind borders we could approach but never cross. Where who knows what monsters might exist. And sure, I thought about flying saucers. But mostly I thought about nothing, about the not-answer that lay beneath even my ability to ask questions. I remembered the sign I'd seen by the giant jackrabbit: HERE IT IS.

And I remembered how, hundreds of miles away and in a different desert, what was left of Route 66 still ran westward, from Arizona into California and across the Mojave to Los Angeles, to the place where it ended at the Santa Monica Pier, by the Ferris wheel on the edge of the sea.

———

There was one more place I needed to visit, but getting there took some time. After I got back from Area 51, I flew to Paris and went completely to pieces, which I am telling you not to sound exotic but simply because it is what happened.

After that, things got better, but they got better slowly, and in the interim I moved across the country and the website I was working for collapsed. So it was not until the following winter that I managed to contact the army and ask for permission to visit the Trinity site. They said yes, don't ask me why. It's where the first atom bomb was detonated. Three weeks later, the second, Little Boy, exploded over Hiroshima. The site is open to visitors two days a year, in April and October, that's it, and I'd missed both days. But the army liaison, Lisa, took pity on me and agreed to drive me out. I went in early February; it was the week of the Iowa presidential caucuses.

Trinity is a hundred miles or so south of Route 66. It's inside the White Sands Missile Range, in southern New Mexico. Another gargantuan expanse of military land, larger than Delaware, so huge that driving across it kills a workday. On the northern side, which is closest to Trinity, the nearest town is San Antonio, New Mexico. There's a restaurant there, the Owl Bar and Cafe, that opened in 1945. Manhattan Project scientists used to drink there in their off-hours; I stopped in for lunch. On the sign outside, the owl's painted wings looked like flames.

White Sands is mostly empty terrain. On the drive out to Trinity, I noticed military road signs depicting animals I didn't recognize, black silhouettes inside yellow diamonds, horselike heads with long, spiral-turned, gently arcing horns. Lisa told me that in the 1960s, the base commanders had imported twenty-five hundred oryx from the Kalahari in order to stage exotic game hunts. Since the oryx's major predator is the lion, and since, as Lisa pointed out, "we don't get too many lions in New Mexico," the herd had thrived such that there was now a basically self-supporting population of wild African antelopes contained entirely within the largest missile-test zone of the American military apparatus. Just: right there. No distance at all from the place where the atomic age was born.

On the drive back, I saw them. Marvelous creatures. Like stout horses, but with startling black-and-white face masks and the tall V of the horns, which seemed to belong to different animals entirely, more ethereal but also more demonic. The herd was set back from the road, just grazing. There were many oryx. I was in a distracted state from having seen Trinity and from having stood, alone except for Lisa, on the spot where, on the morning of July 16, 1945, the first mushroom cloud had risen over the desert, an explosion of such power it shattered windows 150 miles away. The ground there glitters with green rocks called trinitite, created when quantities of sand from beneath the bomb tower were sucked up into the blast and vaporized. When they came down to earth they recrystallized into a radioactive substance scientists still don't fully understand. Green flakes of it appear around the many small holes that dot the site. I wondered if the holes were related to the bomb, but Lisa said no, they were rabbit holes, rabbits have reclaimed the land around ground zero.

So when I saw the oryx, I was not, mentally, all the way online. What I was thinking about was a poem by John Donne. It's the poem that Robert Oppenheimer, who ran the Manhattan Project, cited when asked why he'd chosen the name Trinity for his nuclear test site, even though (as Oppenheimer himself noted) the poem has nothing to do with the Trinity.

It's a poem about traveling west. "Hymn to God, My God, in My Sickness" finds Donne on what he believes to be his deathbed, surrounded by doctors, and because it's the early seventeenth century, Donne starts imagining the doctors as "cosmographers" and himself as a map, the sort of map an explorer might make, filling in the world's blanks:

> Whilst my physicians by their love are grown
> Cosmographers, and I their map, who lie
> Flat on this bed, that by them may be shown
> That this is my south-west discovery,
> *Per fretum febris*, by these straits to die.

Per fretum febris: by the wasting away of a fever. That was Ferdinand Magellan's cause of death, when he died while trying to sail around the earth. (He really died while trying to convert the Philippines to Christianity by force, but that was a subcomponent of the larger expedition.) Magellan had discovered the strait that made passage between the Atlantic and the Pacific possible; Donne is reimagining this as the passage between life and death. To go west is to die, and yet

> I joy, that in these straits I see my west;
> For, though their currents yield return to none,
> What shall my west hurt me? As west and east
> In all flat maps (and I am one) are one,
> So death doth touch the resurrection.

Travel far enough west, on a map, and you come out on the other side, in the east. In the same way, Donne says, if you travel into death, you emerge into resurrection. History's unreturnable current moves one way, but creation is a sphere, not a plane, so nothing is really final, nothing is lost.

Then I saw the oryx. They made no sense there. They made the opposite of sense. This isn't a generic desert landscape. You would recognize these ridges, these grasses, this violet-gray light as New Mexico in a photo from the moon. In the same way, the oryx are unmistakably from where they're from. The image didn't fit. They had nothing to do with the atom bomb, nothing to do with war, nothing to do with anything I'd come to see.

And yet. What shall my west hurt me? They were beautiful.

I watched them, as we drove away on the straight road out of Trinity, until they disappeared behind the lavender curve of the world.

The Little Gray Wolf
Will Come

A talking cat lives outside his door. Every night, after his mother puts him to bed, it comes. If he opens his eyes he can almost catch its shadow, pacing along the gap where the light shines in through the door. The light is magical, he thinks; it holds enchanted things. He thinks of the cat, and happiness, and bread sprinkled with sugar.

He lives, by day, among the trees in the yard, with the other boys from the *kommunalka*. Climbing, fighting, catching insects, waging wars. His family shares a communal apartment with four others. In this part of Moscow, that makes them lucky, he knows: The flat upstairs holds twelve. Fifty people under one roof. It is 1952 and there are no social classes in the workers' paradise, but his father is a machine-tool adjuster. Families who live in Maryina Roshcha are not well-off. Bandits operate in the area; at night, the lights are dim.

His family, the Norsteins, are Jewish. The word doesn't mean much to him, but sometimes old women spit and call him Christ killer, and sometimes his friends do the same.

One day after class, his drawing teacher pulls him aside and tells him not to come back. He cries when this happens, because he loves art more than anything. He does not understand that Stalin is stoking anti-Semitism for political purposes. He only feels that the mood of the world shifts unpredictably, and sometimes the days are bad.

He knows who Stalin is because he sees his picture on the street. Joseph Vissarionovich says there will be no bread tomorrow. Comrade Joseph, who won us the war. He knows what the war was because he remembers it, a little, the fear and the fireworks and the close-typed lists of the dead. The war is why his aunt Bella came home alone and pregnant, after serving with the air force on the front. He was very small then. When the baby died, Aunt Bella gave him her milk. There was so little other food, so little of anything. "Auntie, Auntie," he would call across the yard. "Give me some milk!" The war is why the nights are still so dark, why the streetlamps are dull and the hallway bulb dimmer than the paraffin stove, barely as bright as a candle.

He doesn't mind the dark. It, too, is magical. When the moon is out he watches the wind sweep the leaves from the ground, like a big arm scooping itself up. He listens to the music playing somewhere, the accordion always sighing out the same song, the tango "Weary Sun." After bedtime the dark belongs to the little gray wolf, who, according to the lullaby his mother sings, will take him away if he sleeps too close to the bed's edge, steal him away and hide him in the woods, under the willow root. The wolf is absolutely real to him. Like the cat, it lives just past the boundary of what he normally sees and hears, in the other realm that surrounds his everyday life.

A bad day: His father is fired. Stalin is moving against the Jews, and the consequences reach all the way down to the machine shop. He feels the tension, sees the worried lines on his parents' faces. Then an hour comes when the world pulls back in thrilling disbelief: Stalin is dead. Later, adults tell him about the transports that the dictator had prepared to carry the Jews to Siberia.

Wood smoke and wax smoke. Potatoes rattling in a pan. Granny Varya, whose son spies for the government. Climbing the poplars, higher than the buildings, climbing hair-raisingly high.

Later, when he is an old man, he will marvel at these memories. His childhood, when the days seemed so long.

And leafing now and then through a book about Siberia: Well, well, Joseph Vissarionovich; but here I am.

———

Well. Here he is, an old man, onstage at the Dom Kino. Cinephiles of Moscow, your evening's entertainment: Yuri Norstein, seventy-four, white bearded, stout, small, urbane, and mischievous. Sitting in front of a pale gold curtain, in a rumpled shirt, with a bump on his nose the size of a pistachio shell. Considered by many a great, if tragically self-defeating, Russian artist. Considered by many the finest animator in the world.

It is 2016. He did not move to Moscow last week; he knows what people say about him. They say he sabotaged his own career at what should have been its peak. They say he has not released a new film in thirty-seven years. As a young man, he made *Hedgehog in the Fog*, a movie every Russian child knows by heart, and then *Tale of Tales*, which international juries have more than once named the greatest animated picture ever made. Then, people say, he threw it all away to chase an unattainable ideal, an animated adaptation of Gogol's short story "The Overcoat" that he has toiled at for nearly four decades and never been able to finish. He takes questions at events like this, and the sequence is always the same. First a few respectful queries about his past work, his process, his inspirations. Then, when some brink of nerve has been crossed: When will you finish *The Overcoat*? Do you think you ever will?

Still: a good crowd tonight for his lecture. In the vestibule outside the hall, his assistant, Tania, has set up the usual table, selling postcards and picture books and refrigerator magnets. The faces of his most beloved characters look out from the racks, in tiny dozens; the same faces he'll project, enormous, onto the screen behind him while he speaks. The little gray wolf. The poet's cat. The hedgehog, the owl, the bull that turns the jump rope. Some people might find it strange to see their dreams living outside their heads. For him it is the other way around: The moments are rare when he is not surrounded by dreams.

He is introduced. Applauded. He takes out a flask of cognac, holds it up for the audience. Drinks. "I hope we will have a *very serious* discussion tonight." Laughter. On the screen he projects an image of himself, sitting beside his pet. "The two people in this photograph," he announces, "are both dogs."

He turns his sad, merry eyes over the crowd. He has given this talk, and many talks like it, many times before. He has to give talks because he has to pay his rent. In 2005 he collected his lectures on the art of animation into a kind of memoir, *Snow on the Grass*; it sold so well he ran out of copies for Tania to stock at the table. His charm onstage is casual, but he knows how to hold an audience. He is romantic: He believes that imagination, embodied in art, offers an escape from what is degraded and alienating in a society that wants to make us machines. But he is also a clown: He likes to shock people, he knows how to make them laugh. He has hidden a bottle of beer in the lectern. He'll reveal it when the cognac runs out.

He speaks of the great paintings, how they move when he looks at them. Here, consider Kandinsky: The lines go up and down like pistons, while the circles float like soap bubbles. Michelangelo's bust of Brutus: electrifying, how it changes from different sides. He has never been to the Accademia in Florence, but in his mind he sees it in three dimensions, so clearly it makes his heart race.

He shows off his grandson's drawings of a medieval battle, thickets of arrows plunging toward stick-figure armies. Such energy, such use of white space! Technical perfection is not the highest aim of art; art needs human vitality, which is why paintings by children can be riveting and why animation done with computers makes him feel physically sick. Small imperfections, which make a work human, make it beautiful. "If my hands shake," he says as he talks about this, "it is not because I am an alcoholic. It's because I'm honest!"

He speaks of his own work. Wolf and hedgehog, heron and crane. Here is the image of the infant at the breast that appeared in *Tale of Tales*. Here is a photograph of his wife, Francheska—his most important collaborator, the art director for his films—in a similar pose, breast-feeding their son, Borya. (Can it really have been fifty years ago? It was:

in the late 1960s.) He remembers how furious she was when he included the photo in his memoir. But he loves it so much; and then, he and Francheska have been married a long time, and they put up with each other, which is to say, she puts up with him. He tells the story onstage, and her long-ago anger tickles him. He laughs.

He talks freely about *The Overcoat*. Why not? The story—it concerns a poor clerk in St. Petersburg who has to save up for a new coat, only to have it stolen as soon as he acquires it—is one of the foundational works of Russian literature, as important, he says, as a book of the Bible. He says nothing about the film's state of completion, but he plays clips, as he sometimes does, from the scenes he's finished so far, and wonder ruffles the crowd.

He doesn't treat it as an unfinished project. He speaks of it as something long accomplished, widely known. Perhaps this is backward, describing the making of a film that technically does not yet exist. But he cares about this work, which has consumed half his life. He cares about how it is received. If the film were a real overcoat, you could see light shining through its holes. But he knows what he has, and he knows what it has cost him. And what artist does not wish to be praised?

From the stage, he looks out at the old movie palace. High ceilings, faded velvet, dusty light. A church of cinema: suitable for such revelations.

———

A church. That is where they send him to work in 1961, when he finishes animation school. Or not a church, pre-

cisely. It has stone walls and a bell tower, a steeple and on-
ion domes; it is set back from the street behind a black iron
gate. But the bureaucrats seized it from the priests years ago
and, exercising their own power of transubstantiation, made
it into something else. Now it is a puppet workshop that only
happens to look like a church: in the same way that Eucha-
rist blood once happened to taste like wine.

He works, posing puppets, for Soyuzmultfilm, the Soviet
state animation studio. He doesn't like the work; he would
rather be doing something else. He is young, headstrong,
frustrated. The studio's films embarrass him. Puerile Disney
knockoffs, whitewashed for communist children.

Listen, animation is not serious art. Not really! His dream,
since he was a little boy in drawing class, has been to become a painter. But the state permits artistic careers only to
those who have successfully finished art school, and when
he tried that, all he managed to do was fail the entrance
exam. This, however, he did very successfully: He failed it
four times. He wound up in a furniture factory, pounding
nails into packing crates. There was one way out: a two-
year training course in animation. He thought it might offer
a roundabout path to art school. It didn't. But what was he
supposed to do, stay at the factory and get sawdust up his
nose? What a waste of time!

If you believe in progress and the revolutionary logic of
history, which treats time as a straight line, then he will
never be an artist, in the same way that the church is no
longer a church. The church has been made into a mere
building, a part of the neighborhood: the snow and the trash
cans, crooked streets and barking dogs. He has been made

into an animation assistant. But he is not sure he sees much reason to believe in progress. And he has never been sure that time is a straight line.

He went to the Pushkin Museum not long ago with his mother, to see the old master paintings the Red Army rescued from Germany after the war. The awe he felt in those rooms! A cloak painted so that you could feel the pull of its rippling in the wind. A staff painted so that you saw clearly how its angle would change as the bearer put weight on it. This, he felt, was what art should be: not entertainment, not instruction, but something that spoke to the highest possibilities of the human spirit. People say that now, with Khrushchev having succeeded Stalin, Soviet artists are finally free to express themselves. But animation directors are so cautious! He yearns to create work worthy of Leonardo, of Goya, yet he spends his days tweaking the joints of a puppet shaped like a ewe.

He isn't shy about sharing his opinions. Animators, like many Soviet workers, are strictly divided into ranks. It is true that within the relatively relaxed, creative environs of Soyuzmultfilm a certain irony tinges the observation of this hierarchy. Good morning, Animator Class 1, how are you today? About the same, Director Class 3, only I wish I slept better. Still, he speaks his mind impetuously enough that he annoys his superiors. Norstein! There is one well-known director, old Ivan Ivanov-Vano, who spots his potential and tries to help him. But Norstein sees his peers moving ahead of him, watches as his classmates from the training course are given their own films to direct. And he bristles, and he shifts a hoof two inches, and he sighs.

It isn't a matter of capability; he can do things they can't.

He can do things no one has thought of. One day, on a film being made with cutouts—essentially two-dimensional puppets, drawings with movable limbs—he startles his colleagues by gathering all the cutouts and tearing the hinges out of their joints. Why rely on hinges when he can make them move more naturally as loose collections of shapes? Sometimes he senses a possibility in this, a faint stirring of potential. He works on one film, *My Green Crocodile*, a lyrical, melancholy fantasy about a crocodile who falls in love with a cow, which makes audiences gasp with delight. But the experience is annoying, because the film is made with puppets, and puppet animation is inescapably limiting. Why go to so much trouble to emulate realistic physical space, he thinks, when if animation offers anything, it's the freedom to create any sort of space you can dream up?

At the studio he meets a young designer. She is dark, quiet, careful, and serious, all things that he is not. He sees immediately that she is a better painter than he is, a more skillful illustrator. Francheska Yarbusova: a film student, helping out at Soyuzmultfilm in the evenings. She had wanted to work on live-action movies, but her adviser convinced her that a woman would never be able to order men around on a set; she should try animation, where the men are imaginary. He is the son of a machine-tool adjuster; she is the daughter of a famous psychologist who made important contributions to the study of the human eye. He is irascible, she is implacable. Their arguments are ferocious. Still, he thinks: Something good may come from this job after all.

It's a good joke, him working where he works. As a boy, he was banned from drawing class because he was a Jew. Now he spends his days making children's cartoons under a dome built for Christian murals. Saints and their serious faces, angels with fiery wings.

———

In his studio the dried flowers rustle like birds' wings. He pads, in house slippers and cargo shorts, through the warren of dark rooms, holding a white teacup: Lipton Yellow Label, splash of milk. Kuzya, the dog, snores by the door. From outside, in the park, he hears birds singing. It occurs to him that Kuzya, who is deaf, can't hear them, and he feels a twinge of pity: What would a life without birdsong be like?

He loves the park, with its soft light, its little ducks and trees. Every morning when the pond is not frozen solid, he jumps in and goes for a swim. "Only not," he sometimes boasts, "in the summer. The water is too hot!"

Now, in 2016, it is spring, and Moscow is noisy with construction. Jackhammers ripping up sidewalks; cranes tipping themselves over buildings like giraffes above watering holes. He hates what Putin is doing to the city. The old Moscow had an organic order to it, like a beehive: church, square, shops, neighborhood, church, square, shops, neighborhood, and again, in simple, untroubled succession. Now everything is haphazard. Every rooftop suddenly needs a café. Skyscrapers shoot up, senseless clumps of them, as though rubles were drifting over the city like dandelion fuzz and apartment towers sprouted wherever they took root. Construction contracts make Putin's cronies rich. Boutiques keep the populace docile. It makes him shake with rage. Many Muscovites keep dachas, country houses within easy reach of the city; his was once forty-five kilometers from the nearest urban development, but the new Moscow threatens to swallow it up. "I keep telling Francheska, 'I'm going to write to these idiots, and I'm going to call them out,'" he says. "I know they could say, 'You're being offensive,' but I'll say, '*You're* offensive!' I'm going to do it!"

At least the studio, where he lives as well as works, is his to arrange as he likes. Not that he owns it. This is capitalism; he pays rent like anyone else. It keeps him young, he thinks, having to chase his living. He has hung bells, many bells, from the low ceilings. Every surface in the small dark rooms is cluttered with books, lamps, dried blossoms, postcards, art: his sketches, other people's sketches, children's sketches, charcoal portraits of nineteenth-century clerks, religious icons, tubes of paint, a large wooden camel, a travel poster from Seville, hangers from Marks & Spencer, a magazine photo of a Brazilian soccer fan with her breasts spilling out, tiny scissors, glass bottles, an old record player, a small green chair, stills from his films, interesting stones, rolls of masking tape hung on hooks, a spotted frog, and hedgehogs, dozens of hedgehogs, painted and molded and carved; people keep giving him hedgehogs because they love his most famous character, the little *yozhik* who goes to visit his friend the bear cub and finds himself lost in a fog. "Enough hedgehogs!" he roars. In his bathroom, he has taped a sign reading PIRATE'S CORNER—Pirate was his last, and deeply loved, dog—to the wall over a phalanx of miniature samurai on a glass shelf. The cup beside the samurai is full of paintbrushes. In the center of the paintbrushes is a single tube of toothpaste.

On Saturday mornings, he opens his studio to admirers, who come to buy his pictures and his magnets and the children's books he has made from his films. Tania takes payment in cash; she prints receipts with an adding machine. Most of the time, his Saturday crowds are small, but sometimes—on the day he released his memoir, for instance—the lines stretch around the block. Occasionally they include foreigners; his friend Hayao Miyazaki, the legendary Japanese animator, sometimes compliments his films in the press, and that brings him some attention, Miyazaki being so well known. But mostly they are Russians, of all ages. He tells them jokes. With a flourish, with an exclamation mark, he signs their books.

Tania has worked for him for more than twenty years, and she loves to goad him, so while their Saturday callers flip through the racks of prints, she will sometimes begin explaining loudly what a terror he is to work for. Sometimes, she says, businessmen come to see him, professional people in suits and ties, and offer him money, as much as he needs to finish *The Overcoat*. "And whenever this happens, Yuri Borisovich begins to TREMBLE. 'Don't worry about *anything*,' these men say. 'We'll take care of *everything*.' And Yuri Borisovich goes into the other room, and he paces, and he hides. And after a while, he comes into the hall like THIS"—Tania imitates a stomping, glowering ogre, puffing out her cheeks and crossing her eyes—"and he POINTS at me, and he POINTS at the door, and he shouts: 'Tania, YOU handle this!'"

Tania Usvayskaya: his former student. A talented artist in her own right, as he tells anyone who will listen, who has published books of cartoons in Japan. Only rarely, and only if he leaves the room, will she deliver the other part of her speech, about his unsurpassed skill as an animator. "Yuri

Borisovich's hands are not like other people's hands," she says. "They move differently. And Yuri Borisovich's brain is not like other people's brains. He thinks in half millimeters. He lives"—she taps her head—"on a different cosmic time-scale." One of the challenges in animating anything by hand is how to keep the rate of motion consistent for objects moving at different speeds. Depicting one person running is easy, but when you have two people, and one of them is slightly faster than the other, making their movements line up from frame to frame requires all sorts of tricky calculations. But Tania has seen him, on *The Overcoat*, do this by pure instinct. He simply knows how much to move each figure, and he can improvise individual running styles for them, too. She shakes her head. "We ask him, why, why not take help? Why do you always make it so hard on yourself? But the only things Yuri Borisovich is afraid of are the things that might really help him."

The trouble with Russia, he thinks, is that it's so hard to *trust* anything. Many things seem real but aren't; other things, like art, seem made-up but are in fact the only sources of truth. This morning, for instance. This morning is perfect. The white clouds over the city are staggering, enormous. Someone will say that if you stand in the middle of Red Square and face St. Basil's, the candy-bright cathedral will look, under the citadel of cloud, about three inches high. Well: beautiful. But Putin's head is always poking in. Every year, for the city's massive May Day parades, the government wants blue skies. So every April, Russian planes seed the clouds to disperse them. And that, people say, is the real reason the air over the city grows so dramatic in late spring, because when the clouds come back, they are changed. He, Norstein, autographs picture books; Putin can't rest until he has signed his name on the sky.

He keeps photos of Putin on the corkboard over his worktable: the all-powerful autocrat, caught making ridiculous faces. Scrunching his head down into his neck while counting money. Jutting out his neck, a blond turtle, to straighten his tie.

Once, on the side of a building near his studio, he found some old graffiti reading, "A dick up the nose of the state." He took a picture of it, which he likes to show to his guests. "Oh, how I wished I had written that!" he says. "Straight up their noses! I might not have written it, but I'll tell you what I did do: I marched up and down the sidewalk shouting it for *days*!"

———

Here they come: the revolutionaries. Marching down the street. A band of cartoon silhouettes, red, flat, wearing workers' caps, with jagged bayonets affixed to the ends of their rifles. Their momentum pulls the angular city behind them into a blur. Capitalists—fat, black-jacketed squiggles with fat round squiggles for faces—wobble out from the buildings, shaking fat fists and bellowing: "Go back, stop this at once!" The workers keep coming. The music is by Shostakovich, and when the cymbals crash, the silhouettes flash. The workers come faster. Running now, rifles akimbo, limbs flying: a red chaos, a sea monster seething with spines. The capitalists gape and totter backward into their towers.

He is making his first film as a director. Finally, after so many years. He is twenty-six now, in 1967, and he feels that he has waited a long time. He and Francheska have moved into their own apartment, his first home away from the *kommunalka*, where he had lived with his mother since his father died. The film is an eight-minute short about the October Revolution. He is co-directing it with another animator, Arkady Tyurin. He and Tyurin share an enthusiasm for the avant-garde political art of the early Soviet era, the period of Tatlin and Malevich, and they have decided to bring the uprising to life by bringing revolutionary paintings and posters from the era of the uprising to life. This is, of course, a way to talk about politics that is also a way to talk about art, and about the relation of animation to art. He has learned a great deal in the years he has spent working on other people's films. He is eager to think about what he has learned, and about how the lessons might tie together to make a career.

One thing he has learned: He likes working with cutouts. The trick, in producing animated films, is how to make the labor manageable. The most straightforward way to make a picture move is to draw it over and over, changing it slightly where movement occurs: Think of the flip-book doodles you might make on the corner of a notebook. But this becomes prohibitively labor-intensive once you start to imagine scenes with many static elements—walls, windows, trees, background imagery—because each of these elements would have to be redrawn, in exactly the same way, every time a character turned her head or took a step. Traditional cel animation gets around this difficulty by placing moving elements on transparent sheets of celluloid, which are then overlaid on one background image. You make several drawings of the dragon flying, then photograph each of them, in turn, atop a single drawing of the castle. Run the photographs at high speeds, and you see the dragon soaring over the battlements.

In cutout animation, the principle is similar, but instead of redrawing the dragon to make it fly, you make a dragon cutout, a jointed drawing with articulating parts, and physically move its wings. This is intended as a way of saving time, but he feels it as an artistic possibility. Cutout characters have a consistent physical identity, unlike characters in cel animation. But unlike in puppet animation, where the puppets are three-dimensional objects inhabiting the same physical universe as people, cutout characters can be integrated into their backgrounds in the same ways drawings can, with the same tricks of depth and perspective. Cutout animators interact with their characters as puppeteers do, but it is as if they were puppeteers inside the worlds created by their drawings.

The film takes its name from a poem by Mayakovsky: "25th—the First Day." He and Tyurin incorporate works by Chagall, by Mayakovsky himself, by the revolutionary era's great artists, then throw them together in hurtling juxtapositions; the pace and the use of double-exposed images recall Vertov's *Man with a Movie Camera*, the groundbreaking work of Soviet silent cinema. But when they come to the end, a problem is waiting for them. They want to use a painting by the artist Pavel Filonov, whose aesthetic system, Universal Flowering, combined aspects of cubism and futurism. They find Filonov exhilarating, but his work has been in disgrace with the authorities since the late 1920s. They are told to change their script. Lectures in dismal offices: some suggestions, comrades, for your ending. Ugly ashtrays, buzzing lights. The people need a film about Lenin. The people have no need for this frippery about art.

They try to concoct a plan that will please the bureaucrats while keeping the film true to their conception. But they are young and inexperienced, and they have no leverage with the studio. They are forced to insert a scene, made by splicing together photographs and old film footage, that shows Lenin giving a speech to a celebrating crowd. It looks and sounds like a newsreel, and it has nothing to do with the study of revolutionary art and its relationship to animation that they have tried to make. He feels ashamed—and his bosses hate the film anyway. He is rewarded for his contribution to the smooth functioning of the propaganda state by being trucked off to produce a fire-safety video for children.

Well, comrade, what did you expect? You have a role to play in society. You make light entertainments for the masses. Isn't it a little late to pose as an aggrieved artist?

He thinks: To do what you see in your mind, you will have to learn to manipulate the system.

He thinks: I don't care what happens to me, I will never compromise again.

———

If civilization is fallen, if the imagination of the artist offers our only model of a better world, then not to compromise is the artist's first duty; a vision adulterated by outside influence is a vision infected by the malady it means to cure. But what if the refusal to compromise results in a masterpiece that cannot be finished? What if the prerequisite for producing great art makes a great artwork impossible to produce?

He begins *The Overcoat* at the start of the 1980s: a good time for him, a moment when his career feels like a fight he has won. *Tale of Tales*, his luminous, nonlinear film about art and memory, has been rapturously received at international film festivals; the authorities have allowed the film to travel, though not him with it. He has been in and out, mostly out, of the state's good graces, but he has on his side a group of fellow animators and artistic administrators that his friend, the writer Ludmilla Petrushevskaya, calls a "mafia of decent people." They know how to maneuver against the censors. When *Tale of Tales* was under review, the authorities assumed that it must be subversive, since they had no idea what it was about. But his friends anticipated this, and arranged for his past work to win an important state prize just before the new film went before the functionaries. That way, the censors could not ban *Tale of Tales* without attacking the judgment of the powerful prize committee; they fumed, but they let the film pass.

He has learned how to obfuscate, how to plot, how to disguise his intentions. He has learned to speak a language in which "yes" means "maybe" and "perhaps" means "never." He writes film treatments that bear no resemblance to the movies he wants to make, then, when the budget is approved, throws out the treatments. And when the bosses complain about unannounced changes, about budget overruns, about blown deadlines: *But of course we can talk about it, comrade, nothing could be simpler. Perhaps we should assemble a committee?* Delay till you can get them on your side. Delay till your film exists and can persuade them. Delay till they have a choice between releasing your film and releasing nothing; let them think about how, if they choose nothing, they will explain themselves.

The story "The Overcoat," Gogol's story, is dear to him. Akaky Akakievich is a lowly clerk in St. Petersburg. This is mid-nineteenth century, the Russia of the czars. St. Petersburg is the imperial capital. The functions of government are divided among a large class of civil servants, each ranked according to a rigid hierarchy, from the meanest scribe to the most exalted minister. One's place in the hierarchy determines one's whole life. So here, already, he feels, is the Russian national disease, the flaw that has unspooled from serfdom on, the flaw communism was supposed to (but did not) correct: the obliteration of common human feeling by a morbid obsession with rank.

Akaky Akakievich's rank is lowly. At fifty—pale, stooped, balding—he spends his life hunched over an inkwell, copying official papers. He has no friends, and his imaginative life is wholly confined to his work: Sometimes he brings pages home to copy in the evenings, just for his own satisfaction. But early one winter, when the snow is swirling and the cold is nipping at the heels of the clerks on Nevsky Prospekt, he realizes that his old overcoat is too thin and frayed to last another season. He will have to replace it. An overcoat is a huge expense. He saves for months. He finds himself, quite uncharacteristically, fantasizing about his new garment: how warm it will be, how rich, how splendid.

At last the day comes when the tailor delivers the coat. Carefully, Akaky slips it on: It's perfect. His small swelling of pride actually dizzies him. Everything seems different now that he has the coat! His colleagues, who normally tease him, invite him to a party. But on the way home, passing through a dark square, he is stopped by robbers. The robbers steal his new coat. In shock, he goes to see a high-ranking official who, he is told, will be able to find his coat for him. But the official only yells at him. It is freezing in St. Petersburg, and Akaky Akakievich, lacking a coat, catches a fever. He dies. After his death, a ghost appears in the city, a ghost that rips the coats off people's shoulders as if it is searching for its own.

He is drawn to "The Overcoat" partly because Gogol's imagination is ideally suited to an animated film. The details are so eccentric and so vivid. There is the tailor, Petrovich, with his deformed big toenail, "thick and hard as a tortoiseshell," who curses at his thread when it won't go through the needle: "You'll be the death of me, you devil!" There is the "rather weakly built" policeman who, Gogol tells us, was once knocked off his feet by a "quite normal-sized, fully mature piglet which came tearing out of a private house."

But he also loves "The Overcoat" for the same reason the story has resonated in Russian culture. Its moral theme, the perversion of empathy by power, is a cry right from the heart of everyday Russian tragedy. He feels this with a passion he is barely able to contain. This is what art is for, this is what it can do: It can show people that fellow feeling runs deeper than the arbitrary distinctions that raise one person over another. Gogol's story includes a moving scene. A clerk is taunting Akaky Akakievich, who responds, as he always does, by muttering, "Leave me alone, why do you have to torment me?" The clerk, who has been laughing, suddenly falls silent. And for a long time, Gogol says, those words will haunt the clerk, even in his happiest moments, because he hears the sound of others underneath them: "I am your brother."

He thinks his adaptation will be twenty minutes long and take at most a few years to complete. But the film grows in the making. A scene that is meant to last one and a half minutes comes in at more than sixteen. Deadlines fly by. Perhaps it will run for sixty minutes instead of twenty. Perhaps a little more. The production runs into problems almost immediately, and the problems compound. He and Francheska have furious arguments—they always fight when they're working, always have fought when she's designed one of his films, but this time the stakes seem higher because Gogol's story is so important. The characters and the setting must look exactly right. They spend months searching for the precise downcast angle of the eyes, the precise worried furrow of the brow, to represent Akaky Akakievich. Production stops for months at a time while he maneuvers behind the scenes to get a promotion for his longtime cameraman, Alexander Zhukovsky, but the elitist buffoons who control the Soviet art system reserve advancement for university graduates. Norstein isn't one, and neither is his friend. The attempt fails, after consuming huge chunks of the calendar. By 1986, he is years behind schedule, and the studio has promised his space to another director. He is evicted. Soon he loses his job altogether. He has no choice but to abandon *The Overcoat* or find a way to make it on his own.

While the structure of his creative life is collapsing, the whole world seems to follow suit. The Berlin Wall comes down. The Eastern bloc disintegrates. Along with the rest of humanity, he watches Yeltsin standing on a tank—Boris Nikolayevich, with his face like beaten dough—and witnesses the end of the economic and cultural regime under which he has labored for his entire adult life.

The problem now is one of how to live. How can he get by, with a stalled film and a back catalog from which he has no clear hope of profit? He can teach classes, for one. He can give lectures. He finds that he is admired enough abroad, in Europe and Japan, for opportunities to present themselves, and now he is free to travel, so: Paris, Tokyo, art schools, film schools, museums. He plows his fees back into *The Overcoat* or toward keeping his small team of artists together. He works on his film when he can. When he takes on foreign investment, the deals go badly, because the investors want a say in what his picture will be like, and he refuses to listen to them. The investors want him to work abroad, where they can watch how their money is being spent, and he does not want to move away from Moscow. It turns out that the tactics he has learned for operating under communism, the oblique stubbornness and concealed perseverance, do not work in the same way under capitalism, where stricter accounts are kept; and he feels frequently unmoored, unsure of the ground under his feet.

In any case, the troubled status of his film limits interest from investors. The endless production of *The Overcoat* costs him his chance at Miyazaki-like international fame, but then, what good would international fame be if it meant rushing or skimping on *The Overcoat*? The story is more urgent than ever; it is only the work that is slow.

And so, slowly, his status in the culture of the new Russia

drifts into something curious; he is half laughed at, half revered. Once a decade or so, he releases a few minutes of new work: a series of commercials for a sugar company in 1994, a set of opening titles for a long-running children's show in 2000. In 2003, his tiny, two-minute sequence about the poet Basho appears in a Japanese omnibus film called *Winter Days*, featuring the work of thirty-five directors. Each of his new pieces is, in its own way, marvelous, but they are all either work for hire, like the sugar commercials, or very brief, like the fragment about Basho.

He thinks that time is strange. He has never quite understood the way other people seem to perceive it. To imagine life as something so finite, so headlong! Art takes what it takes, and memory has a way of looping back on itself; things that are forgotten are gathered up again and remembered, things that have gone slowly suddenly go very fast. Sometimes an unfinished work—there are portraits by Rembrandt like this—seems old when it is new and then, when it is old, seems so modern it can steal away your breath. Sometimes, at his talks, he shows the crowd a clip from the scene in which Akaky Akakievich holds his old coat up to the light, to see whether the fabric can be mended. The footage is in black and white. Akaky's big, fretful head turns in the wavering candlelight. He wipes his nose. He has been out in the storm. Shining droplets roll off the brim of his hat. He raises the coat and bunches the fabric in his fingers. He puts it over his head like a tent. His fingers slide out through small holes. It is as simple as that. He is quiet, careful, and serious. The scene is so mesmerizing, and so unlike anything the audience has seen before, that unless the crowd is full of animators, no one thinks to ask how a two-dimensional cutout could create realistic bulges and wrinkles in cloth.

———

How can a two-dimensional cutout inhabit a three-dimensional world? Animation is traditionally filmed by a camera that points downward, into parallel sheets of glass: This is the system that Disney, for instance, used for more than fifty years, from the 1930s all the way through *The Little Mermaid*, in the late 1980s. The lowest sheet holds the static background painting; the top sheet holds foreground elements, typically characters, either cutouts or drawings on celluloid. A minimal setup might have only two or three panes, but in a more complicated one, layers of glass between top and bottom might be used for objects in the middle distance, or to create an illusion of depth. The camera is suspended above the stack of panes, so that when it takes a photograph, it resolves the separate layers into a single image, just as your eye might if you looked through a series of windows, each with part of a picture painted on it.

A complex multi-plane system, such as the one Disney developed, offered early animators a solution to one of the new medium's trickiest problems: how to simulate advanced camera movement. Animators wanted their work to incorporate the visual grammar of live-action films, but a two-dimensional image under a camera does not behave like three-dimensional space. Tracking shots, for instance, were almost impossible to achieve in early hand-drawn animation, because zooming the camera in on a flat background drawing would make distant elements grow larger at the same rate as closer ones, which is not how we perceive forward motion in the real world: When we drive down the highway, the far-off mountain and the road sign do not grow at the same pace. With a multi-plane animation stand, however, animators could simulate tracking shots by raising foreground and middle-ground planes toward the camera while leaving the background plane in place. An animation stand of this sort would typically be operated by several technicians working at once, and would require an enormous number of calculations to make sure that rules of perspective were maintained.

He is allowed to make his second film as a solo director in 1974, when he is thirty-three. For his text, he takes an old Russian folktale, a *skazka*. But when he thinks of the look he wants for the movie, he finds that his thoughts keep straying to some ideas he has about Asian painting, ideas that have been with him for a long time. The year his father died, when he was fifteen, he came across a book of Japanese poetry. He was thrilled by its combination of extreme concision and extreme openness, the way it painted tiny, vivid scenes that seemed to contain vast meaning. Now he thinks: Isn't the haiku a perfect template for an animated scene? It offers one resonant action, one perfected moment: The old frog jumps into the pond. The firefly lights up inside the soldier's helmet. His love of Japanese poetry has led him, over the years, to Japanese painting, and then to Chinese painting, and he has been thinking about the ways in which these traditions treat perspective and background: not as a mathematical extension of foreground, but as something free-floating, suggestive. Something unfixed. The hint of a mountain in faint brushstrokes, ink flowing behind smoke.

He thinks that he wants to explore the potential of

indefinite background depth in an animated film. He thinks that perhaps the way to turn animation into the kind of art he values is not to make it self-consciously "adult," not to make it political or place it in explicit dialogue with avant-garde aesthetic movements, but instead to intensify what it traditionally is: uncomplicated, lovely, with access to strong, direct feeling. He imagines a film that is technically marvelous, that is beautiful, but that places the most sophisticated techniques in the service of a haiku-like simplicity. What if it were possible to make films that could be loved by adults and children alike, because they made no distinction between work intended for one and work intended for the other? At their most childlike, they would possess a visionary beauty that linked them to fine art; at their most experimental, they would have the sincerity of lyric and the radiance of childhood memory.

With Francheska, he has been exploring ways to merge his physical cutouts with their drawn surroundings. They have found that if they make the cutout from celluloid instead of card stock, and leave a margin of transparent cel around the outline of the character, they have more control over how the cutout blends into its environment. They have also decided to forgo static background painting altogether. Instead, they experiment with building each background element from multiple layers of cel, then arranging those layers across different planes on the animation stand to create a sense of texture and physical depth, what he calls "a play of the air." So everything is a cutout, and everything is a painting: Francheska, it turns out, manages this brilliantly. At the same time, he is working with Zhukovsky to design a new multi-plane animation stand. It is radically, audaciously simple: three panes of glass that can be moved freely, independent of one another, and a few slots for additional panes, which cannot be moved. Unlike the laborious system used by most large studios, including Soyuzmultfilm, their stand can be operated by just two people, an animator and a cameraman. Instead of being optimized for mathematically precise, classical perspective, it is designed to allow the relation between foreground and background to remain unstated, like that of a Chinese ink painting.

So: In a dark, overgrown garden, full of ruined pillars and fountains, live a heron and a crane. They are lonely, and they would like to live together. But they are also vain. The crane thinks he is the handsomest bird in the garden; you can tell from the smug way he examines the tips of his wing feathers, like a lothario gazing at his fingernails. The heron is a bit of a snob. She walks with her head pointed up in the air, and when she sees the crane, she scans him from head to toe: "Hmph!" He brings her a bouquet of dandelions and asks her to marry him; she blows the dandelion fuzz in his face and says no. But then she thinks: Why did I reject him? I don't want to live alone, so she runs after him and says that she will marry him after all. But now the crane is wounded and angry, so he rejects *her*. As soon as he does, he thinks: But why did I say that? I *do* want to marry her; I should go after her and tell her. And this continues, with each bird alternately acting as the pursuer and the pursued, through many transformations.

The story is a gentle satire of human pride, simple enough for a child to find it funny; the narration, by the acclaimed actor Innokenty Smoktunovsky, is a small masterpiece of baritone suavity. But the film becomes darker as it goes. The heron and the crane begin to seem trapped in a ritual they are powerless to escape, and at the same time their suffering begins to seem more real and less cartoonish. Some of this has to do with the way the setting behaves. The garden is a place of strange yellow mists hanging over faraway fields. The black tree line floats over the horizon. Time seems suspended because space does. The sudden rains that blow through when the birds have an argument feel like iterations of the same recurring storm. In the last scene, the heron walks angrily through one such storm while the crane follows her, trying to shield her with an umbrella. We see them from the side, in profile, and from some distance away, behind long slashes of rain, so that they are only silhouettes. We can't hear the dialogue, but the heron seems to snap at the crane to leave her alone. He falls back. Then he scampers forward, gives the heron his umbrella, and runs off into the storm. The heron, chastened by this gesture of kindness, takes a few tentative steps after him. Mist from the rain covers her up, and though the narrator tells us that the story keeps going, the movie ends.

—

Moscow keeps going. Moscow ends. It is 1976 and he is back in Maryina Roshcha, his childhood neighborhood, to see it before it disappears. The state is sending bulldozers to knock down old houses from before the revolution. The people who live here are being moved somewhere else; soon, when the new apartment towers are finished, people from somewhere else will be moved here. Brezhnev has ideas about how the populace ought to be housed: out with wooden matchboxes, in with concrete piles.

The autumn day is warm. He walks, with Zhukovsky, among the old, sunken houses, in their thickets of dark trees. Zhukovsky takes pictures. Already the place looks half-abandoned. In the yards are piles of broken furniture, plaster statues missing arms and heads, car parts, scattered firewood. He sees a beautiful bentwood chair under a poplar tree, propped up on an old nail crate. A cat slinks by. Zhukovsky speaks to it.

Later, when he sees the photographs, he will think: What a fine silver sheen we give to the departing world.

He is working on a new film. He has commissioned his friend Ludmilla Petrushevskaya, the well-known novelist and playwright, to write the treatment. Petrushevskaya's bleak, intelligent literary work has been banned by the government, but animation isn't literature; why should anyone care if a writer wants to waste time on something as safe as a children's movie? Petrushevskaya has a new baby, and for weeks the writer and the animator have been walking in the park together, pushing the stroller and arguing about ideas.

His last film, *Hedgehog in the Fog*, was a triumph, a picture-book story that left children breathless and animators baffled: How did he make this? The hedgehog sets out on his journey with a tiny bottle of jam wrapped in a spotted kerchief, only to find himself lost in a fog that acts as if it is alive. He is followed by a funny, scary owl who lurks behind him and watches him and mimics his movements. The owl has eyes like round moons and a curved yellow beak, and he looms over the hedgehog with wings spread, as though he plans to have him for dinner. But the owl is also intrigued by the hedgehog; when the little *yozhik* looks down a well shaft and calls out to hear his voice echo, the owl pauses his pursuit to do the same. The fog swirls around them. The owl vanishes, but then reappears right next to the hedgehog. It calls out; then the fog swallows it up again.

It is the fog that astounds other animators. It's too dense and deep to be a drawing, but it cannot be a cutout, and if it is a trick of light and filters, how is it controlled? It opens onto incredible visions, which the little *yozhik* watches with wonder-struck eyes. It parts to reveal a huge white horse, an enormous fish, a bounding dog. It explodes in a glitter of butterflies.

Hedgehog is immediately loved by almost everyone who sees it. But now, in the park, Petrushevskaya tells him that he has come to a dead end. He cannot possibly make a film more beautiful than this one. He needs to look in a new direction, she argues, toward the mundane, away from the magical. He needs to look toward the stuff of everyday life.

He thinks that he would like to make a film about a poet who is misunderstood. But he is also thinking about memory, about the way lives are built up from fragments gathered and mixed together. When you look back on your own life, you never see it as a straight line; it comes to you in a series of moments, loops that play out of order and blur together at the edges. He thinks: Perhaps I could capture the way that feels, that mingling. Perhaps the way to make animation into art is to animate the experience of time.

Petrushevskaya writes a proposal that is deliberately vague. The idea they are working on is not ready for the censors, and in any case he is not yet sure what sort of film he wants to make. So she concentrates on finding the right tone. "This is to be a film about memory," her draft begins.

"Do you remember how long the days were when you were a child?"

They write draft after draft of a treatment about a poet. But when he begins to write the shooting script, he is drawn back to his visit to Maryina Roshcha. He goes to see it again, only to find that the bulldozers have been in before him and left it in ruins.

He had thought of calling his film *Tale of Tales*, after a poem by the Turkish writer Nazim Hikmet. Now he thinks of a new title, one that looks back to his childhood: *The Little Gray Wolf Will Come*.

He and Francheska begin working on designs. They have terrible arguments. He gives her sketches to work from, and he wants her to work quickly, so that her drawings have a spontaneous energy; she prefers to linger over each image until it is perfect. He stomps and thunders. She goes on strike. One night he dreams that he is flying over the earth with lightning bolts shooting out of his chest, killing people on the ground. Francheska tells him that this is all the nastiness coming out of him. But slowly, over months, the look of the film emerges, and a loose structure takes shape.

What he comes up with is a work longer than his other movies—twenty-nine minutes—and far more ambitious. It will have no single plot, but will be made up of parallel stories, or fragments of stories, that emerge and subside and come back again. A girl jumps rope with the help of her friend, an enormous bull who stands on two legs. A fisherman rows out to sea. In the time of the war, a ghostly procession of soldiers drifts through the air. A mother nurses her infant, humming a lullaby. A poet works on a manuscript.

The little gray wolf moves from story to story, watching with big, frightened eyes.

The stories look so different from one another that they might take place in different worlds. The jump-roping girl and the poet live in a warm, bright seaside idyll with almost no color in it: They look like ink sketches flickering on parchment. Another story, set in a snowy winter garden, is vividly saturated with color: There is a little boy eating a green apple, and his coat is sapphire blue.

The atmosphere is melancholic. In the time of the war, young women and young men are dancing under a streetlamp to the tango "Weary Sun." One by one, *blip blip blip*, the young men disappear. Loose papers, blown in by the wind, circle in the air. The women grasp for them, to read the names of the dead.

The little gray wolf makes a campfire near a tumbledown *kommunalka*: his, Norstein's, own childhood home. The doorway to the house glows with what looks like magical light. The little wolf walks timidly inside, and finds himself, unseen, in a room where the poet is writing. The poet's cat is sleeping on the table. The magical light seems to emanate from the poet's pages, lying on the edge of the table. The little wolf's curiosity gets the better of him: He takes the manuscript and runs into the trees. Now he finds that instead of a manuscript, he is holding a crying baby. In a panic, he rocks the baby and sings a lullaby, the one every Russian child has heard before falling asleep:

Baby, baby, hush-a-bye,
On the edge you mustn't lie,
Or the little gray wolf will come,

And will nip you on the tum,
Take you off into the wood
Underneath the willow root.

When the authorities review the film, they say: A sugges-
tion, comrade, about your title. They think he should call it
Memories of My Childhood. He sits in the office of the head
script editor, and while the embarrassed representative of
the state examines a crumb on the table, they agree that he
will instead use the film's original title, *Skazka skazok: Tale
of Tales*. It isn't a bad name, he thinks, only slightly jarring.
Skazka is also the name for a fairy tale. A communist bu-
reaucrat's office seems like a strange place to settle on "once
upon a time."

—

Once upon a time there was a writer whose fear of God was
so great that he died of it. Nikolai Gogol was an odd, thin,
furtive, nervous man—tall, hawk-nosed, slightly stooped;
you picture the cloak forever swirling behind him—with
a biting sense of humor. In 1828 he came to the capital,
St. Petersburg, from a farm in Ukraine and once there proceeded to write a series of brilliant, bizarre stories: not only
"The Overcoat," but also the satirical play *The Government Inspector*, and "The Nose," a story about a man who
wakes up one morning to find that his nose is missing, and,
worse, that it is traveling around the city in a hat and cape,
impersonating a powerful official. In 1842, he published
the first part of his greatest work, the novel *Dead Souls*. He
intended to write two more installments. But Gogol became pious as he aged, and he fell under the influence of a

spiritual elder who convinced him that his literary work was a sin. One night in the winter of 1852, he threw the unfinished manuscript of the second part of *Dead Souls* onto the fire. He took to his bed and died a few days later— of starvation, it is commonly thought, though the official registry lists the cause of his death as "a cold."

The irony is not lost on Yuri Norstein—how could it be, a great Russian artist failing to finish a masterwork adapted from a great Russian artist who died with his masterwork unfinished. Sometimes it seems the process is working in reverse: He set out to adapt Gogol, and instead, Gogol adapted him. But he has no interest in God and no desire to starve himself. "His children tease him," Tania says. "They say, 'Papa, Papa, why do you live this way, why do you make things so difficult? Come on vacation to Greece with us!' But Yuri Borisovich says, 'No, no, I need to be in Moscow. I need to touch the flowers. I need my cross-country skis. I need to feel the wind in my face!'" He likes to swim in his pond and he likes to sit with Kuzya in the studio, and on weekends he likes to visit Francheska at the dacha, where she now spends most of her time. He likes being applauded at his talks. He likes drinking cognac. He likes to storm and yell and fire his assistants, too, but he always hires them back before they get through the door. He looks through books of nature drawings and fantasizes about visiting the Arctic. He thinks that for all the damage people do to it, the world is too fascinating a place to turn away from.

There are long stretches when he does no work, while he summons his creative energies. But when the time is right, Tania says, he works quickly: "Yuri Borisovich takes his little tweezers and goes *tchk, tchk, tchk*, and just like that, a scene is finished."

He likes to tell a story about a time when Francheska surprised him. He has always been in awe of her intuitive connection to nature. One year, they brought home a bundle of nettles that turned out to be full of caterpillars. The caterpillars crawled all over the room; soon chrysalises hung from every available space. One morning Francheska told him, "A butterfly is about to come out of that chrysalis." And as he watched, "my heart pounding with excitement," the shell cracked and a pair of wet wings came through. The wings began, slowly, to beat. Francheska explained that the butterfly was drying itself, preparing to fly for the first time. "She knew in advance each action of the butterfly," he says, and it happened just as she told him. When the time was right, the butterfly stepped out of the chrysalis, and then it began to fly.

Many years ago, when he was fifteen, he was chosen to attend a special art class for talented students. The class met two days a week in a stately old mansion in Moscow, near the planetarium. The spacious quiet of the studio was something utterly new to him. After the dark, crowded *kommunalka*, it opened his eyes to a different world. He discovered Greece through the alabaster statues in the art room: Laocoön, silently screaming; Socrates, bald and with a nose like a potato. He remembers the sound of the easels rattling, the clinking of the watercolor brushes in their saucers. It is good, he thinks, to have memories like these. He keeps them among his sources of enchantment—along with bright light, and sugared bread, and a talking cat whose shadow he can almost see.

Man-Eaters

I

Of the twelve tigers I saw in India, one might have been a ghost; two were in water, eight were on land, and one was sleeping in a tree. One stepped out of high grass, crossed the road in front of me, and disappeared into grass on the other side. One walked along a low ridge on the edge of a different road, oblivious or indifferent to the tourists taking her photograph. One looked out from a cover of branches and red leaves, so perfectly concealed that from thirty feet away he kept stereoscoping in and out of sight. Three were cubs, just four or five months old. Three were juveniles, aged around one year. The rest were fully grown. All were tired, because the days were hot, and because the days were dry they moved and breathed and slept in a film of clay-colored dust.

Every morning we left before dawn, to have the best chance of seeing a tiger. At that hour the lodges didn't serve breakfast, but at four forty-five or five o'clock or five fifteen they put out tea and ginger cookies, and sometimes porridge or fruits. Shadowed safarigoers in camouflage pants and intricately pocketed wrinkled vests gathered in hushed groups around the piles of their camera gear, sipping Darjeeling from china cups. Later, after we had driven for three or four hours, we would stop and the guides would spread a white tablecloth on the jeep's hood and on this they would lay out a full breakfast: hard-boiled eggs in metal tins and green apples and basmati rice and triangular sections of cheese sandwich and salt in fluted glass shakers. Tea was steeped in boiling water, from kettles that drew power from the jeep's battery. If we had stopped at a forest rest area there would be stalls where you could buy hot chai for twenty rupees and Coca-Cola for fifty rupees and also T-shirts, and books of wildlife photography still wrapped in cellophane. Tourists browsed among the tables or threw bits of egg to the stray dogs lying in the dust between the jeeps. I bought a Coke from a boy selling them from a dirty Styrofoam cooler, then looked out at the field of black bushes behind the rest area and wondered how close the tigers came.

As it happened, I never saw a tiger near a rest area. As it happened, the only wild animals I saw near rest areas were langurs, big coal-faced monkeys that congregated in troops along the sides of forest roads, infants clinging to their mothers' necks and staring out with calmly startled eyes. Families of gray langurs would sometimes go leaping through the bushes, and I liked watching them because I liked the front-sprung, bucking gait with which they ran, tipping from hind limbs to fore. I liked the langurs, too, because their unbothered presence near a rest area seemed to suggest that there was nothing, after all, so strange about the scene, that the act of shopping for baseball caps and art books in the middle of a jungle preserve contained no insurmountable irony, that the Coca-Cola and the banyan trees and the cheese sandwiches and the monkeys were merely pieces in a puzzle whose edges were by necessity somewhat blurred. Eventually, my experience in the jungles of Uttarakhand and Madhya Pradesh made me mistrust the convenience of this reasoning; it was comforting while it lasted.

I had no trouble imagining a tiger creeping up behind the T-shirt stand, in any case, because in the presence of a tiger what most astonishes is not its size or its power or even its beauty but its capacity to disappear. I'm sure you've heard about the stealth of tigers on nature shows. It's no preparation for the reality. You will not see a tiger that does not choose to be seen. Maybe a professional guide can spot one, or one of the forest villagers who live around the reserves; for a regular human with untrained, human senses, there's no chance. The way a tiger arrives is, there is nothing there. Then a tiger is there. Outside one of the exits from Bandhavgarh, the densely forested jungle reserve in central India, there is a sun-faded sign. It shows a picture of a tiger, and next to the tiger the sign reads: PERHAPS YOU MAY NOT HAVE SEEN ME, BUT PLEASE DON'T BE DISAPPOINTED. I HAVE SEEN YOU.

The arrival of a tiger, it's true, is often preceded by moments of rising tension, because a tiger's presence changes the jungle around it, and those changes are easier to detect. Birdcalls darken. Small deer call softly to each other. Herds do not run but drift into shapes that suggest some emerging group consciousness of an escape route. A kind of shiver seems to run through everything, a low hum that sounds—

literally, in the murmured Hindi conversation of the guides—like *tiger, tiger, tiger*. This zone of apprehension follows the tiger as it moves. Often, the best way to find a tiger is to switch off your engine and listen. You might then hear, from a distance, the subtle changes in pitch and cadence that indicate a boundary of the zone. But even then, it is impossible to predict where, or if, the tiger will appear.

The first tiger I saw came out into a rocky canyon in Uttarakhand, in the foothills of the Himalayas. We were parked on the rim, looking down. For several minutes before the tiger showed herself, unease warped through the canyon. An unidentifiable impulse made the human occupants of the jeeps on the canyon rim stand on their seats, gripping their binoculars with both hands. Two peacocks that had been dancing on the canyon floor folded their tails and slunk away in silence. And it was very strange: Because the tiger had been, so long as she was invisible, a hazard of pure atmosphere, a permeating energy that filled the whole jungle with dread, when she walked out into the open, she seemed curiously small and specific, no longer a magic aura but a creature bound by a body, with a body's limitations. Above all she seemed indifferent. She had not come to justify the myth we were writing for her. She was not interested in the mood she created or in the sounds her audience made. She was hot, and here was a muddy pool, so she waded into it; that was as far as her participation went. Somehow her aloofness made her even less conspicuous. When she first appeared, I had to have her pointed out to me. I was scanning the canyon floor only for her, yet she had taken several steps out of the cover of the tree line before my eyes would register her existence.

2

At Bandhavgarh, I shared a jeep with Jerry and Verbena, an English couple on holiday from Wiltshire. They were in late middle age and very tall, and they lived near Stonehenge, in a house they described as full of dogs and guns and old furniture. Verbena had been to India before, in her youth, which from her brief anecdotes I imagined as a time of freedom and acoustic guitars and truth seeking, flowers in her dark hair, wild horses, trains to Goa. Her voice was clear and deep, her pronunciation received, her posture immaculate. Would you mind, Brian, she said, if on the way back we stop at that lovely little shop that sells crafts made by the local women? I would quite like to have a look around. In Agra we went, didn't we, Jerry, to a studio where we saw the most beautiful marble tabletop. The marble was inlaid with stones in what really were the loveliest patterns. I was so tempted to buy it, but of course it wouldn't fit our lifestyle, with the dogs. And then, too, in Agra, the prices are always exorbitant.

Jerry was making his first trip to India. His accent was West Country ("China" rhymed with "joiner") and though his manner was mild, even gentle, there was something about him, a stooped ruggedness, that suggested a military past. His blue eyes, watery now, seemed acquainted with long-ago deserts. He kept bees. He knew about the rifles hunters used in the nineteenth century. Had made trips to see famous examples. It had more to do with artistry then, he'd say, gunsmithing. He and Verbena had met late in life, there were grown children from previous relationships, but in Wiltshire they went tramping together through wet woods and hills and built big fires in the hearth and looked up birds in bird books, and at Bandhavgarh they wore matching white neckerchiefs and loose camouflage shirts and tactical sunglasses, and they passed water back and forth and reminded each other to put on sunscreen.

Every morning and every afternoon we drove from our lodge to a checkpoint outside Bandhavgarh, where we joined the line of jeeps waiting to enter the forest. Guards in khaki uniforms moved down the line checking passports. They made ticks on their clipboards. Our guide filled out entrance forms.

They do love a bit of paperwork, Jerry said affectionately, don't they, the Indians.

Until recently, our guide told us, it had been easier to gain access to the reserve. Then, in 2014, it was found that the amount of jeep traffic was harmful for the tigers. Tigers were mobbed by jeeps. Jeeps bristling with tourists and photographers surrounded tigers at road crossings and watering holes. The government announced new rules. Fewer jeeps would be allowed in. Guides would no longer be allowed to share a tiger's location by radio. Core areas were declared off-limits.

The new rules had the intended effect of thinning out the crowds and reducing stress for the tigers. They also produced unforeseen consequences. Fewer jeeps in the parks meant fewer visitors, which hurt tourism. The eco-lodges, which were licensed to operate jeep tours in the reserves, often hired local people, and those jobs were coveted, because they paid well and offered the chance of advancement. Now lodges were closing; people were being put out of work. Fewer tourists in the park also made it easier for poachers to operate, so more tigers were shot, and this problem was exacerbated by the fact that villagers were less motived to help the cause of tiger conservation when their share in the tourist economy was reduced. Deprived of jobs at the lodges, they might turn a blind eye to poaching, or assist in poaching, or even become poachers themselves.

The guard waved us through. We drove into the jungle. Already, just after sunrise, it was 90 degrees; afternoon would hit 115. Sunscreen stung the corners of my eyes where sweat blurred into them.

Jerry and Verbena had seen a documentary about tiger poaching and they knew how much it cost to have a tiger killed. It cost three hundred American dollars. Our guide confirmed this: For $300, you can hire a local soldier to shoot a tiger. Then, if you have the right contacts, you can smuggle the dead tiger into China. It will follow an overland route, across Tibet, through the mountains. At each checkpoint and border crossing, the tiger will be passed to someone else and a fee will be paid, a fee that doubles with each handoff as the dead tiger draws closer to its destination. It will be necessary to preserve the tiger, and perhaps also to butcher it, along the way. A tiger's pattern of stripes is unique to it—if you shave a tiger, you find the same pattern on its skin—and some wildlife reserves keep records of their tigers' markings, so skinning the tiger will help to hide your tracks. In Lhasa, Tibet, you can sell the skin for $10,000. When the rest of the tiger reaches Beijing, it will be sold to a black-market shop for $100,000 or more. Chinese traditional medicine creates the world's largest market for poachers of endangered species, and this is particularly true where tigers are concerned: Tiger bone wine, a rice wine in which the bones of tigers have been steeped, is credited with far-reaching health benefits, and when the bones come from wild tigers, which are valued over tigers raised in captivity, wealthy Chinese will pay astonishing prices. Other parts of the tiger are equally lucrative. Tiger penises, for instance, are prized for their power to enhance male potency. The word "Viagra" is taken from *vyaghra*, the Sanskrit word for tiger.

It turned out that I was bad at spotting tigers. This wasn't for lack of trying. Jerry and Verbena were enchanted by the little birds that swung in clothesline arcs beneath the canopy or perched on fallen branches by the road. They tracked each bird with their binoculars. They craned forward to read the passages the guide showed them in his books. They agreed that the little gentleman really did have the most extraordinary plumage, he must be on his way to a party dressed like that, in his special ruby cravat. I ignored the birds and spent this time scanning our surroundings for tiger shapes. Nevertheless, when a tiger did detach from the ambient background plane of branches and shadows and dead leaves, I was almost always slow to see it, slower even than my companions in the jeep who were focused on something else.

We were stopped twenty yards from a watering hole. Two little tiger cubs, around four months old, were alternately dozing and playing by the side of the pool. The air was full of the feeling of a tiger's presence. A jungle fowl was crowing. I was scanning the trees with binoculars, and Verbena said, Do you know, we had a cock that sounded just like that when I was growing up, his name was Mr. Mustard, and Jerry said, Why Mr. Mustard, love, and Verbena said, Because he was really quite vicious, he had a tyrannical personality, and then the naturalist in the front seat turned with his binoculars and said There, and Verbena and Jerry turned and said Oh my yes oh hello gorgeous, and I saw nothing at all. Only by following the line of their binoculars did I finally spot the gigantic male who had come out of the trees and lain down in the shade near the water. His big flank inflated and collapsed. His muscular tail switched at the air like a cow's.

No doubting what kind he is, Jerry said with a chuckle.

My God, Verbena said, look at his great balls.

We drove under a canopy where soft black tumors that were beehives hung upside down from branches where sun streamed through. Black bees mulled below the hives. I believe I shall have a swim when we get back to the lodge, Verbena said. And then perhaps I will use that coupon that they gave us for the spa. A cool dip and a bit of a massage really would be the loveliest thing right now. Ah! I wish we never had to leave this place.

They were leaving for Delhi the next afternoon, she said. They were taking the train, because it was cheaper than hiring a driver or buying a plane ticket from Jabalpur. Verbena felt that they had perhaps miscalculated in purchasing a second-class fare, because they had ridden second-class from Agra, and on that trip they had been forced to share their carriage with a rather large Indian army officer. This had been all right during the day, but it became a serious problem at night, because the officer snored loudly, indeed snored so violently that you could feel the vibration of it throughout the carriage, like the cup of water in *Jurassic Park*, Jerry said. Verbena had asked the desk manager at the lodge to see about upgrading them to a private first-class compartment for the trip to Delhi, but there was no guarantee that one would be available, and Verbena was anxious about this, as well as sad about saying farewell to the tigers, which she had grown to love.

The jeep stopped at a village and our guide got out. Jerry took off his neckerchief and poured a bit of water into it from one of the reusable aluminum water bottles the eco-lodge had given us. He wiped the sweat from his forehead. The village was clustered around a grassy clearing with a wide tree. There were piles of bricks around the tree and a giant tire, which looked as though it belonged to a piece of construction machinery. A small boy wearing a shirt and no pants was squatting in the tree's shade. Two young women in brilliant saris walked down the side of the road, carrying baskets. The jeep began to drive and Verbena leaned forward. Are we leaving without the guide, she asked the driver, and when he said we were, she turned to Jerry and said, I haven't tipped him, I thought he was coming back.

Uh-oh, Jerry whistled.

The driver asked if he should turn around.

I don't know, she said. Will we see him again? Will we see him tomorrow?

The driver shrugged.

Did you give him something, Brian, she said. How much—I wonder if we *ought* to turn back.

I had given him five hundred rupees as he got out of the jeep. She looked back, but the village was no longer visible in the haze of dust behind us.

All right, she said. I suppose that will be—unless we do see him tomorrow—we can say that is all right.

When we got back to the eco-lodge waiters in collarless

shirts and black trousers brought out tightly wrapped cool washcloths for our faces and glasses of cucumber water for us to drink. We sat in the shade of the long portico outside the dining room and drank cold sweet water and cleaned the dust from our faces and hands. Through the glass wall of the dining room, we could see waiters setting out white napkins beside each china plate. The napkins were folded like fantails. The desk manager peeked out at us from his small office room. Vish, Verbena called, Vish, did you have any luck with the train? Vish had not had any luck with the train. Oh too bad, Vish, Verbena said, that really is too bad, but it's all right, Vish, thank you for trying.

We'll get stuck with some loudmouth, then, Jerry said, not unhappily.

Verbena was looking at BBC News headlines on her phone, and somehow this led, with the sense of a boundary being approached, to their asking what I thought of the new American president.

I said I thought America had lost its mind.

I don't like him, Jerry said carefully, but I do understand the people who voted for him. I do understand that grievance. The way working people have been left behind. He's a poor messenger, in my opinion, but his supporters, they have a point.

He seems, himself, quite unstable, Verbena said. But if you could imagine a better person with the same message, a smarter person, there is something really quite appealing about that. I don't like Trump, I find him frightening. But there is a feeling that the same ways of doing things will no longer work. It isn't only in America. I was surprised when Brexit passed in the U.K. But I do have to admit I was also pleased, because I do, she said, her voice growing colder now, yes I do believe Europe has failed.

3

I liked watching the forest guide go about his work of tracking tigers. He was small and wore a neat mustache and a dark green uniform and he coiled a loose bright houndstooth scarf around his neck and went barefoot. When the jeep was moving fast, he covered his mouth with the scarf to keep out dust. When the jeep stopped to listen for alarm calls, he pulled himself up out of the passenger seat and sat on the side railing with one knee tucked up and a bare foot resting on the door. Occasionally he murmured in Hindi to the driver. The forest was loud with the alien-sonar sounds of jungle birdcalls. The guide listened intently but without urgency. For the tourists packed into the jeeps—the Europeans and Americans in their new safari clothes, the Delhiites in soccer jerseys and Spider-Man T-shirts—seeing a tiger now, this afternoon, might be the difference between a successful vacation and the waste of a small fortune. For the guide, though, the jungle was a crossword he attempted to solve every day. When he spoke in English about tigers, it was always in the singular: the tiger, this tiger, he. He knew that he would find this tiger sometimes, and that much of the time, even if he did everything right, this tiger would not appear.

Now he raised his arm and waved the driver forward with two fingers. We came to a place where a few thin men in long button-down shirts were burning dead leaves on the side of the road. Villagers, the guide said. Forest department have them to do this. The leaves burned in long low piles. The warm air smelled of smoke. The guide slouched on the side rail of the jeep with his chin buried in his scarf and quizzed the villagers about tigers. The villagers held out their arms and chopped the air to indicate direction. The tiger was not here. They had heard alarm calls. The tiger was there.

We saw the jeeps before we saw the tiger. Tourists were standing on their seats craning forward with their phones aimed at something in the trees. Photographers crouched over cameras whose huge lenses, wrapped in camouflage or dusty green covers, were propped on the vehicles' crossbars. The jeeps' drivers kept switching on their engines to jockey for position and when this happened there was a great deal of gesturing and shouting among the guides. Clouds of dust came up when the jeeps moved. Finally I saw the tiger. It was a male, a small one, resting in a pile of fallen leaves under a tree.

The tiger got up and walked toward the dirt road. He came very close to the jeeps. The tourists were excited and began to take pictures faster.

I looked at the guides. None of them seemed alarmed. Tigers in the parks did sometimes kill people, I knew, forest policy and habitat destruction having created a scenario in which conservation itself might inadvertently produce man-eaters. The jungle corridors linking the reserves had been destroyed; many parks had become islands where highly concentrated tiger populations competed for limited territory and prey. When tigers did attack humans, however, it was not tourists in jeeps who were at risk but the villagers whose lives overlapped the boundaries of the reserves. Only a few weeks earlier, in the north, a tiger designated T-28 had dragged a village woman into the forest near Jim Corbett National Park, devoured her, and then killed her father-in-law when he tried to come to her aid. In early 2014, I had read, a tiger at the same park, Corbett, had killed and eaten nine or ten people over several weeks (nine certainly; the tenth might have been killed by a different tiger). The killings created such a panic that a group of villagers stormed a national forestry office. Man-eater attacks often served as flash points for conflict between forest dwellers, conservationists, and government officials. Villagers thought conservationists prioritized tigers over human lives. Conservationists opposed killing problem tigers except as a last resort, and their donors, most of whom lived in cities and overseas, often opposed killing tigers under any circumstances. So did tourists. Twitter campaigns had been waged to save man-eaters.

In the mangrove swamps of the Sundarbans, I had read, around the large tiger reserve on the border between India and Bangladesh, tigers killed forest dwellers at a rate of one per week or more. The attacks had been going on for decades. Probably thousands had died. The jungle in the Sundarbans is waterlogged. Men from the villages paddle small boats into the swamps to gather honey and wood. Women and children collect prawn seeds along the banks. Tigers glide through the water like crocodiles and burst out of it when they attack. For years, villagers in the Sundarbans wore clay masks on the backs of their heads, because it was thought Bengal tigers would strike only from behind. The mask trick worked for some time. Then the tigers figured it out, and the attacks began again.

This tiger crossed the road without looking at us.

On the way back to the checkpoint we met another group of village men. They were stooped under a tree gathering fallen yellow flowers. They piled the flowers into the middle of a blanket. Some of the men bent double at the waist and some of the men squatted. When they saw us, they scooped up handfuls of yellow flowers and brought them to me in the jeep, holding them cupped in both hands. They want for you to be eating this flowers, the guide said. For you, boss, one of the villagers said. I took a few of the flowers. They were fibrous yellow spheres, slightly elongated at the tip. The guide told me their name, *mahua*, and said that the villagers used them to make wine. He showed me how to rinse them with water from my bottle. He poured a little pool of water into his upturned palm and swirled a flower around in it. He popped the flower into his mouth. I did the same and began chewing. The flower was spongy. It had a musty taste. The villagers smiled and nodded as I chewed. From my raised seat in the jeep, absurdly, mouthing a flower, I smiled down at them.

Yes, boss, the man said, as if humoring my ignorance of the world and all things in it. Yes, boss.

4

Our rooms were in cottages elevated fifteen or twenty feet above the ground on stilts. Sometimes rhesus macaques, small pink-faced monkeys with shaggy gray fur, would be sitting on the terrace outside the door, and when you came up the stairs they would leap over the railing into the nearest tree. Inside the cottages were large and light. The rooms had been designed to evoke the British Raj. The walls were white and the faded chairs had wicker arms. From the window, if I pulled back the curtain, I could see out across the forest to the hills.

When I came back from safari I showered, then lay on my back on the bed and watched the lizards that clung to the wall in the places near the ceiling. Sometimes one of the lizards would start to run and its feet made a dry scuttle against the wall as it moved a little and stopped, moved a little and stopped. The ceiling fan turned in slow circles. It was useless to think about "nature." Nature was inconceivable, any vision of it self-negating; how could you have thoughts about the system that enclosed all possible thought? A tiger had no concept of nature. A tiger saw what was. That was why tiger tracks lined the dirt roads all over the forest. The roads made it easier to get from one place to another, and what difference did it make to a tiger who put them there? It was a mistake to think you could imagine nature as something distinct from the part of nature that was human activity, for the same reason it would be bizarre to invent a separate category for all of existence minus squid or silkworms. Yet I realized that in coming here to look at tigers, what I had wanted was to see the wilderness, to be close to the thing itself, and instead I had a strange sense that I was still at home streaming nature videos on YouTube. Except on YouTube the wilderness might have felt more like itself, might have been more recognizably a wilderness, than here in the physical jungle, where you could not help but see everything—the breakfast sandwiches, the access roads, the villages, the confusion—a nature video would have artificially kept out.

It had to do with language, perhaps. If nature could only be grasped through approximations, through terms we could use to frame an experience that was otherwise terrifyingly subjective (what we see is not nature itself but nature exposed to our method of questioning), then here in the eco-lodge our terminology was that of London and Delhi and Los Angeles; we were closer in every important respect to Paris than to the village a few hundred yards away. In Paris, Hermès had dedicated part of the previous year's collection to the big-cat organization Panthera, founded by the billionaire investor Thomas S. Kaplan, whose foundation's website credits him with a "strong passion for wildlife conservation." This was the language we spoke. We, too, felt a strong passion for wildlife conservation. We, too, wished to preserve nature for the next generation. We saw this as a matter of initiatives and campaigns, fund-raisers launched at Sotheby's, outcomes measured in pure numbers and broadcast through mailers declaring "a rare success story." We believed in cautious optimism but much work left to do. This way of thinking, it seemed to me, quickly ran the risk of making the object of reference so abstract as to be unobservable even in its presence.

One day I had been shown a newly built wall. It separated, I was told, the reserve from one of the villages. If a tiger killed a cow or an ox outside the reserve, the villagers were entitled to compensation from the government. If it killed one inside the reserve, they were not. Villagers whose cattle were killed in the reserve had been caught dragging the carcass into their own yards in order to claim the payment, and so the government had built the wall, not to stop tigers from attacking the villagers or their cattle, but to stop the villagers from claiming payments they were not owed. Until 2006, it had been illegal for forest dwellers even to own the land they lived on; the law had been changed over furious objections from conservationists. I was beginning to perceive that not everyone living in this scenario might feel a strong passion for wildlife conservation. I was beginning to think that preserving nature for the next generation might seem a less academic notion in New York than on the threshold of the actual jungle—how under certain circumstances it might sound like a mystifying collection of words, and how it might in fact sound more mystifying the closer to "nature" one came.

One night, before dinner, the lodge showed a movie about Jim Corbett. We were at Jim Corbett National Park; the park had been named for him. Corbett was a legendary hunter who became a conservationist and, in the 1930s, helped establish the park as India's first tiger reserve. The screen was set up beside the pool. Waiters circulated with trays of beer and cocktails. Lights shining from the pool were waveringly blue things on the walls and the trunks of the trees. Jim Corbett was famous for hunting man-eaters. In the early twentieth century, in the villages of the Kumaon hills—not far from where we were now—there had been a shocking wave of tiger and leopard attacks, costing more than a thousand lives. Corbett had shot many of the man-eaters. Big cats that eluded all other hunters, that in some cases thwarted entire army units, he tracked and killed, often alone and on foot. In 1907 he shot the Champawat Tiger, one of the deadliest man-eaters on record, which had consumed more than four hundred people. In his old age, he wrote books about his exploits. The first, *Man-Eaters of Ku-maon*, was a worldwide bestseller in the 1940s.

The film showed a tall, thin man with a shy face and a diffident mustache, captured in grainy black-and-white photos wearing kneesocks, shorts, and a pith helmet. He had a little hunting dog, Robin, which he trained to ride in his coat pocket.

Corbett's ancestry was Irish, but he had been born in India in 1875. When he spoke, which he did softly and sparingly, his accent and diction sounded "chi-chi," half-Indian and half-British. His background left him in a peculiar position, not quite one thing or the other. He had grown up among the Kumaoni villagers and felt close to them, but with them he was inescapably a white man, a sahib, separated by complex codes of privilege and obligation. Among native Britons, by contrast, he was looked down upon for not being British *enough*. He was "country bottled," as the saying went. Colonial societies produce these baffling hierarchies. Were you born in London? Then you aren't one of us. Nevertheless he was devoted to the British Empire. In his old age, after India became independent, he moved to Kenya; easier to leave his lifelong home than to live in a country that was no longer a British possession. By that point he was famous. He dined with Princess Elizabeth, at the Treetops Hotel near Nyeri, on the night her father died and she became Queen Elizabeth II. He wrote in the guest book,

For the first time in the history of the world a young girl climbed into a tree one day a Princess, and after having what she described as her most thrilling experience she climbed down from the tree the next day a Queen.

It had been Corbett's devout loyalty to the empire that spurred him to go into the jungle after the man-eaters. It was his duty, he believed. Colonizers were supposed to improve the lives of the people they colonized; that was the justification for the whole imperial system. Of course it's clear now that the justification was fraudulent, and it was clear to many people in the early twentieth century, but it wasn't clear to Corbett. The irony in this case was that the empire had almost certainly been responsible for creating the man-eaters in the first place; deforestation at lower altitudes had driven tigers into the hills, where game was scarce enough that weaker animals turned to hunting humans to survive. Corbett's heroism spiraled helplessly into the logic of the crisis it was trying to avert: To uphold the empire meant hunting man-eaters, but upholding the empire also meant there would be more man-eaters to hunt. Critics of twenty-first-century conservation movements have a term, "conservation colonialism," to describe the way in which the overwhelmingly urban and international conservation paradigm, however well-meaning, unwittingly replicates the processes of colonial degradation. I had read Corbett's books, and I found the parallels unnerving. If Corbett, whose bravery and sacrifice were genuine, had ultimately been a servant of the vicious system into which he was born, which of us could be sure of doing good?

5

Have I told you about the tiger who fell from the tree? Mr. Sharma asked. Ah, yes; well. It was a rather droll occurrence, which happened to be witnessed by a friend of mine, on a drive very much like this one. In fact, if you'll look just to the side of the jeep—yes, indeed. It happened in that tree, that one there.

Mr. Sharma indicated a wide, bushy tree of medium height, made up of many spindly branches. I don't know, he said, if the tiger was hungry or merely bored, but he saw a monkey in this tree, and he decided to climb up and try to make a breakfast of it. People are fond of saying that tigers do not climb trees. To that rule, we here encounter a rather notable exception. In fact, I believe I may have a video—yes, here it is—of this *interesting* incident on my smartphone.

He handed me his phone, whose screen held a miniature double of the tree I had just been looking at. In the branches of this second, smaller tree, a gray langur was staring with mild disbelief at a tiger that had somehow climbed to within a few feet of her. The tiger looked much more startled than the langur did. The langur had a baby around her neck, but she seemed in no hurry to escape. She seemed not so much afraid as offended. The tiger climbed above her and glared down at her. He had maneuvered himself into pouncing position only to discover that there was nothing to stop him from falling headfirst to the ground. Finally the langur took two easy swings out of the tiger's striking range. The tiger flinched and lost his balance. He flipped over onto his back and tumbled down the tree. For one pitiful moment, he clung to a cluster of low branches, hind legs dangling. Then he dropped ten feet to the ground.

Under the tree, the tiger scowled and yawned.

Look, I said. He's annoyed there's a camera running.

Indeed, Mr. Sharma said. I have never seen a tiger more desperately conscious of his dignity.

Mr. Sharma and I were being driven through one of the inner zones of Jim Corbett National Park. Mr. Sharma was the eco-lodge's head naturalist. He wore rimless glasses and a lodge-branded khaki ball cap and his round cheeks were roughened by salt-and-pepper stubble. Of course when I meet anyone from your country I cannot help but wonder what they think of this character, President Donald Trump, he had said, and when I told him, he said, Ah! Then it appears we can be friends.

The jungle here was darker and seemed older than any I had visited. Mr. Sharma regarded the hushed forest, the towering trees, the masses of knuckled roots with an air of elegant possession, as though we were touring a particularly fine wing of his art collection.

It turned out that I was not merely bad at spotting tigers. In the jungle's half-light, I often saw things that weren't there at all. A peacock was really a bush. A leopard became a dapple of shade on a stone. As we drove among the tree trunks, Mr. Sharma drew my attention to the calling of a fish owl, one of the large nocturnal birds that hunt the forest streams. The owl's call sounded nothing like the *who, who* of the owls I was familiar with. It was a low moan, *mmmm*, faint but insistent, the sound of a person stunned with pain. Very hard to spot in this light, Mr. Sharma said, but the owl is somewhere near.

Then I saw it. It was perched on a fallen tree limb a short way ahead. It was the most beautiful bird I had ever seen. Its body was brown, with a white outline, and the feathers of its head were white. It was beautiful because of its marvelous tail, which fanned out behind it, and because of the angle of its head, which somehow implied a gentleness and thoughtfulness quite different from what most owls' heads express. I stared. Just when I was about to point it out to Mr. Sharma, we drew a little closer, and I saw that the owl was only a broken branch extending from the fallen limb.

A few minutes later, the elephant charged us. We had come around a bend in the road. To our left was a wooded slope thickly covered with dead leaves. To our right a narrow track led into a bamboo grove. Bus, bus, bus, Mr. Sharma murmured to the driver, holding out his hand: Stop, stop, stop. We had seen, throughout the day, trees broken by elephants, branches ripped off and stripped of leaves, trunks splintered and snapped. Now, in the jeep, we looked around. I thought I saw movement in the bamboo grove. I was peering in that direction when Mr. Sharma bellowed and an unmistakable trumpeting came from the other side of the jeep and the jeep lurched, and I turned my head and an elephant was running down the slope toward us.

Uphill, she looked even huger than she was. Her trunk swung from side to side, nearly scraping the ground. The jeep moved away from her, slowly at first, then the engine roared and we went fast. She doubled her speed. She was really charging now. I was in the backseat. She was a few feet behind me. When we swerved onto the track that led into the bamboo grove, she broke off the chase and stared after us, ears flapping.

The jeep stopped. My heart was pounding. We were twenty feet ahead of the elephant. We looked back at her. Dust drifted across the road. Now, Mr. Sharma said, as calmly as if he were in a library, let us wait a moment and we shall see if she settles.

The elephant's tail swished. The lower part of her mouth, a strange, soft beak, opened and closed. She scooped up a trunkful of dust and hurled it over her shoulder, so that dust billowed down across her back. Mr. Sharma said something to the driver and we drove a few feet in reverse, closer to her. She kept her hard black eye on us. With her trunk, she began stripping leaves off the tree she stood beside and thrusting them angrily into her mouth. She chewed the leaves. We moved a few feet closer.

A smaller elephant, a juvenile male with two little tusks, walked carefully around the corner and joined her at the tree. Then an even smaller elephant walked around. A baby. The baby elephant looked wobbly and happy, the way baby elephants do.

I sensed movement again in the bamboo. Then, all at once, I saw them. Among the thin green reeds, elephants were walking. Elephants of different sizes and at varying distances to one another were visible as if through a screen. The herd was all around us. I stood up to take pictures, then sat down with my hand on my head and stared. Mr. Sharma smiled in contentment.

It was after nightfall when we came to the town of Ramnagar. Ramnagar was not a village but a small city. There were motorcycles and cars and phone-repair shops and fruits laid out on blankets on the side of the road. In fact, Mr. Sharma said, Ramnagar is named not after the Hindu god Rama but after an English administrator, Henry Ramsay, who was the commissioner of Kumaon in the nineteenth century. You see at that time it was quite difficult for the people in the area to engage in trade, because to reach the nearest center they would have to pass through a rather miserable landscape. They had an unfortunate tendency, on such journeys, to contract diseases, or to be eaten by wild animals, or to be waylaid by dacoits, who were a species of highwaymen. Ramsay saw that what was wanted was a trading center for the people of the hills here, which they could reach without being molested or eaten. And so he caused Ramnagar to be built, and for many years, under the English, it was a well-run and orderly place, which prospered according to schedule. And then (he smiled, with the gentlest imaginable sarcasm) the English left, and we messed it up.

Traffic squeezed together in a narrow cobbled road that led uphill toward the town's limit. An oxcart was trying to pass across the road to an alley. Cars had been forced to stop for the ox, and motorcycles were nosing among the cars. The drivers honked their horns. The ox's muscles slid a long way when it moved. I call it managed chaos, Mr. Sharma said with a laugh, because for all that each traffic jam seems insoluble, by some miracle they are always quickly resolved. I find it rather a pleasure to see collective human intelligence solving the problems collective human intelligence creates.

People passed along the roadside, young people, old people, men in soccer shirts, women in veils, men in jeans and aviator sunglasses, parents with children, children alone, shirtless children, milling by roadside stalls; the stalls jutted out into the road; there were no sidewalks. Someone started setting off fireworks and a thin, vanquished silver drizzled over the rooftops. Music played from half a dozen radios. I felt relaxed, for the first time in days. That human intelligence could solve the problems human intelligence created was precisely the notion I was growing to disbelieve. For the moment, doubt seemed to press less hard.

The oxcart reached the alley. The traffic jam resolved itself. Streetlights hissed between power lines. Above, on the hill, behind a wall with sawtooth spikes, the jungle was black, a void in the radiant jostle of everything.

6

The first time Jim Corbett hunted a man-eater, it nearly killed him before he saw it. Corbett had followed the blood trail of the Champawat Man-Eater's latest victim, a young woman, into the jungle. The trail led to a small pool. Here Corbett found more blood and bone splinters, as well as deep pugmarks—paw prints—so fresh that reddish water from the pool was still seeping into them. From a distance, he had noticed an object near the pool that puzzled him. Now he crouched down to examine it. It was part of a human leg.

It was 1907. Corbett was thirty-one years old; this was his first time tracking a man-eater. For a moment, the carnage overwhelmed him. "In all the subsequent years I have hunted man-eaters," he wrote, "I have not seen anything as pitiful as that young comely leg . . . out of which the warm blood was trickling." He felt an awesome isolation. The Kumaoni forest is a place of green shadows under dark canopies, towering banyans whose roots spill toward the ground like ropes of melting wax. The tiger was somewhere nearby. A chill crossed the back of his neck. He looked up; a bit of dirt was sliding down the face of the fifteen-foot bank in front of him. In his narrative he remembers the plopping sound the dirt made as it dropped into the pool. From fifteen feet, the tiger had been looking down on him, about to pounce.

He climbed the bank and followed her, stepping carefully through blackberry vines. The ferns ahead of him shook, then went still. Then ferns farther along would begin to shake. When he came to those places, he found streaks of blood. The tiger was dragging the girl's corpse with her, pausing to feed while Corbett made his way over the rough terrain.

Then, from some way ahead, the tiger started growling. A tiger's growl sounds like a Harley engine idling; you feel it in the wall of your skull. "I cannot expect you who read by your fireside," Corbett writes, "to appreciate my feelings at the time." It was beginning to get dark.

He shot the tiger the next day. The end was dramatic, as it usually turned out to be. He'd arranged for men from the village to drive the tiger toward him, banging pots and pans and firing guns in the air. He hit the tiger twice, but not fatally. He was out of bullets. He seized a shotgun from the village *tahsildar* and pursued the wounded tiger onto a large, flat rock. From twenty feet away, he fired. She fell forward with her head slumped over the rock.

What's more striking than the killing is what Corbett did the night before, as darkness was falling. He went back to the pool to bury the girl's leg. Her family would need some part of her body for the Hindu cremation ceremony, and he wanted to make sure the tiger wouldn't find it before they could.

In 2014, a group of amateur Corbett researchers traveled to the north of India and made their way to a village called Phungar. They were trying to figure out precisely where Corbett had started from on the day he killed the tigress. (Corbett is almost clinically detailed in his description of landscapes, but he often omits place-names, which can make it hard to follow his movements.) For years, the group had thought Corbett set out from a different village, Gaudi, because of a claim they had read in a book. But though Gaudi was near the area where the tiger must have been shot, when you actually went there you found that it couldn't have been the right village—the geography didn't make sense.

In the nearby village of Phungar, however, they met an old man who said he had information about Corbett's hunt. The old man's name was Dev Singh Bohra. As he spoke to the researchers, he alternated long drags on the German cigarettes they gave him with bites of chapati. His father, he said, had witnessed the hunt for the tiger. His father had been born at the end of the nineteenth century and was a young boy during the time of the man-eater. His father was perhaps ten years old when Corbett came to Phungar. His father's older sister, he said, had been killed by the tiger while gathering oak leaves near the village. The tiger had carried her into the forest on the day before the final hunt. Corbett had found her leg beside a jungle pool. Her name was Premka Devi. She was fourteen years old when the tiger killed her. Corbett hid her leg so the family would have it for the funeral.

Dev Singh Bohra gave the researchers directions to the spot his father showed him, the hill with the flat rock where Corbett shot the tiger. Starting from where he told them to begin, the group—one of whose members, Preetum Gheerawo, wrote about the search in a book called *Behind Jim Corbett's Stories*—was able to follow the account in *Man-Eaters of Kumaon* to a site that corresponded exactly to the large, flat rock Corbett described in his book. Dev Singh Bohra told them how his grandmother had made her way through the crowd when the tiger was brought to the village. She had beaten its corpse with her fists. Phungar, then, was the village from which Corbett had hunted the tiger—the village whose men, at great risk to their own lives, had driven the tiger toward him. The nephew of the Champawat Man-Eater's last victim was still living there in the year the Indian space program launched its first probe into orbit around Mars.

———

We were in the van, driving to the airport. We drove over broken pavement, past hulks of construction equipment, past fields lined with bell-shaped mounds of straw and dung. We passed crumbling stone farmhouses, turquoise tour buses, tall trees freckled with bats. We passed women making bricks at an outdoor kiln. The women's saris were every bright color you could name.

I was thinking again about man-eaters, though I didn't say so out loud. Nor did I mention the last tiger I saw at Bandhavgarh, the twelfth I saw in India. I was the first to see it, before Jerry and Verbena, before the driver and the guide, even. In fact my glimpse of it was so fleeting that I never had time to point it out; no one else saw it at all. We were driving past a shadowed glade with a wide, dark pool on

which dead leaves were floating. Beside the pool, on a raised
ridge littered with more leaves, I saw a large animal. It was
walking away from me. In the shadows it looked brown,
almost monochrome, different from how I thought a tiger
should look. Yet it moved almost like a tiger. It was almost
the size of a tiger. I think it was a tiger. I think it was real.
I am not sure that it was.

In the Dark:

Science Fiction in Small Towns

I. ATLAS DRUGGED (2012)

On Easter Sunday I fell down our back staircase and had to be rushed to the hospital in an ambulance, so the following Tuesday I took more than the recommended dose of Vicodin and went to see *Wrath of the Titans* at the cineplex in our town's Walmart parking lot. I needed an escape, and I thought if I took enough painkillers maybe it would seem like the Titans were starring in a Sofia Coppola movie. I kept picturing a thousand-foot-high flame minotaur aiming a gaze of numbed-out longing toward the space slightly left of a cyclops, "Wind Cheetah" by T. Rex kaleidoscoping in the air. Chained to the chalky / chalice of night. My right arm was in a sling and was basically useless.

We'd moved eight months earlier, my wife and I, to Carlisle, a Cumberland Valley town of eighteen thousand in south-central Pennsylvania. Siobhan is a college professor, and in Carlisle there's a good liberal arts school, Dickinson College, on a couple of neatly mown quadrangles off the center of town. That was how we'd come to acquire a large, run-down Victorian house on a not-quite-seedy stretch of Hanover Street, across from a funeral home and a Papa John's Pizza. I'd grown up in a small town, in Oklahoma, but I hadn't been prepared for the in-drawn Appalachian Valley character of Carlisle, the bleak quaintness of its row houses, its colonial steeples, its intricately diseased old trees. It made me uneasy, though we came to know wonderful people there. The town had been a frontier outpost before the frontier as we think of it existed, before the Louisiana Purchase; it was the place George Washington rode out from to suppress the Whiskey Rebellion. Now even the historical markers were faded, and the factories were long since closed.

Every fall, because Carlisle stood at the junction of two major highways, I-76 and I-81, the sky filled up with migrating vultures. You'd see them sunning themselves on the roofs of churches, in groups of a dozen or more. At night they roosted in the neighborhoods. Once I left a party, late, and sensed something odd in the darkness. I realized what it was: The trees were full of vultures. Alien rustlings crept among them, which meant they were watching me.

It was particularly galling that I'd injured myself in our house, because the house had been one of the reasons we'd decided to move to Carlisle in the first place, one of the borough's few unequivocal lures. It was the kind of house—big, brick, not literally on fire—we'd never have been able to afford anywhere else. As it turned out, we couldn't afford it there either, because nothing in it worked; everything had to be replaced. Redo this, tear out that. Local builders looked at us and saw dollar signs swirling like Heffalumps. You can try and last another six months with this pipe, but you're gonna thank me if you put in copper. Our contractor was a wild-eyed Jimmy Buffett superfan who went by the nickname "Moon." He spent a good part of each day narrating his long-ago sexual exploits, many of which he'd compiled on the Parrothead circuit. Often these stories made him emotional. He'd stand there with his lips pursed, thumbs tucked into his tool belt, shaking his head as if to say, life, my friends. It was nobody's fault.

We had no furniture and no money to buy any. We sat on camp chairs in the living room and slept on a mattress on the floor. We moved walls. We hung ceilings. One day everything smelled like polyurethane, the next day like tung oil. The backyard was a jungle. I don't mean "we'll spend a weekend weeding and then plant hydrangeas." I mean there were creatures out there that had lairs. If H. R. Giger had been into horticulture, he'd have planted a garden like that. I needed to clear it, but gardening on that level is like submitting to psychoanalysis. You have to be prepared to confront what you find in the depths.

I'd never fully understood why the house had a back staircase in the first place. Maybe servants had used it? That made no sense, I mean logistically it didn't, because the back stairs opened onto the second-floor hallway just a few feet from where the front stairs emerged, an arrangement that would have hilariously undermined the Victorian labor hierarchy it was meant to reinforce ("Go to your *own* staircase, Martha; I'll see you at the top . . . in four seconds"). On the other hand, if we'd wanted a house that made sense, we wouldn't have bought one whose electrical wiring had been spun by silkworms during the Rutherford B. Hayes administration. Our next-door neighbor was a man named

Mr. Piety, who'd formerly been the religion editor for a newspaper in St. Louis. He told us how he'd answered the phones: "Religion! Piety speaking." You took the good with the frankly bewildering, in Carlisle.

———

Vicodin is a weird drug in that, for me at least, it has absolutely no effect, not even the minimum advertised effect of reducing pain, yet when I take it I become acutely conscious of precisely this absence of effect and develop a feeling of numb acceptance specifically embracing the drug's utter virtuelessness. *It's okay*, I think. *It is so okay that this isn't doing anything right now.* This realization does make me feel somewhat more mellow and washed-out about whatever else happens to be going on, possibly just because it gives me something else to (not) focus on. Which I guess qualifies as an effect, although kind of a watery, delicate one. Someone once told me, and I could see how this was the case, that hydrocodone turned pain into a movie you were watching or, if you were lucky, a song you could hear from the next room. As this paragraph probably makes clear, I'm not really cut out to take drugs of any kind, and for the most part I don't, but this week I was making an exception.

Wrath of the Titans was a late show. By the time I arrived at the theater, there was only one other person in the lobby, and he worked there, a lava-lamp ovoid of male youth in a heather-blue cineplex-issue polo shirt. His name tag said: BOB. Okay: BOB. BOB sold me a ticket, and here I ran into a complex bit of trouble, because I tried to use a free-ticket voucher I'd gotten as a reward for participating in the theater chain's discount-card program, only it turned out that the voucher didn't apply to 3-D movies, which *Wrath of the Titans* was, and BOB, who spoke slowly and with an anxious, mouse-like precision, had to explain to me that the cineplex's concession-counter computer interface would allow the face value of discount-card vouchers to be applied toward a larger order total, but the ticket-counter interface would not, meaning that I could use a voucher for a small popcorn toward the cost of a medium popcorn, but not a voucher for a regular movie ticket toward a 3-D movie ticket, although, BOB told me sadly, "we've been hoping for an upgrade for a while."

I wanted to ask if it would be possible to use a regular movie voucher toward the cost of a medium popcorn, i.e., if the concession-counter interface was sufficiently advanced to enable trans-categorical discount offsets, but this seemed like a lot of words to say at one time, so I slid my credit card over to BOB across the slightly mottled and somehow interestingly dense-feeling gray laminate countertop. I did this tranquilly.

Since you asked: I fell down the back staircase because I was wearing socks and carrying dishes and we'd just had that staircase refinished and the top was slippery and I took a bad step, just one of those things. Trust me when I say I'd have made a great Marx Brother, apart from the weeping. I had no permanent damage, just a better-than-average excuse to look up "hematoma" on Wikipedia, plus this arm I couldn't move for a few weeks. A medium degree of medium-term pain, which I was dutifully killing, or at least filtering. Not much compared with the trials of Perseus.

Weird thing about BOB: Maybe eight minutes after he sold me the ticket, after I'd one-armedly hauled my stub and transaction receipt and cellophane-wrapped 3-D glasses and medium popcorn and Pepsi back to auditorium 6—it took two trips—and discovered that I was the only person in auditorium 6, and started to wonder if perhaps I was the only human being in the entire cineplex, not counting BOB, so that auditoriums 1–5 and 7–8 were airing their explosions and murders and desperate kisses to the empty air, while I was processing all that, deep in the coming attractions, BOB wandered into the theater, carrying one of those orange-cone flashlights that ushers walk around with, and saw me, and did a freaked-out jiggle in place.

"Oh shit, someone's in here!" BOB said, and scurried out.

I wondered about this, at the time, less than I should have. My only immediate reaction was to look at Facebook on my phone. On Facebook I saw that back in my hometown, in Oklahoma, my high-school friend Kara had uploaded a picture of her kids, and in the background of the photo, behind her two sons, you could see a piece of art she'd hung on the wall. It was a giant poster that read INSANITY IS MERELY AN OPINION.

I think the Vicodin had mostly come online at this point.

———

I have a dumb affinity for cornball sword-and-sandals epics: thus *Wrath*. For cornball SF and fantasy in general, really, although like most former child nerds I have somewhat particular taste. I prefer stuff that's actually good, of course, but am often happy with stuff that definitely isn't, as long as it seems to reflect somebody's odd extruded personal vision rather than just, like, orcs. What I don't like is genre work that's neither great nor endearingly awful, but merely competent and serviceable about meeting expectations. I felt tremendous fondness for the original 1981 *Clash of the Titans*, which I'd seen as a kid, loving in particular the golden owl, Bubo; years later, when I read "Sailing to Byzantium" for the first time, and got to the part where Yeats asks to leave his mortal body and be refashioned as a golden bird, Bubo was what I pictured him becoming. The movie I was seeing tonight was only thinly related to that film, though, being the unasked-for sequel to an unnecessary 2010 reboot. It was a sure bet to be terrible. The question was whether it would be terrible enough, and in the right way, for me to maybe enjoy it by accident. A lot of the time getting by in this world requires outmaneuvering your own intentions.

Stirring music. Camera gliding through deep space. Constellations wheeling in 3-D. Intro voice-over: Man's fate is written in the stars. If, for instance, you're an accomplished English character actor, your fate may be to intone exposition over opening credits for money. Blame the stars!

The early scenes were a mixed bag, badness-wise. Whether because of the opioids, or the effect of solitude, or the fact that BOB had screwed up the volume on auditorium 6's surround-sound interface, the whole thing came at me in a numb, murmurous rush, through a faintly buzzy sheen of overexposure. On the other hand, shit kept breaking that plane of coolness—violent, mythic shit that tended to erupt right when I was hoping for a big Sofia Coppola zoom out followed by a Pastels song. Perseus (Sam Worthington) would be talking to Zeus (Liam Neeson) about what Hades (Ralph Fiennes) said to Ares (Edgar Ramirez), when suddenly Perseus (Worthington) would be snatched up into the air by a two-headed fire-breathing demon-dog (MacBook Pro) and hurled into a marble column (Doric). Beast swarms of various descriptions kept pouring out of the mouth of Tartarus, right toward me, in 3-D. Piety speaking! The Vicodin membrane wasn't quite strong enough to keep it all out.

They take a lot of damage, these heroes. Having recently experienced a degree of blunt-force trauma myself, I wasn't entirely prepared for how it would feel to watch half-naked, very vulnerable-seeming human bodies crash through stone walls, or bowling-ball into temples, or fall to the ground from fifty feet in the air. One thing you can say about the Greek myths is that they're often astonishingly beautiful about killing people. My favorite moment in *Bulfinch's Mythology* comes when Perseus (Worthington), the selfsame hero of *Wrath*, is denied hospitality by the giant-king Atlas. This makes him furious, so he pulls out the head of Medusa, and

> Atlas, with all his bulk, was changed into stone. His beard and hair became forests, his arms and shoulders cliffs, his head a summit, and his bones rocks. Each part increased in bulk till he became a mountain, and (such was the pleasure of the gods) heaven with all its stars rests upon his shoulders.

Like reality, though, *Wrath of the Titans* mostly sticks to hurling people into very hard objects. And occasionally lighting them on fire, impaling them on a trident, snapping their necks, electrocuting them, choking them to death, and transforming them into disintegrating sand sculptures.

At the same time, though? Nobody feels any pain. The heroes are mainly demigods, which is like being on Percocet at least. They're anesthetized by their own awesomeness. By and large, *Wrath* adheres to the timeless law of damage in action movies, which is also the idea the NFL dined out on for years—that slashing can wound you but concussive force can only move you around. No deep-tissue bruising for Perseus after being swung around like a private wrecking ball by the ogre that jumps him in the labyrinth of Tartarus, only a razor-thin cut where its horn-shard grazes his pectoral. Everything is sort of numb, although the Jesus and Mary Chain is nowhere to be heard and the only whispered personal revelations are between Heston-bearded gods played by aging male Oscar winners. It was okay, I decided. I had a wrecked elbow and a complicatedly dislocated shoulder and the back of my thigh looked like a map of ancient Greece, but I felt fine, and Perseus & Co. kept getting hit by comets, but they felt fine, and we were all floating in the dark, waiting for the fire-minotaur to show up, feeling fine together. Insanity is merely an opinion.

———

It's a little odd, given the movie's title, how few Titans actually put in an appearance. We're not really talking about the wrath of the Titans, plural, so much as the wrath of one Titan, Kronos, who is admittedly no slouch in the wrath department (make no mistake: he's furious), but still, a really appalling amount of potential wrath gets left on the table. Mnemosyne, for instance, is a Titan who I would think could dispense very terrifying wrath—she's the mythological personification of memory. Kronos can lay waste to the desert (although why, it's already a desert), but memory is what really kills you. Especially since Perseus's whole motivating backstory has to do with anguish over his lost home, his dead wife and daughter. Imagine what Mnemosyne could spin that into, if they'd flown in, say, Cate Blanchett and given her some scenery to chew. *Don't tell me you've forgotten already?* she'd sing. "Should the pillars of memory / topple out of my reach, / I must remake the air," Pablo Neruda wrote, which is an incredible action sequence if you've got the CGI budget for it.

We floated there, Zeus and Andromeda and I. By any standard of human achievement predating about 1900, *Wrath of the Titans* is a deathless miracle, a visual wonder you could escape into for days. The sight of Kronos, father of the gods, lumbering across the plain, this living mountain of brimstone, would have upended civilization in Queen Victoria's day. The Goya painting of the same character is terrifying because it's an expression of mad, almost will-less appetite, a staring animal driven to consume its own child. The Kronos of *Wrath*, by contrast, is simply a malignant machine. No pity, no fear, hardly even the capacity for desire, just a numb, annihilating force rolling forward, leaving nothing feeling behind.

By any applicable standard from almost any prior point in human history, it was completely transfixing. By today's standards, it was just a dumb, fun-enough thing, a minor example of the influence of *Shadow of the Colossus* on movie-monster scale. Where we're at, I thought, the machine has long since passed by. I thought about tweeting that, but it would have hurt to get my phone out.

Afterward, the lobby was deserted. Not even BOB was around. The lights had been dimmed, though the mini-arcade was still bleeping in its corner, partying contentedly in its medium-tech ghost town. I felt sure that I was the only customer at any cineplex in America at that moment, and that BOB was waiting for me to leave so he could close all of them. I hoped that somewhere, maybe in a bigger city, he could try out his upgraded interface.

I adjusted my arm in its sling, tried unsuccessfully to pull my jacket on, and called Siobhan to come pick me up. Our house was five minutes away, so I had five minutes to kill in the parking lot. Panera Bread was closed. GameSpot was dark. The lights from Walmart looked a long way away. I thought about anesthetics, how they differed from analgesics—painkillers—how you could trace that through the words' Greek roots. I didn't know which one to file this night under. You could make the case—people had—that American culture itself was now mostly one or the other. But that, too, was merely an opinion, and I didn't think it was mine.

In my case the Vicodin wouldn't wear off for another couple of hours, if it was even doing anything. Then I would take some more. I looked up and the stars looked back down like an interested audience. Chained to the chalky / chalice of night. The moon was as white as a bone.

2. COMPUTER LOVE (1989)

We had orange carpet in our living room in Oklahoma, where, on regular weeknights, I would stay up and watch *Star Trek: The Next Generation* instead of doing my algebra homework. My seventh-grade algebra teacher was a sneering, straw-haired, lip-smacking wearer of short-sleeve dress shirts named Mr. White, whose strategy for handling classroom disruptions was to flex his biceps one at a time and say, "I call this one Thunder and I call this one Lightning. Let me know if you'd like an introduction." Mr. White spent the first part of every class bivouacked behind his desk reading *Whitetail Bowhunter* magazine, which gave me time to get caught up, imperfectly, if I'd skipped a problem set the night before.

In our living room, on the wall across from the TV, my parents had hung a couple of 1930s advertising posters for Royal Mail cruises. When the black reaches of space appeared during *Star Trek: The Next Generation*'s opening credits, you could see the cruise ships' reflections in the TV glass: the *Enterprise* sliding at its usual bold angle out of starry darkness, SOUTH AMERICA BY ROYAL MAIL, with its big blue ocean liner and flaming tropical sunset, shimmering like a nebula around it. Also reflected: me in pajamas on the couch. Sometimes my dad would watch with me; sometimes the rest of the house was asleep.

I wasn't a Trekkie; not really. The minutiae of setting, the language of the truly devout, left me cold. I didn't know the rules of tridimensional chess or care about Romulan politics. I'd tried watching the original *Star Trek* and found its cartoon-bright universe—the soundstage brawls, the sonar blorps, the happy overacting—almost incomprehensible. For some reason, though, *The Next Generation* awakened in me a feeling of serious, almost overwhelming yearning, that suffocating childish escape wish that's the wake of a certain type of fantasy. That feeling that in a different world you'd be yourself. I carefully recorded each episode on our VCR and typed out labels on my enormous electric typewriter, a Christmas gift from a year or two before. One VHS tape held two *Next Generation* episodes, so I had to fast-forward through the first in order to get the label timings. "Who Watches the Watchers 0:00:00" b/w "Déjà Q 0:58:59." Having the correct timings seemed vital, possibly because so many *Next Generation* episodes themselves hinged on matters of fine timing, radiation leaks with critical exposure imminent, warp jumps that had to be calculated to the nanosecond (yet somehow always involved a character yelling, "Now!"). Except to get the episode lengths, I don't think I ever played the tapes. None of my friends watched the show, or at least we never talked about it. For me, the series was a fleeting, unconnected ritual, a regular hour when everything hushed and got bright.

One of the problems with revisiting science fiction is that every voyage into the future eventually becomes a voyage into the past. I recently rewatched the entire run of *Star Trek: The Next Generation*, all 178 episodes, and I found that traveling to the show's twenty-fourth century sent me hurtling backward at about warp 9. That's partly because the series is bound up so strongly in my memory with those misfit hours of adolescence. It's also because *The Next Generation* itself is helplessly, indeed movingly, of its time.

You can't help but notice this, watching now. The first sign is that for a franchise that famously defines space as an extension of the Old West, *TNG* very quickly dispenses with almost any sense of a frontier. Captain Kirk's *Enterprise* was a ship of phaser-happy explorers forever pressing onward toward the next fistfight on the next undiscovered planet; in comparison, Captain Picard's *Enterprise* is a calm, sleek vessel of end-of-history galactic administration—a faster-than-light embassy, complete with chamber music concerts. There's very little fighting; there's a great deal of personal growth and a staggering amount of trade-pact negotiation. Many, many episodes turn on the decidedly nonstandard TV plot of "something has gone wrong with a diplomat." There's an only-global-superpower, world-policeman feel to most of this: The Klingons, the wild, violent others of the Kirk series, are now allies of the Federation. Everything's running smoothly. The crew's heroic quest is just to keep it that way.

So they transport medical supplies. They help colonies fix their weather-control systems. Gene Roddenberry's guiding vision of the Star Trek franchise was, famously, that it would offer an optimistic vision of humanity's future. The Soviet Union collapsed a couple of years into the filming of *The Next Generation*, and the show's optimistic future became startlingly coterminous with the optimistic present of the George H. W. Bush presidency. Where else but space could you find a thousand points of light? The grand adventure of the NCC-1701-D was no longer to spread civilization, or even defend it; it was just to keep the machinery oiled. Remember 1991, America?

And it breaks. There is something bizarre and significant about how often the *Enterprise* breaks. Geordi La Forge, who is the chief engineer but who still has to crawl on his hands and knees through the ship's cramped interconnecting Jefferies tubes to spot-fix most problems himself—well, let's please note that after a couple of weeks of welding between-decks trifusium relays in order to prevent cascading sensor-pattern overruns from harmonically generating a reactor-core breach, I myself would not retain the tenth part of Geordi's amiable disposition. One of my uncles was a tech enthusiast who lived in a geodesic-dome house and built (and subsequently crashed) his own airplane. One Christmas, not long after I discovered *Star Trek*, he gave us a towering beige computer—it must have run MS-DOS, if that—and gave me a quick course in hacking the autoexec.bat file. I was the only one in my family who used this PC, which I remember as physically fortresslike. It was always broken, always, and always broken in some complicated and hard-to-define manner that meant you could use it, but not use it *all the way*. It would work, but loading programs, or whatever I was trying to do with it, would be elaborately difficult. If the constant malfunctions Scotty had to cope with on the first *Star Trek* series were drawn from large-scale stuff, war experience and manufacturing and the rapid expansion of infrastructure, Geordi's troubles seem to reflect the small-scale nightmares of late-eighties personal computing. Machines— nanobots, space stations, the ship itself—are constantly becoming sentient. This thing has a will of its own! Whole episodes revolve around arbitrary glitches and bugs. (For instance, every episode in which anyone goes into the Holodeck, for any reason, ever.)

The Next Generation drew something like twenty million viewers a week in its heyday, a colossal number by today's standards, and the penetration of the show's keywords— "energize," "engage," "Number One," "I am Locutus of Borg," "resistance is futile," "make it so"—was light-years beyond what you'd expect from a syndicated SF show. But in a way, it's no wonder. The *Enterprise* crew was driving a misfiring IBM PC in the service of a quasi-neoliberal agenda, and so, at the same time, were we.

———

But why, then, that yearning? No one lies awake at night longing to be transported to a convincing imaginative extrapolation of early-nineties social themes, or if they do I have yet to find their chat rooms. It's obviously the case that the great obsession of American television—family—was also in play on the bridge of the *Enterprise*. It's in play on almost all TV shows, of course; there are exceptions, but even most shows that don't revolve around actual families revolve around impromptu families centered on work or sitting around in a coffee shop or whatever. I suspect that this has equal amounts to do with the centrality of family in American life and with the mechanics of staging a television show: When you have a regular cast whose interactions form the bulk of any plot, there's always going to be a tendency to portray their relationships as overridingly important and to indulge the little bit of wish fulfillment that says they can satisfy all their emotional needs in one another.

Like *The West Wing*, say, *The Next Generation* offers a fantasy of smart friends working together and supporting each other; it's designed to make you want to join them. When you're a skinny thirteen-year-old who's nervous a third of the time and bored another third, the idea of roaming the constellations with Captain Picard, whom adventure follows like a shadow and who always knows what to do, is bound to have a powerful appeal. And as the show advanced through its run, *The Next Generation* became very good at fusing its thematic concerns with the kind of intense fan service a long-running SF series probably can't do without. Loneliness barely exists in it; characters on-screen by themselves are usually about to be attacked by glowing balls of light or semitransparent children. By the third or fourth season, the show runners had realized that *TNG*'s two major themes, the android Data's ongoing inquiry into what it means to be human and Picard's personification of enlightened humanism, could just as easily be explored around a poker table, or while feeding Data's cat, as they could during computer meltdowns and alien standoffs. Data's little visor and Troi's relationship with her mother and Picard and Crusher's wistful breakfasts and Geordi's dating woes and Picard's discomfort around children—all of this stuff seemed peripheral, but assuming you wanted to hang out with these people in the first place, it was a delight.

But *The Next Generation*'s appeal went beyond the image of your brilliant best friends saving you a seat in Ten Forward. As a preface here, think about the Harry Potter series. One of the reasons J. K. Rowling's books exerted magnetic power over every sentient creature on earth is that they resolved, indeed fused, a cultural contradiction. She took the aesthetic of old-fashioned English boarding-school life and placed it at the center of a narrative about political inclusiveness. You get to keep the scarves, the medieval dining hall, the verdant lawns, the sense of privilege (you're a wizard, Harry), while not only losing the snobbery and racism but actually casting them as the villains of the series. It's the Slytherins and Death Eaters who have it in for Mudbloods, not Harry and his friends, Hogwarts' true heirs. What results is an absolutely bonkers subliminal reconfiguration of basically the entire cultural heritage of England—and thus the backstory of much of the modern world. It's as if Rowling remakes a thousand-year-old national tradition into something that's (a) totally unearned

but (b) also way better than the original. Of course it elec-
trified people.

Star Trek does something similar, though with an American contradiction that's arguably even more fundamental. It
was already possible, by the early 1990s, to trace the terms
of the current partisan divide in America. Conservatives—
think in Jonathan Haidt–ish terms here—value tradition,
authority, and group identity; liberals value tolerance, fair-
ness, and care. Or whatever; you can draw the distinctions
however you'd like. The point is, The Next Generation depicts
a strict military hierarchy acting with great moral clarity
in the name of civilization, all anti-postmodern, "conservative" stuff—but the values they're so conservatively clear
about are things like peace and open-mindedness and concern for the perspectives of different cultures. "Liberal" values, in other words. You could say, roughly, that the Enterprise
crew is conservative as a matter of method and liberal as a
matter of objective. They sail through the universe with colo-
nialist confidence sticking up for postcolonial principles.
Starfleet has a Prime Directive . . . but it's explicitly noninter-
ventionist! This is so weird that it's almost hard to notice; your
mind slides over it. But it's fascinating in numberless ways.
Picard is both indisputably the most patriarchal Star Trek
captain and indisputably the least likely to punch anyone in
the face. No one is more individualist than the individuals of
the Enterprise ("If there's nothing wrong with me, maybe
there's something wrong with the universe"—Dr. Beverly
Crusher, "Remember Me," 1990), but their individualism has
led them to reject most forms of private property (because it
actually holds them back, they're so boldly individualistic)
and embrace ultracentralized health care. It's nuts, but it's

also a vision of the American psyche that, if you can get into it, makes a lot of fine things suddenly seem possible, and makes some debilitating anxieties simply fall away.

———

The thing I can't shake, having taken in all 133 hours of the series, is that Data's positronic brain doesn't have a wireless connection. When *The Next Generation* wants to impress you with the superhuman information-retrieval capabilities of a twenty-fourth-century android, it shows him, uh, reading really fast. Not that you expect a 1980s TV show to be accurate with respect to near-future technology, but there's something about *TNG*'s enormous pass on networking, its total failure to see interconnectedness as part of the Federation's eventual culture, that seems more revealing than any of the predictions—warp fields, the iPad—it did get right. There are episodes, kind of a lot of them, in which Data has to be shut down for one reason or another, and one of the other crew members pushes the hidden catch on his head that opens his cranial access panel, and a little square of hair swings up off his scalp and you see his metallic skull. And there are tiny banks of Christmas-type LED lights blinking on it in an arrhythmic sequence. The main impression you get is of the *enclosedness* of Data's head, its armored separateness. The model for a thinking computer is not a cloud of decentralized cognition but a hard shell containing a single distinct self.

By contrast, when Picard is kidnapped and assimilated by the Borg, the species of hive-mind albino cyborgs that poses the major existential threat to the Federation, what's emphasized is the physical violation this entails, how Picard's body is ripped open to receive the Borg implants that erase his individual consciousness. *The Next Generation* is surprisingly anxious about the idea of sharing thoughts in general. With the exception of the telepathic Betazoids, who are mostly represented positively, creatures who communicate through mind reading or centralized consciousness are seen either as villainous or as so remotely alien that they can't be comprehended. Networking, either organic or technological, transgresses *Star Trek's* ideal of individualism, in which the thrust of personal development is always toward independence, uniqueness, and competence. Technology is meant to be a tool you can use or not; it's not supposed to change the way you think. No one is ever alone on the *Enterprise*, but there are depths to which togetherness can't penetrate.

Star Trek: The Next Generation aired its final episode in 1994, the year before I got my first e-mail address. Watching it again over the last couple of months, I've had moments when I wasn't sure whose future I was supposed to be projecting myself into. Series lore suggests that we, the current denizens of Federation Sector 001, Sol system, are going to grow up to become the self-reliant, fencing-class-taking, light-to-casual computer-employers of the twenty-fourth century. On the other hand, I've seen a race of electronically linked humanoids who share information in a vast decentralized net to which they all have access; who see data as a neutral atmosphere, like air; who use technology to share thoughts and impressions at all times; who are never out of contact with one another; and who react to the briefest removal from their shared consciousness with an itchy, frantic eagerness to get back. Remind you of anyone? They fly around in giant cubes and occasionally erase whole civilizations, like Apple Maps.

I have no idea whether the heroic (but responsible!) individualism of the *Enterprise* crew is a relic, a quaint throwback that was already being assimilated by the Internet while *Star Trek* was busy articulating it, or whether the type of humanism Captain Picard represents can survive the transition to online culture more intact than *TNG* wants us to think. Part of me desperately wants to believe the latter. What I'm certain of, though, is this: I am Locutus of Borg. Resistance is futile. And—another part of me wants to add—oh, God, make it so.

3. IN THE DARK (1993)

What I remember first about that year is the darkness of the nights. We would pile into a car and if we all had late enough curfews we would drive out of town, past the last light, on some country road we didn't know the name of, fields and stars as far as we could see. When there was a lightning storm on the plains we'd drive toward it, watching slashing omens craze across the sky; otherwise light was what instinct led us to avoid. My friend had an ancient and indestructible Oldsmobile, the color of a polluted lake, and we drove it down alleys as fast as we could, we crashed it into other people's trash cans. We bought grape slushes at Sonic and snuck into the park off Canterbury Avenue, across from the golf course, where we'd sit under the trees and tell each other stupid and wonderful things. We had been there as children hardly any time ago; now, in the dark, it was transformed. If you've ever been seventeen, and especially if you've ever been seventeen in a small town, you've had your own year of dark nights. But when you are seventeen, and especially when you are seventeen in a small town, you believe that there is opening before you a mysterious and uncharted realm that exists for you alone. You and your friends are conspirators in a shadow country.

I didn't watch *The X-Files*, which premiered that fall, on September 10, 1993. I was wasting time at an advanced enough level not to need help from television. But *The X-Files* was there, in the background, for that year and for several years after it. In my memory of that time it seems to be running, muted, on every TV in every room I enter after dark. We are huddled around a phone trying to figure out whether there are such things as girls we might call, and in the other room we see the back of my friend's mother's head and Mulder's and Scully's faces staring out at us. Years later, when I watched the show in sequence, I never minded the incoherence of the main storyline, which infuriated longtime fans, because I was already used to imagining the series as a montage of empty atmosphere, and in fact had fallen half in love with it as such. The show's cinematography, lush by today's standards and astonishing in 1993, looked shadowed and moody, and because Scully's expression was a striking combination of horror and numbness and bravery and trauma, none of which we had experienced and all of which we wanted to pretend we had experienced, it seemed only natural that the show would slide along the margins of our secret world.

The names alone were thrilling. Mulder and Scully: Somehow the words were both left field and all-American, weird and out of time and stylish. They could have been in *Bringing Up Baby* or they could have been rock stars or they could have been murder victims in a film noir. (That year, I went to every old movie that played at the Poncan, our town's converted vaudeville theater.) And they were deep; they were haunted with overtones. "Mulder" with its echoes of "mull" (to ponder) and "molder" (to decay, to turn to dust); "Scully" with its baseball reference wrapped around the obvious "skull." Not watching the show, I still knew its basic program, that the heroes were FBI agents investigating the paranormal, that Mulder was the intuitive one who believed in telepathy and aliens and Scully was the skeptical one who didn't, and it resonated because something like that conflict was at work in our lives, too. If we made fun of *The X-Files* for the simplicity of its contrast between "belief" and "science," it was because our own experience was just that simple, and because unlike Mulder and Scully we had no language in which to discuss it.

I took pride in being furiously rational. At the same time I often felt that my sanity was a mirage and that with one second's concentration I could dispel it forever, like smoke. Mulder and Scully argued about whether the craft that went down in the woods of Wisconsin was a UFO, while we drove at midnight to the old Robin Hood Flour plant by the train tracks, a looming tower of rusted cylinders deserted before we were born, and argued about whether to break in. Mulder and Scully uncovered monsters in the timberlands of Oregon and Virginia and Maine, while in Ponca City we told stories about the murderous spirit who haunted the Indian reservation in the form of a beautiful woman. Known as Deer Woman, she could run alongside cars on the highway and if you looked over into the next lane and made eye contact, she would steal your soul. Which sounds ludicrous, right until the moment when you are seventeen and driving at night down an empty country road.

We had been lied to so often that we spent half our time seeing through lies, but inexplicable things still happened. We had been told not to understand things we understood, and at the same time we knew there was more to the world than anyone was willing to tell us. The truth was somewhere, and perhaps it was mundane and perhaps it was magical, but then when you are seventeen in a small town, the felt distance between those terms is perhaps less than is commonly supposed.

And then there was the big thing, the one that was omnipresent in our town, the one *The X-Files* groped toward but never quite knew what to do with. When our life sciences class arrived at the unit on evolution, our teacher, who was also the wrestling coach, made it clear that he was continuing under protest. He held a piece of chalk as he said this, and stabbed mildly at the air with it. We were all free, he said, "to not necessarily buy into what's in the book." Half the class nodded and looked grim.

One weekend I followed my girlfriend to a raft retreat organized by her church, in some hills three hours from town. My friend and I lost our way looking for the cabin. We got there in the middle of the night. There had already been a bonfire and a sing-along with the youth leader's guitar and now the teenagers were spread out in the dark summer air, under humid masses of trees, communing with the Spirit. They each held an arm up, like unsteady radios. There was excitement when we appeared because an angel had come down to dance with my girlfriend (she was the pastor's daughter, the angel always danced with her) and we were the first audience for the story. No, you couldn't *see* the angel, but you could tell it was there, she wasn't just reaching her arms out, she was holding on to something. You could see where its fingers were pressing her skin. I went rigid with contempt, at which point the youth leader, whose name was R.J., got out his guitar again and tried to win me over by sing-talking. "It's like what Bono said," he hummed. "Fuck the mainstream." I spent the night in a rough wooden bunk in a room with five or six earnest boys from farm towns, and if this had been an *X-Files* episode, if the roof had split open and the floodlights of a UFO pounded down on us, I'm not sure which of us would have felt vindicated.

———

Of course what I didn't know then was that *The X-Files* rigged its own central question, that the dichotomy of science versus belief never resolved in favor of science. Scully was always wrong, always, and most episodes let you know she was wrong before she even appeared on-screen, before she had a chance to speak. The liver-eating immortal bile-mutant would slither through the air-conditioner shaft toward its victim in a shot whose objectivity was not tainted by the presence of a perspective character, and then we'd cut to FBI headquarters, where Mulder, in his Ambien-furred morning voice, was saying, "Hey, Scully, what if the killer's some kind of bile-mutant," and Scully would look stricken and respond with a theory about swamp gas or atmospheric contaminants, a theory so self-evidently lame that the viewer was not even expected to remember it. Scully's wrongness and the show's determination to see the paranormal everywhere unwittingly reversed the whole polarity of the series: It became clear before long that what Scully meant by "science" was not "the scientific method" or "testing hypotheses based on observable evidence"—an approach that might lead you to believe in ghosts around the thirtieth time you saw one—but simply "the canon of currently accepted scientific knowledge," which bizarrely became the show's most irrational article of faith.

You could argue, and I would almost agree with you, that beneath all the obvious post-Watergate, post-JFK government-conspiracy machinery, the real subject of *The X-Files*' stylized paranoia was the American city's anxiety toward small towns. The show out-noired noir by recognizing that the most extreme context for modern alienation was not the mean streets of the detective story but a white-collar bureaucracy that extended infinitely above the protagonists—literally into space—and that could control them without their knowing how or why. But in practice, Mulder and Scully spent most of their working hours, especially in the stand-alone "monster of the week" episodes that made up the bulk of the series, pursuing mysteries in Lake Okobogee, Iowa (where Ruby Morris was abducted by aliens in "Conduit"), or Delta Glen, Wisconsin (where the agents investigated a cult in "Red Museum"), or Miller's Grove, Massachusetts (where cockroaches attacked humans in "War of the Cophrophages"). The strangeness and isolation of small towns was a theme the series returned to again and again. One of the show's most beloved episodes, "Home," takes place in a small Pennsylvania town where a hideously deformed, inbred family molders in a disintegrating house, a nightmarish vision of the freakish underside of Capraesque normalcy. Darin Morgan, the show's cleverest writer, had approached the same subject from the opposite side in the second season, when, in "Humbug," he sent Mulder and Scully to a town populated by circus freaks whose behavior is surprisingly pleasantly normal.

In this show about not knowing, then, the agents confronted two distinct sets of frightening unknowns. On one side was the shadow government represented by the Smoking Man. On the other was the evil that lurked beneath the surface of every American town. Often, Mulder and Scully's role was simply to act as interpreters between their own antagonists, rendering chaotic eruptions of village horror comprehensible to men in marble corridors in D.C. Think of all the shots of the heroes in their oversized 1990s glasses laboring at their field reports, or again of all the shots of them cruising through a hostile rural enclave in businesslike topcoats and a sensible rented Buick.

The X-Files was probably the first great TV show to be galvanized by the Internet and the last great TV show to depict a world in which the Internet played no part. Its fan culture found a home online early in the series's run, but though the role of computers became both more central and more realistic as the show progressed—in season 1, an operating system became sentient and took over an office building; three years later, Scully's word processor made the switch from green text on a black background to black text on a white background—it was possible at least through the fifth season or so to see the web as a distraction, something with no important bearing on anyone's life. Remember when you could turn it on and off?

It used to be a critical commonplace to say that the Internet destroyed the old American monoculture, because it freed us to be absorbed by our own interests, to spend our time downloading obscure anime rather than caring about Madonna or ABC. But the Internet also created a new type of monoculture: It made every place accessible to every other place. We no longer assume, now, that the peculiarities of our own environments are private. Our hometown murders might appear on CNN.com. The world of small-town *X-Files* episodes is still that older world of extreme locality, where everyone in town grows up knowing that *the rules here are different* and *we handle it ourselves*. Children vanish or trees kill people or bright lights appear in the sky, but there is no higher authority to appeal to and it has nothing to do with what goes on a few miles down the road. In my hometown we knew that the spillway by the lake was where you painted a memorial if your friend was killed in a drunk-driving crash. It's the same thing. Here is here. And this is just the opposite of the here-is-everywhere world inhabited by the conspiracy, which is global in scale, utterly connected, and ruled by pseudonymous men whose flat-affect, no-eye-contact meetings were almost the personification of a chat window.

> SmokingMan1963: how do u want to proceed
> FirstElder: u need to take care of the girl
> SmokingMan1963: haha the pieces are already in place
> FirstElder: i hope so
> FirstElder: for ur sake
> SmokingMan1963: haha lmao
> SmokingMan1963: u don't trust me?
> SmokingMan1963: ?

The small-town grotesques in the series lived with secrets. The Syndicate curated them. Almost more than belief and science, the sustaining tension in *The X-Files* is between two manifestations of the American psyche, one fading and the other just taking form, as they encounter each other for the first time and recoil in horror.

————

One day in the spring of my senior year of high school, Timothy McVeigh blew up the federal building in Oklahoma City. I was not at home, having left that morning on a trip to visit colleges. It was the first time I had been on an airplane.

There was something wrong with the government. In Oklahoma, we all knew that. Some injustice or some imbalance, some flaw too deep to be named, seemed inherent almost in the landscape. The silos spoke of it and the trucks spoke of it and the big sagging hay bales spoke of it, and the oil wells rolling their shoulders on the horizon thought of it but didn't know what to say. The TV above the *Super Mario Bros.* machine at Mazzio's Pizza played a never-ending montage of police swinging batons, Los Angeles burning, the white Bronco gliding down the freeway, oil fires in Kuwait, and when our fathers sometimes pulled their tables together they smiled terse smiles over their pizza and talked about taxes and said it was coming on time for a change. Donald Trump was a fading minor celebrity and the idea that he might one day enter politics would have been too inane even to be comical, but a wave was building, a long way away. If we borrowed our parents' cars and forgot to hit the preset for KMOD or KOSU, we might catch ourselves listening to hypnotic radio hosts who claimed that Bill Clinton was mad, a cokehead, a murderer, none of which we could prove or disprove, it was all so far away. The margins of knowledge receded into a distance that left the feeling of wrong intact but removed the explanation. The structure of things was a skeleton whose skin was falling away.

This is why I stopped at saying I would *almost* agree with you if you thought *The X-Files'* paranoia had mostly to do with cities and small towns. For all their differences, the series's two realms shared a basic assumption about America, which was that in essence it was still meant to be the country found in Frank Capra movies: white, Christian, centered on families, governed by old men. This was a status quo that was already doomed, though still superficially in effect, when the show began. Mulder and Scully function as its representatives, figures of a weird reactionary beauty, struggling to understand and then prevent the profound transformation breaking out across their world. Earth is not alone, aliens are among us, our way of life is under threat; is it so hard to locate within these sources of terror the sense of a vanishing historical phase? ("Fight the future" was the tagline of the first *X-Files* movie, in 1998.) Think of the way, for most of the show's run, Mulder and Scully have chemistry but not sex: Sex implies procreation, hope, a continuity that their experiences have destroyed. (When Scully discovers that she has a child in season 5, it's an alien hybrid, created from harvested eggs.) Instead, they move in the dark with a sort of numbed longing, whispering to each other through cell phones, waiting for the world to end, not a hair out of place.

———

In 1995 I left for college on the East Coast, where I spent four unhappy years watching beige snow pile up on sidewalks. The day the plane landed in my first year I had a melodramatic impression that my life was over and in fact it was, at least as I remembered it. I spent a great deal of time remembering, an absurd amount of time for someone so young. I did not know—because I had still not watched *The X-Files*, had still seen it only in the background of things—that Mulder's obsession was just as wrong as Scully's: There are forms of resistance that hasten the disappearance of the thing they are trying to preserve. Mulder's sister was abducted by aliens when he was twelve, and his monomaniacal quest to find her underlies the plot of much of the series. But it leads him into a world of conspiracies and lies that destroy his ability to experience life as he knew it before she was taken. Trying to prove the reality of his loss makes the loss the only thing that's real to him. The show repeatedly underlines the self-defeating tendency of Mulder's work. Innocents die (Scully's sister in "The Blessing Way"), monsters are freed by the system (Eugene Victor Tooms, the liver-eating mutant, in "Squeeze"), the truth retreats from view (in "Gethsemane," for instance, when the conspiracy manipulates Mulder into suspecting that everything he's learned about the conspiracy is a lie planted by the conspiracy). The futility of Mulder's heroism is probably the aspect of the series that's proved most prophetic. Mulder's life's work was essentially to become a Chelsea Manning or Edward Snowden, revealing secret government misdeeds to a public he trusts to correct them. He would have loved WikiLeaks. But WikiLeaks, far from forcing a great moral reckoning, only subsided into a continuum with Russian state hackers. It became a tool of the state repression it set out to expose. The accounting Mulder assumed would happen never took place.

"What is more precise than precision?" Marianne Moore

asks in a poem. "Illusion." In the same vein Albert Einstein said that all true science begins in "the sensation of the mystical." But *The X-Files* was never interested in science. I remember as clearly as anything a night when one of my best friends showed up at the ice cream parlor with a goldfish. His parents had just been divorced and he was assigned to do a school project with a girl and in a helpless gesture of sympathy the girl brought him a fish. She hadn't thought as far as a bowl so they were taking it around in the plastic bag from the shop. It was the most beautiful thing. We ate our sundaes and it hovered on the table, this bright discrepancy. Recently I asked my friend about this and he couldn't remember that it had ever happened, or he said it seemed vaguely familiar but he couldn't recall any details. His girlfriend at the time, who is now his wife, had no memory of it at all. Neither did anyone else I talked to.

Was it real? Did my memory invent it? What about the owl I saw once, which landed in front of my car, with a silent clatter of wings, one night in Ponca City? I stopped the car and it looked at me in the headlights. I remember its furious eyes. I remember the gray-brown half-moons on its white belly. I don't remember precisely when or where I saw it. For years I've wondered if I really did.

My friend who did or did not have a goldfish was the one who eventually introduced me to *The X-Files*. My father told me not long ago that we did have an owl that year, living in our backyard. He saw it many times, he said, gliding at night over the creek that ran behind our house. I never saw it again.

Once and Future Queen

I. ELIZABETH IN ENGLAND

Her City

London, late summer, the trees inheriting autumn, the pavement a history-book map tracing a dwindling empire of rain. Traffic pushing through the evening, along the parks, around the monuments, a stream of headlamps parting for angels and cannons and kings. England in September: The sky is gray but the air is blue. Beside the river, the crowds lined up beneath the Eye are craning their heads back to take pictures of the sky's steel miracle, the plexus of spokes and beams; above the river, the crowds inside the Eye are craning their heads forward to take pictures of two little gingerbread castles, Parliament and Big Ben, lit up for the night like sweets wrapped in gold foil. Twilight, a rider on a different Ferris wheel, coming slowly to the earth. Faces of walkers along the Thames, and of cyclists along the Thames, and, half glimpsed, of drivers along the Thames, moving in and out of shadow like a word on the tip of your tongue. Buildings shining out of puddles, upside down. This present moment: darkening London, settling itself down to begin, once more, the work of becoming yesterday.

At night the city is illuminated. Each gargoyle on a wall grins in its own clear spotlight. Globes of light run in the water like smears of melting pearl. Walking east beside the river, we have passed towered bridges and merloned battlements, feeling as darkness comes on the presence of an older London, that low-slung city whose arms open out toward the sea. Even at this distance, the sea is palpable. You feel it in your sense of scale, a width just past perceiving. The men who laid these stones were masters of the sea. The strength of this city is the ancient strength of the sea. Englishmen, when they sleep, dream of the sea. In old days, these waters were crowded with masts. Ships with huge sails set forth from here to make war upon the world. England's safety is its ragged coast, its rocks, its cliffs, its place at the convergence of the tides. England pulls the sea around her like a mantle: these waters our robe of ermine, these stars our imperial crown. This is the order that outlasts one night and the next. That outlasts circumstance. What you feel around you, in this cool air, is not what's passing or what's past. It's what's perpetual. Sea and stone, the steadiness at the core of things, the solid facts of place and ritual. No need to make a fuss. It is enough, if you trust your role in the order, to hold your gaze steady. Sometimes it is enough in this world to be patient, and do your duty, and bide your time.

Her Handbag

She carries a five-pound note, crisply folded, for the church collection plate. Sometimes ten pounds; never more. She carries lipstick, which at least twice she has been seen to apply in public: once in 2000 and once in 2014, first at the Royal Cornwall Agricultural Show and then at the opening ceremony of the Commonwealth Games. Her mirror she keeps in a small metal makeup case that her husband gave her on their wedding day. Her wedding was in 1947. The country was still under austerity measures then. She bought the silk for her dress with ration coupons. The silkworms that spun it came from China. On the day of her wedding her train was thirteen feet long. Her white satin dress was sprinkled with embroidered flowers. Her wedding was devised as a symbol of England's rebirth, its recovery from near destruction in the war. The emperor of Ethiopia sent her a golden tiara as a gift. The nizam of Hyderabad sent a wreath of diamond roses. On the morning of the wedding, the tiara she planned to wear as her "something borrowed"—it belonged to her mother—snapped. A police escort rushed her jeweler to his workroom. He fixed it just in time. As she stepped down from her carriage outside Westminster Abbey, light shone on the loose pattern of wheat ears, an ancient symbol of fertility, made from the ten thousand seed pearls sewn to the gown's skirt and bodice.

Her bags are made by a company called Launer, from calf leather lined with suede. She favors long handles because she is often called upon to shake many hands in a row, and she finds it most comfortable to slip her bag over her left forearm as she does so. For many years the contents of her bags were a mystery, but then someone wrote a book about them, a book based partly on information divulged by sources in her household, and now most of the newspapers in England have run stories about what she carries in her purse. She carries her reading glasses. She carries treats for her dogs. Sometimes one of her staff cuts out a crossword puzzle for her, and she carries that. In her father's time it was considered shocking for a servant to speak to the press. In 1950, her former governess, Marion Crawford, whom she loved, published a book about her and her sister. The book was called *The Little Princesses*. Neither she nor her family spoke to Crawford again. Crawford moved to a house near the road to their estate in Scotland. The family would pass by without acknowledging her. Crawford attempted suicide, writing in her note, "I can't bear those I love to pass me by on the road." When Crawford did die, in 1988, thirty-eight years after *The Little Princesses* was published, neither she nor her sister sent a wreath to the funeral.

There are so many claims on her time. Because she is often required to be gracious while also being greatly in demand, she uses her bag to send coded signals to her staff. Placed on the table, it means *I wish to leave within five minutes*; on the floor, it means *discreetly extricate me from this conversation*. At luncheons and dinners, she likes to hang the bag from the underside of the table, on a hook she carries with her for the purpose. More than one guest at an occasion of ceremony has registered surprise, before the meal, at the sight of the queen of England spitting into her hook's small suction cup.

Her Standard

There is, or was, as recently as a few years ago, a bluff-faced man in a dark blue uniform, looking something like a constable—plump of cheek, erect of bearing, wide of eye—whose job consists in raising, lowering, and caring for the queen's royal standard at Buckingham Palace. When he receives word that Her Majesty's motorcade is approaching, he climbs by a narrow set of back stairs onto the palace roof, carrying the bundled flag under his arm like a rugby ball. He positions himself upon the roof in such a manner as to be able to identify the motorcade from some way off. When he makes visual contact, he salutes—a lonely, invisible figure—then runs the standard up the flagpole. The black iron gates swing open for the line of automobiles. As the queen's state limousine drives through, he pulls the cord that undoes the bundle, allowing the flag to spill out into the wind. Her Majesty is officially at home.

There are other standard keepers, because the standard must fly wherever the monarch is in residence, and the queen has other homes. Indeed, she has other banners. Her personal flag is not the same as her royal one. Her royal standard in Scotland is not the same as her royal standard in England. The protocol of her flags and the protocol of her family's flags are coordinated by professionals within her household and within a multitude of international governments. The papers now, in this September of 2016, are full of the news that later this month, her grandson William and his wife, Kate, will fly to Canada on a royal visit to the Yukon Territory. Complex conventions govern the standard that will fly over their visit. William's personal standard in the Yukon Territory is based on the escutcheon of the Royal Arms of Canada, defaced with a roundel bearing his cypher, a *W* surmounted by a cornet, and a label charged with a red shell resembling that of the coat of arms of his late mother, Diana, Princess of Wales.

But the standard keeper at Buckingham Palace is responsible only for the standard that flies over Buckingham Palace, Her Majesty's standard, and that, in his view, is quite enough for one man to worry about. He folds the flag according to a special method, in a special room. He keeps it dry. He airs it out when Her Majesty is away. He ensures that each of its four quadrants remains lustrous in color and free from dirt, from rents, from moths. It is the little rift within the lute, Tennyson says, that by and by will make the music mute, and if the standard keeper does not quote these lines to himself as he goes about the performance of his duties, he would surely recognize them as an apt motto for a man in his line of work.

He knows the flag's four quadrants like the back of his hand. First and fourth quadrants: three gold lions passant guardant on a red field, representing majestic England; second quadrant: red lion rampant on a gold field, representing bold Scotland; third quadrant: gold harp on a blue field, representing tuneful yet curiously lion-averse Ireland. He thinks with satisfaction of the black cabs all over London. When they drive tourists past the palace, what do the cabbies point out? They say, if you ever want to know if the queen is at home, just look for that flag there, that one. What is that moment but his own small kingdom? He faces the camera, in the royal documentaries in which he appears, with bashful pride, looking a little amazed, a little transfixed by the dignity of his office and the responsibilities vested in him.

Her Outfits

Someone or other is always trying to kill her. She sees no point in tracking individual threats; one has people for that. She does not regard the possibility of being murdered as a reason to alter her schedule. It is an inconvenience of life, like long speeches and bad weather. Nineteen eighty-one, for instance: a month before her eldest son's wedding to Diana Spencer. She was dressed in the ceremonial red tunic of the First Battalion Welsh Guards, riding her favorite horse, the black mare called Burmese, in her annual Birthday Parade. As she rode past the crowd on the Mall, a seventeen-year-old boy named Marcus Serjeant fired six shots at her from a replica Colt Python revolver. The shots were blanks, but in the moment, no one knew that they were. Burmese spooked at the noise and nearly bolted. She leaned forward in the saddle, calm, and soothed the horse while the police went after Serjeant. The boy said later that he would have liked to kill her, but he had been unable to find real bullets. He said that he wanted to be famous, like Mark David Chapman, who had assassinated John Lennon the year before. Once Burmese was settled, she straightened her tunic and continued with the parade.

In 2005, Ayman al-Zawahiri, then the number two leader of al-Qaeda, proclaimed her an enemy of Islam and a target for jihadists. In 2007, Ugandan terrorists posing as a television crew filled two broadcast vans with homemade bombs, intending to blow her up at a Commonwealth summit in Kampala. In 2014, an al-Qaeda-affiliated magazine published an article urging lone-wolf assassins to kill her at the horse races, her love of horses being widely known. In 2015, four men were arrested for plotting to stab her to death at the Royal Albert Hall. As a girl, to keep safe from German bombs, she slept in the dungeons at Windsor. At fourteen, she recorded a radio address to persuade the United States to join the fighting. Her father, the king, held dances throughout the Blitz, leading conga lines through palace staterooms. What is there to do but carry on?

It is right, of course, to take precautions. Sensible precautions, for her, come in the form of mint jackets, pink dresses, yellow hats. She is famous for her wardrobe of bright monochromes: pink tweeds and lime-green woolens, magenta silks, lemon veils. But her ensembles are not matters of style only. Her clothes are an issue of state security. She makes herself a block of vivid color because she is so often in crowds. Her protectors must be able to see her. Predecessors of hers, it is true, wore brilliant devices on their shields, yet were sometimes lost in battle. Still one prefers to believe one might trust one's guards to look out for the lady in violet.

Her Heir

Prince Charles is now sixty-seven years old. He has the bearing of a man who has fought bitterly, with the tooth and claw of detachment and protocol, to survive the immense good fortune into which he was born. A scholar manqué: heavy but intangible. Proceeding down the sidewalk with his fingertips pointing downward into the pocket of his double-breasted suit jacket, umbrella hung over the opposite forearm. A man with camel coats, bowler hats, a face like a shaved fox: pointed, defeated, amused. Age-mauved cheeks achieved sunlessly, as if, by the same principle through which ice can be scalding, he had burned himself by spending too much time in the rain. There are men who command a room with their presence, men whose vitality bullies the air. Charles compels attention through a mechanism inverse to this, a kind of charismatic absence: Reality warps toward his titles as toward a reluctant black hole. Then he regards reality, with his loose, sad eyes, as if he wishes it would go away again. We are sure, he seems to say, to disappoint each other. A pity: but there it is. No use pretending.

There is speculation that when his mother dies, Charles will allow the succession to bypass him. He cannot possibly wish to be king. He would be the oldest monarch ever crowned in Britain. He could not help but appear, to his subjects, as something pitiable, an enthroned anticlimax. So why not let the job sift down to the younger generation, which looks more suited to it? In fact he does not have a choice. The assumption of kingship is not volitional. Should you be next in line when the reigning monarch passes, sovereignty enters with your next breath. And then, when his mother dies, the only monarch most of her subjects have known in their lifetimes, the grief will be international and paralyzing. It will not be a time for violating tradition, or making personal stands.

What he could do is abdicate. His great-uncle did, Edward VIII, to marry his American divorcée. An act still viewed with shame within the family. Charles is made of different stuff, in this sense: That the faithful performance of duties he dislikes is the measure of strength that authorizes him, in his own estimation, to dislike them. The less he wants the throne, therefore, the less he will be free to give it up. He will have to be king because he will hate it so much.

So: a man for puttering in gardens. A man for planning

with great care the slight repositioning of a retaining wall. A man for books of medium age, read in uncomfortable chairs. Not a cruel man, but self-protective, unpracticed in kindness. When his first wife threw herself down the stairs in misery, he went out to play polo: a normal day already the limit of what he could deal with. (He tries to be better for his boys.) A man who loves nothing more than to write an editorial about wool. He has done so, in fact, this very month, for the *Telegraph*, on its uses and capacities, its neglectedness in the era of synthetics. "The much bigger contribution that wool could, and should, be making in our lives." This is his Britain: a land of practical craftsmen, pride in workmanship, the preservation of old ways. Shoes lasted in Northamptonshire, tweed woven in the Hebrides, slippers furred by Draper, umbrellas ribbed by Brigg. What if I told you that candles use less energy than lightbulbs; what if I told you that music has not advanced since the motet? Sent into the world this way, to face Brexit and BBC News with the help of a Stuart horticulture manual and a malacca walking stick. To face modernity's submarines, with his twin rows of suit buttons gleaming like Lord Nelson's gun ports.

Her Castles

Hawthorn flowers only once each year, but in Glastonbury, where legend says that Joseph of Arimathea brought Christianity to Britain, some hawthorn flowers twice: once in the spring, like the common plant, and once in the winter, at Christmas. The flowers are white and quilled with red-tipped stamens. Their scent is hideous; medieval peasants said that the smell of hawthorn was like the smell of plague.

But they are beautiful. Legend has it that Joseph thrust his staff into Wearyall Hill, where it sprouted branches and grew into a holy thorn tree. Legend says many things in Glastonbury. It says that once, when these lands lay under water, the hill now called Glastonbury Tor was called the Isle of Avalon. It says King Arthur is buried there, or the Holy Grail is buried there, or both are buried there. It says that thousands of years ago men made a gigantic map of the stars, a kind of terrestrial zodiac, out of the landscape itself, by lining up hedgerows and trackways: Its remnants, legend says, may still be traced. It says that the Tor is an entrance to another, older world. It says that Glastonbury is a gateway to Annwn, the land of the dead.

Each year at Christmastime, the pupils of St. John's Infants' School gather at the Church of St. John the Baptist. They sing carols. The vicar makes a speech. Then the school's eldest child cuts a flowering sprig from a twice-flowering holy hawthorn tree. The sprig is wrapped and sent to the queen at Buckingham Palace. Each year, the thorn blossoms travel with the royal family to Sandringham, their estate in Norfolk, where they spend Christmas; and each year the sprig sits at the center of the table, among crystal decanters and silver candlesticks, at Her Majesty's Christmas dinner.

Stability, tradition, the repetition of symbolic gestures, the preservation in politics of an identity with roots sunk in myth: These are advantages monarchy offers over more republican forms of democracy. In the United States, for instance, the election of each new president occasions panic and fury from the losing side, because the question of what the nation *is*, how the nation is to be imagined, is forever an open one. It is possible to go to sleep in a country in which one believes and wake up in a country one no longer recognizes. To her subjects, she offers herself as a check against paroxysm, as a continuity. This symbolism has limited efficacy, perhaps, but it has efficacy, and over a long time its influence is enormous. An empire or an island, in Europe or out, what we are is to be found not in a party or a manifesto but in the cohort of things that last.

At Windsor Castle, her place near London, there is the legend of an oak. Shakespeare, who put on plays at Windsor, wrote about it. It might have started with him, or it may be an older story, one not written down until the time of the other Elizabeth. Versions of the tale vary, but it begins in the forest of Windsor, where there is a tree that men fear to walk by at night. Long ago, a huntsman named Herne died there, hanged from the branches. Now he appears under them, a glowing ghost, with a stag's antlers sprouting from his head. Or else he comes at the head of a wild hunt, lightning flashing, his horse trailing demon hounds, monstrous owls circling. With faery frenzy they wheel about the sky, and those who see them are cursed, or made to join them, or doomed to die. A midnight storm out of hell: centered on a tree not an hour's walk from the castle walls wherein ten generations of ladies and lords have lain sleeping.

Not a story to take seriously, perhaps; but it would be a mistake, too, to lose all sense of the ancient magic of Britain. The queen is the land, and there are ways of being with the land that are not ways of London. In London her privy councillors kiss her hand and walk backward out of the room; she receives a sculpture of a Bengal tiger from the high commissioner of Bangladesh; tourists pose outside her windows taking selfies with stuffed sheep. It is a relief to ease into the country. *Two maidens fair rode to the wood, and dew was on their gown, sir.* At Balmoral, her castle in Scotland, you can hear the floors creak. You can hear the wind. In the evening the lights come on one by one, like children being born. At Balmoral, she pilots her Range Rover and looks at oxen and watches grouse being shot. She ties a kerchief around her head and wears a tartan skirt and goes walking with her corgis in the mist. She leans against rail fences. She asks after the planting. On the snouts of huge horses, she lays an appraising hand.

Her Husband

He makes her laugh. That is what people say about him. Always in a tone of faint apology: Oh, well, he may be an antique, cadaverous, a racist, a snob, a bully to his son, scornful, impatient, brittle, and close-minded, but Her Majesty needs to unwind somehow, doesn't she? There is, in the business of ruling, a great deal of inevitable false consciousness. To be royal at all is to accept that you are better than everyone else. Myself, our family, this bloodline, chosen by God to stand above the nation. But in a democracy it will never do to say this out loud. So one makes a great clamor about service. One places oneself humbly at the disposal of those over whom one is elevated: I wear these diamonds not for myself but for you. For this sort of twaddle Prince Philip has no patience. Why should he remember the names of the tribes in some tiresome jungle, or worry about the mental health of unwed mothers, when a Rolls-Royce is waiting to take him home to his guns and his claret? His little jokes slash away at false egalitarian cobwebs; they must feel bracing, if you happen to be royal, in the way that the exposure of a hidden but operative logic always does. My dear, these people are beneath us. He makes her laugh: standing behind her, telling it like it is to the world's smallest audience.

As a boy he loved to swim. After his grandfather's assassination, his family was forced to flee Greece, and he spent years bouncing from one half-strange relative's palace to the next. Boarding school in England, boarding school in Germany. Shouts from the cricket field, Hitler salutes in the halls. He celebrated his ninth birthday at Wolfsgarten, a grand *Schloß* in the German state of Hessen, riding his new bicycle and bouncing a colored ball in the pool. He played there with Christoph of Hesse, the fiancé of his sister Princess Sophie. Christoph: dashing, enthusiastic, obsessed with fast cars and airplanes; he died in 1943, an *Oberführer* in the SS. Philip's next-oldest sister, Princess Cecilie, joined the Nazi Party in 1937, along with her husband, Georg Donatus, the hereditary Grand Duke of Hesse. They were killed in a plane crash soon after. Hitler sent condolences; Göring attended the funeral. Philip attended it, too, in Darmstadt, walking behind the coffin through streets draped with swastikas.

What language did you speak at home, Your Highness? Home? At the Cheam School, in Hampshire, the pool was outdoors. The shock of it in cold weather, the roar of it in your ears; slap of hands on water, chilling gulps of air. He won one medal for swimming, another for diving when he was eleven. When his father died Philip inherited his gold ring, his ivory-handled shaving brush, and his debts. His mother, who was Queen Victoria's great-granddaughter, was diagnosed with schizophrenia and sent to a sanatorium. He went years without hearing from her. During the war she lived in Athens, where she sheltered Jewish refugees. At eighteen, as soon as he could, he joined the Royal Navy and went to war against his own brothers-in-law.

The world is very large. The life of a monarch encompasses many things. After Elizabeth married him he began finding himself in new countries, odd, uncomfortable places, meeting chieftains and suchlike. Damnable odd fellows! Accept this sword, made from a great whale's tooth. We present you with this bow, this hide, this dish of ants. Remember their names, remember the modes of address. Blessedly the younger generation are now as capable of hying off to God knows where as he was once, in the Stone Age, which takes off some of the strain. Soon his grandson and the Middleton girl will leave for the Yukon Territory—imagine, a royal tour of the Yukon! Snow and ice and not a dram of good scotch in the place. Securing the allegiance of those very important royal subjects, polar bears at the end of the earth!

Well, they'll have enough to keep them busy. No shortage of ninnies who want to bask a minute in the aura. Never a lack of locals to placate. So often the royal couple's duty is to make others feel important. Easy enough when your importance has never been in doubt. But he has been homeless in the finest castles in Europe; he has nurtured the small flame of his own prestige through terrible nights. The map he read by it never showed him these decades of vague, agreeable service. It helps, of course, to know he is doing his duty. But duty, around the small grain of his mortification, is a pearl that never quite closes. Give him the playing field, the decks of his old ships: places where he could trust reason and ruthlessness and where—quasi-orphan that he was—he knew whom he needed to impress. Hold your nerve. Prove your worth. Privation, like war and sport, is clarifying. It is only when you get to the top of the pile that they blame you for knowing which way is up.

Her Daughter-in-Law Who Is Dead

When Diana turned eighteen her parents bought her a flat in London, so she moved to London and lived there. She lived with three friends whom she charged eighteen pounds a week. She painted the walls in pastels. She organized the cleaning schedule. She hung a sign on her bedroom door that said CHIEF CHICK. She had recently taken a cooking course where she learned to make chocolate roulades and borscht, and she sometimes made a roulade for her friends, but her favorite foods to eat at home were Harvest Crunch bran cereal and store-bought chocolates. She worried that she was getting plump, but then she always worried about that. She liked practical jokes. She dated schoolboys, or she dated recently graduated Etonians who were now junior officers in the guards, or she dated heirs of minor noble titles who had finished up at Oxford and were spending the year traveling. Sometimes she did their laundry. She drove a Honda Civic at first, then a dark red Austin Mini Metro. She found a job in a kindergarten, but she wanted extra money, so she got work cleaning houses through an employment agency called Solve Your Problems. Within two years she would be married to the heir to the throne of England.

It was her sister who found the flat. Sarah was older, wittier, more charismatic, and already established in London, where she worked for the real-estate agency Savills. Diana had spent her life in Sarah's shadow. In London, she would go to her sister's flat and Sarah would say to her friends, oh, that's only Diana, give her your dishes, she'll do the washing up. Sarah paid her one pound an hour to vacuum, iron, and dust. It was Sarah, too, who first had a romance with Prince Charles. Or a romance of sorts. They met at Ascot and dated for nine months. Sloane Rangers: She called him "sir" for nine months, and he never corrected her.

The apartment in London cost Diana's parents fifty thousand pounds. Her parents were divorced. They had been married in Westminster Abbey, and the queen had attended the wedding, but the marriage had been bad, and they split up when Diana was small. Both her mother and her father had since remarried. Her father was an earl, the 8th Earl Spencer, and he was now married to the daughter of Dame Barbara Cartland, the bestselling romance novelist. When Dame Barbara came to visit she would bring Diana armloads of her books—she published more than seven hundred—which Diana went through like candy. Diana's mother was the daughter of a baron, the 4th Baron Fermoy. Now she was married to the heir of a wallpaper fortune. She lived with him on a thousand-acre farm on a remote island off the coast of Scotland. Diana's father had won custody of the children in a legal battle. He lived with his wife at Althorp, the Spencer family's ancestral manor in Northamptonshire.

It was at Althorp that she met Charles, during a shooting weekend while the prince was with her sister. She was sixteen then. He brought his Labrador and wore rain boots; her first thought on seeing him was, what a sad man. She felt podgy and undistinguished, but she was lively and he found her charming. After dinner, he asked her to show him the picture gallery. Sarah caught up to them and insisted on showing him the etchings.

Who can say why anything happens? The kingdom needed an heir. The choice of Charles's wife had to be guided by certain proprieties. The Duke of Windsor had been dead less than a decade; Wallis Simpson was still alive, though afflicted with dementia and unable to speak. The king who put love ahead of duty was a living memory for many Britons. The family knew what a slender step it was from *A king can marry anyone he pleases* to *Then why are royals special?* Order depends on obligations. Charles was in love with someone else, but the someone he was in love with could not pass through the moment's filter of decorum. Diana could. That was who she was to them. She was the woman who was permissible.

Whom are you allowed to love? Isn't that always the question? Power begins as a means of realizing desire, but power once obtained necessitates desire's curtailment: first in small ways, then in larger and larger ones, until, generations on, there is no distinguishing between power itself and the restraint required to preserve it. We will make these alliances, honor these covenants, uphold this church, practice these courtesies. A few big houses and the forms of self-abnegation remain long after the day when command of the armies passes to someone else. But desire is imperious. What the heart wants is beyond the grasp of Parliament. She was meant to understand that in joining them, she was consenting to their way of seeing things, their symbols, their duty. But having entered into royalty, unwittingly, as nothing more than the outward proof of Charles's inner surrender, she appeared to the rest of the world as the image of the very vitality royals were supposed to give up: the sacrificial virgin, startlingly unsacrificed. She thought she could stay herself. She thought she was going to be happy. She thought—imagine—that her children would be *her children*. They could never have anticipated that degree of naïveté. It was as if the spirit they had staked their survival on suppressing had emerged, fully formed, in view of all the world's cameras.

If you don't behave, my girl, Philip told her, we'll take your title away. But what good is a title if it dictates everything you can do? The threat she posed to them went deeper than media savvy or a grasp of modern celebrity. There was one thing their entire system, as she saw it, could not allow her to be, and that was what she was determined to remain: a real person.

2. THE DUCHESS OF CAMBRIDGE IN THE YUKON TERRITORY

Her Entrance (Whitehorse International Airport)

She comes out of the plane and of course it is like this: steps, soldiers, tarmac, cameras. A bouquet waits for her at the bottom of the stairs, presented by a girl in a wheelchair, and then another, offered by a young Syrian refugee. Two small posies of orange blooms. She bends to speak to each girl, smiling. Hands to shake: the governor-general of Canada, whose name is David Johnston; white-haired men; red-haired women; husbands, wives; a soldier in camouflage; she holds the orange flowers at her waist, moving slowly down the line, smiling. The day is cold. She is wearing a deep green coat whose provenance—it came from Hobbs and cost £279—will be broadcast across the Internet before she arrives someplace warm enough to take it off. Behind the big government plane, surprisingly close, the pines begin, then the low line of purple mountains, resting against the horizon like a reclining nude by Matisse. The press cordon is some way off, facing the white-tipped peaks: so the photographers can have them behind her, in their shots.

She stands under the Yukon flag while the governor-general—David Johnston; his name is David Johnston—gives his speech. This vast country humbles and inspires us. Welcome to our beautiful land. Then William inspects the rangers: men with rifles over their shoulders, in red jackets and camouflage pants. Not quite professionals: standing in ragged military lines. William is much taller than the tallest ranger. She waits, under the flag, with the many dignitaries. Waiting is a part of what she does. There is an art to waiting. It can be practiced, like anything else. How to pay delighted attention to rituals whose tedium could kill a snail. When to lean back and make a small joke to the dignitary beside you, or when to chuckle at your dignitary's small joke. Alternately, when to look on with profound respect as William, say, puts a wreath on the ground while gazing at a torch. This is not a trivial thing. Waiting performed properly can invest an empty ceremony with meaning. The people with whom she waits will remember standing near her, waiting with her, for the rest of their lives.

The pool photographers are outside the press cordon, kneeling or lying supine on the tarmac with their big lenses aimed at William or, more often, at her. William is stopping in front of each individual ranger, asking questions. She is too far away to hear the questions or answers. She can hear the photographers confined in the press area yelling at the pool photographers to quit blocking their line of sight. "Oi! Get down, mate, lower, lower, lower!" The purpose of this phase of the royal tour is to emphasize the crown's commitment to Canada's First Nations peoples and communities. Many of the rangers William is speaking to are First Nations people. Yesterday—was it just yesterday?—she stood on a wooden bridge in the Great Bear Rainforest, watching screaming seagulls dive onto rotting salmon carcasses. The smell was astonishing. The ceremony took place afterward in a First Nations village called Bella Bella. William unveiled a plaque. The premier of British Columbia—her name is Christy Clark—gave a speech announcing the formation of a new environmental trust in honor of the royal visit. Then aboriginal men in sweatshirts and big jeans came to present William and her with a pair of red and black canoe paddles. One of them, a man called Ian, told her that if you dipped your canoe paddle into the water, it meant you would one day come back.

Life is quite fascinating when you think about it. There was a time when simply flying to Mustique seemed exotic. Now she is here. But then, given what her life is now, sometimes it is her past experiences, the experiences of so-called normal people, that seem exotic. She has borrowed books from a library! She has ridden the Tube alone. She has worked on yachts, other people's yachts, for money, serving drinks. She has bought frozen chicken at Waitrose, and stood in line for it herself, and cooked it herself. How could she help feeling, at times, as if she, too, were a tribal emissary, newly appointed to bring greetings to the crown from some vast and unfamiliar continent? This is a Roomba, Your Highness, my people use it to tidy their floors. My people, the upper-middle class.

When they were young and she was first in London, she and William and their set used to spend Tuesday nights at a club called Boujis, in Kensington. Pulsing purple dance floor, sleek booths, champagne in buckets. A bottle of vodka cost £250, but the owner let them drink for free. The royal comp, people called it. Their favorite shot was called the crack baby: passion-fruit juice, vodka, and champagne, served in a test tube. A crack baby cost £8 without the comp. She wore short print dresses and when her car pulled up outside the club she would climb out of the backseat into a shimmering horseshoe of paparazzi. No one knew then, though people wondered, whether she would someday be queen of England.

William has finished reviewing the rangers. Now it is time to move, slowly, toward the line of black SUVs waiting to carry them to the town. Shaking hands, smiling just so. She meets some rangers herself: interested in each of them, no hurry. How did you first decide to volunteer? What a joy it must be to spend time in this marvelous landscape. Outside the airport, just visible, the crowd that has come to see them from Whitehorse is waiting behind steel barricades. A faint cheer rises when they spot her. Quite a small crowd really, but then, this territory is a wilderness: not forty thousand people in the space of two United Kingdoms. And they have all braved the cold. She will keep her window down as the SUV drives past, regardless of the chill. They will see her wave to them. She was not born to her position but she knows how to do her job. She knows, by instinct, what William's mother never understood, and what William's grandmother only partly does: that to be royal is to be yearned for, and that yearning is a thing to be managed. They will project onto you the fantasies whose reality they most long to see confirmed. They will love you if you reflect those fantasies back to them. But if you respond to their yearning with yearning, if you turn to them with your own need as they turn to you with theirs, you will lose your power to protect yourself, and then, voilà, thanks for playing, good night. Diana left herself too open. The queen keeps herself too removed. She intends to repeat neither mistake. Royalty is the technique by which longing is redeemed through confidence.

Her Pageant (Kwanlin Dün Cultural Centre, Whitehorse)

The time has come for her to thank the breakdancers. She walks out of the cultural center into the night: still wearing her green coat. The performers have been ushered onto a round, stepped patio surrounding a fire pit. The fire's rust-gold circle glows like a Byzantine icon. Sky strewn with infinite stars. Singers and storytellers and musicians stand close together, warming themselves by the blaze. She begins at the near end of the circle, taking hands and smiling. Sincere appreciative smiles. Such a marvelous welcome to the territory: William and I are really touched. So fortunate to have this chance to learn more about your culture. What a marvelous show. William is with her, clasping nearby hands. This afternoon they were at a university being shown a volleyball exhibition. Now they are standing under the dark

Yukon sky. When she comes to the breakdancers she says, "William has some moves of his own, you know," and he agrees, Yes, it's true, I wanted to get up and dance with you. Breakdancers laugh. William may not have his brother's sense of mischief, but he can be teased: one of his really good qualities.

The river is close behind them, a darkness veined with glimmer, like what you see when you suddenly close your eyes. Whitehorse: because the foam of the rapids made the first gold prospectors think of running horses. But now the sound of conversation drowns out the sound of water. She has been a performer herself and understands something of how these people are feeling. They are silly, happy, easy to put at ease. She knows how to speak to them. Once, when she was thirteen, she starred in a school play called *Murder in the Red Barn*. Her character, Maria Marten, met a fortune-teller who told her that "a rich gentleman" would fall in love with her, marry her, and take her away to London. "It is all I ever hoped for!" she whispered. Soon a lover indeed appeared, a tall young man named William. Video from the play has been posted on the Internet; some people have been inclined to view it as a real prophecy. (The William of the play murdered her, however, and hid her body in a barn.) People search for significance in the events of her youth because her life looks, from the outside, like magic, and things that look like magic are easier to explain the more like magic they look. Here is a girl on the road, here a gypsy midwife; see, it was a fairy tale all along.

They search, too, because she is a contradiction, a mote of instability in the unchanging order she is meant to renew. If anyone can be a princess, can a princess mean anything?

Yes: if we convince ourselves that fate took a hand in choosing her.

She knows what it is to be a performer, but she is not performing now. It is all a matter of consideration for others. She has always had an instinct for carrying things off. Her family's party-supply business is sometimes the butt of jokes, but they are successful because they know how to make people feel good. It is a rare gift, the ability to take any situation and ease it toward the pleasantest outcome, the kindest, the most beautiful; to make it a little more relaxed, a little more memorable. Royalty, in that regard, is only one variable among many, a matter of perspective. At St. Andrews, she and William were both Sallies: residents of the hall called St. Salvator's. They were friends before they were anything more. William, of course, was the center of attention then. The world's most eligible bachelor: girls forever flinging themselves at his feet. One night at a party, her friends noticed that he was having trouble extricating himself from a particularly determined girl. No one was doing anything to help him. She strode across the floor, threw her arms around his neck, and pretended to be his girlfriend. In light of everything that happened afterward, who is to say whether that was a performance or not? Perhaps a true performance calls its own reality into being, the way a great painting teaches you how to see it. Conniving, people called her. But haven't things worked out for the best?

They have come almost to the end of the line: time now to make their goodbyes. Soon they will be in an SUV on their way to the hotel, and they will check in with Maria, the nanny, about their children, who have stayed behind at

Government House in Victoria, and they will hear from Miguel, the secretary, about what to expect from tomorrow's events.

Their tour so far has carried them through several small storms. The crown's outreach to First Nations communities has hit a snag in the form of First Nations communities who would prefer not to be reached out to. Some First Nations communities see the whole tour, their tour, as empty theater. Last night, at a ceremony at Government House, William added a symbolic silver ring to the Black Rod, the ebony staff that represents the presence of the queen or her representative in the legislature of the province. The Black Rod had three symbolic rings already, symbolizing the government of British Columbia, the government of Canada, and their link to the government of Great Britain. But this symbolic ring, the new one, was particularly important, because it was meant to symbolize reconciliation between the government and aboriginal people. But one important chief boycotted the ceremony. Another who participated made a speech about cultural genocide. Poverty among First Nations people remains high; the government continues to push forward gas drilling and dam projects that the communities oppose. William has struck a humble tone: We are here to learn and listen. Everywhere they have gone, the people have been delighted to see them. Still, there is perhaps the smallest strain in the mood of the occasion, the slightest hint of a mismatch between the ceremonial and the real. Last night she wore a red dress and a maple-leaf brooch lent to her by the queen. The headline in the *Daily Mail* ran, "The Lady in Red: Kate Stuns in Dazzling £1,000 Preen

Dress at Historic Ceremony of Reconciliation with Canadian First Nations."

The cars are ready. It is time to begin the slow progress toward them. Across the fire, where the press is cloistered, cameras are watching her. They will watch her exit, as they have watched her pass around the flames; as, indeed, they watched her enter. Once she might have wondered how the photographers could have been in place for her arrival, when she left the airport ahead of the press. But there are always photographers. Photographers travel faster than light, expand like gas, and clone themselves like cells. The incentive to take her picture creates its own quantum effect. If she woke up, to her own surprise, on the moon, having teleported accidentally in her sleep, she would find her first amazed look documented from every angle by the photographers already massed around her, who had camped out all night for the shot.

Her Gallery (Media Van to Carcross, Yukon)

This photographer wants to know about Indian chiefs. He has some questions, if you don't mind. He calls them "chieves": "Chief" rhymes with "leaf." The duke and duchess are off on their morning tour of Whitehorse, but the photographer is going on ahead to their next stop. He's on a van to some little village, bumping through Yukon backcountry. In no mood to be patient: up too early, coffee scalding, schedule confused, gear jostled. White bent nose, two flyaway croissants of gray hair. Khaki vest hanging open around the thunderous sag of his belly. Englishness somehow aggravated by profound distance from England: If I'm frank, mate, these yokels are useless. Sucking his lower lip, thumbs hooked through his vest's utility loops. He is here for *The Sun*, or the *Standard*, or the *Mirror*, or the *Star*, shouldering his tripod through the hind end of godforsaken nowhere to beam the royal latest back to civilization, and like his colleagues, battle-tested palace correspondents from the *Standard*, or *The Sun*, or the *Star*, or the *Mirror*, he packed light: He left his illusions in London. Every event on a royal tour has two purposes, the palace one and the real one, and the real one is always the same. Have I got to spell it out, sunshine? Art therapy for drug-addicted teen moms is fine and lovely, sure; you think we're selling an excessive number of papers? No? Then find out what the duchess is wearing.

Carcross: short for "Caribou Crossing." The future dread majesty of the British Empire and his future queen are en route to look at Native dancers. They will be greeted by a chief, perhaps more than one, the media guide isn't clear on that, and what the photographer wants to know is: Will these chieves be wearing their feathers? Or you know—their full . . . gear and things? Beads and . . . with their big sort of headdresses and all? He gestures down his back: their feathers. He has identified a young volunteer from the Yukon government and is addressing loud inquiries to her as the coach jostles forward. Emerald Lake is visible in the window, but Gaffer is no neophyte and is not looking out the window. In the clear light of his mind's inner eye, he sees a Plains Indian from a 1950s Western, wearing a full warbonnet, probably holding a tomahawk, with bright war paint under his eyes, and he sees a photograph, *his* photograph, of

Kate Middleton standing next to this astonishing speci-
men: That photo would *play*. Her so delicate and prim, surrounded by let's say two or even three fierce chieves. He can
see it shining down from the front page of *The Sun*. Tee-
pees and buffalo! So when he is told no, he is thousands of
miles too far north for that sort of costume, the traditional
dress of the local First Nations is something quite different,
he does not surrender his vision without a fight. When the
van stops, he clatters out, hugging his gear, and makes for
the next press liaison he sees. Excuse me—miss? Yeah.
Quick question about these chieves . . .

Her Exit (Montana Mountain)

Morning: She puts on a bright red Carolina Herrera coat-
dress. Amanda styles her hair in a simple twist. She and William have a long day ahead, but there is a reward at the end of
it: They will fly back to Victoria and see their children. This
leg of their tour, the Yukon leg, is the only stretch when their
children are not with them. Their children have been marvelous. Photos of George and Charlotte looking darling have
circulated almost as widely as photos of her have done. Little
Charlotte toddling. George peeping out of the plane with
huge safety muffs over his ears. When the prime minister of
Canada came to greet them at the airport, George refused to
give him a high five. Everyone who saw the photos melted.
No one can predict what children will be like, yet her position, impossibly, requires that her family be exemplary. She
has walked this tightrope without the slightest wobble; she
has made it look effortless, the way she has made so many
things look effortless, and has created a perfect family, a

catalog family, a family whose very being suggests the golden future ahead. How to make people love you: Keep them at a distance, but give them back their dreams.

SUVs to Whitehorse. They tour a museum, the Mac-Bride Museum. It holds a stuffed albino moose, interesting pictures of the gold rush and the Klondike, and the cabin of someone called Sam McGee. Sam McGee was a prospector who was made famous in a poem by Robert Service. Robert Service was a poet who worked as a bank clerk in Whitehorse when he wrote his best-known poems. In "The Cremation of Sam McGee," the prospector dies and his body is burned; in real life, McGee was still alive when the poem was written. Many years later, he returned to Whitehorse, where he found shopkeepers selling urns filled with what were supposed to be his ashes. The museum also has a telegraph office. Here an old man helps them tap out a message in Morse code. The telegraph machine is connected to Twitter, and the message they tap out is published as their first-ever personal tweet. It reads, "The Duke and Duchess of Cambridge, September 2016, Whitehorse Yukon." William jokes (but he is teasing) that the telegraph operator has made a spelling mistake with their tweet.

Arts festival on Main Street. A tall totem pole is being dedicated to the healing of former students of the residential schools, which attempted to forcibly assimilate First Nations children into white Canadian culture. First Nations children were taken from their homes, beaten for speaking their first languages, made to convert to Christianity, in many cases abused, in some cases experimented on. The Truth and Reconciliation Commission has declared that the schools were a form of cultural genocide. She considers the totem pole solemnly. The street festival is full of music and balloons and food smells. She walks through slowly in her red dress, squeezing hands and smiling. Flowers are placed in her hands. She looks behind her and laughs with delight. Here is a baby in a fuzzy white snowsuit; here is a little girl with a tiny Canadian flag stuck through her headband. She stops and asks their ages, really interested: a mother speaking to mothers.

A quick change of clothes, then the SUVs set out for Carcross. The SUVs are Yukons: commendable attention to detail. She is wearing slim dark jeans, suede cowboy boots, and a gray cardigan coat by Sentaler. The drive takes almost an hour.

In the village, they sit on a log bench beneath a yellow and red totem pole and watch tiny Native children perform Raven and Wolf dances. The children caw and howl. Then the children sing songs. The children are from the Tagish nation and the language of their songs is called Tlingit. She and William smile and laugh with the children. Then the chief—his name is Andy Carvill—gives a speech. He asks William to help his people protect their land. He presents them with a carved totem of a killer whale. All around her are First Nations people in their traditional dress: bright robes and vests, fur hats, round shields, turquoise paint. Some wear masks; the masks are ferocious, snarling, really impressive examples of aboriginal art.

A steep road brings them to Montana Mountain. She climbs out into the clearing. The clearing is high on the mountain, on the site of a condemned mine. It is time for the mountain-biking demonstration. They were not, originally, supposed to watch mountain biking on the site of a condemned mine. Originally, they were supposed to bike down the mountain themselves, William and she, with young people from Carcross and the Tagish nation. They are here to support an organization called Single Track to Success, which teaches young people to build mountain-biking trails. Young people from Carcross and the Tagish nation have built world-class trails on the mountain. Serious bikers travel from far away to ride on them. She and William would have enjoyed biking with the young people. She has been biking, and swimming, and skiing, and playing tennis, her whole life. In school she was on the field hockey team; she and William are both athletes. Sport is important to her whole family. Two years ago her sister, Pippa, and her brother, James, rode their bikes three thousand miles across the United States, in support of the British Heart Foundation. Her family have always believed in supporting charity and trying to push themselves. William's and her representatives, however, felt that the bike trails were too dangerous, that from a public-relations standpoint it would be disastrous if the future king of England were to faceplant down the side of a moraine. And furthermore they felt that the scenery on the trails was not dramatic enough. William's press secretary in particular felt that there should be peaks for William to be photographed in front of. So the Single Track to Success organizers had to build a fake trail in a high, flat clearing, so that she and William might support them by walking slowly around it.

The makeshift trail is a circular track scraped into the dirt. Orange safety cones divide the track into different zones. Children, some quite small, are riding in circles around particular sets of cones. Adult volunteers urge them along. "Not much longer now! Keep those feet turning, Abby! Guys, Survivor Island starts now!" It is unclear whether the children know who she and William are. A handsome young representative of the Yukon government appears to escort her around the track. His name is Currie Dixon. Another representative, a woman, walks with William. They all walk slowly: asking grave questions. She has no choice but to take the demonstration with total seriousness. Twenty cameras are trained on her. She gestures, then nods, walking slowly around the track, frowning. The air up here is clear and thin. Many spectacular peaks. The future king of England stands dramatically before the mountains, just as his press secretary had hoped. Yet the photographers all want pictures of her coat. The press will later report that the coat she is wearing retails for £707. The coat will be far more widely talked about than either the bike-trails program or William's kingliness.

They come to the end of the track and linger, making further small conversation with their representatives. Then it is time to greet the volunteers. Several onlookers are standing nearby, holding floral teacups. How did floral teacups make it to the top of the mountain? The scene has the quality almost of a dream. Someone is playing music: "Royals," the song by Lorde, drifts thinly toward the peaks.

A woman's voice cries out. "I loved your mother!"

There is polite laughter among the onlookers. "William," the voice calls again, "I loved your mother! I've been watching you since you were born!"

Less laughter now. The voice belongs to a small, owlishly round First Nations woman in a long black Canada Goose parka. The woman is standing near the Single Track to

Success van. Two green mountain bikes are racked upside down on top of the van. "William!" the woman calls. The woman is holding up her cell phone, pointing the camera at William and at her.

William walks over to the woman. He speaks to her for a moment, then gives her a hug. The ecstatic woman rubs William's back. William throws her, Kate, a glance. She walks over to speak to the volunteers near William and the woman. She is smiling, gracious: not a flicker of concern. William steps back from the woman's embrace. The woman opens her arms and asks for another hug. She is standing next to William: also greeting the woman. The woman does not want to let William go. Everyone is staring. She asks the woman a question, and during the answer she slides herself between William and the woman. William moves away. The woman grasps her and hugs her in William's place. She hugs the woman back loosely, bent slightly at the waist. She allows the woman to hug her until William is well out of reach.

Then she slides toward the other volunteers. Still smiling. "Give my love to the babies!" the woman calls.

It is time to go. The SUVs are ready. It is true, the woman knows their itinerary: In a few hours they will be back with their children. They will drive down the mountain, to the airport where she met David Johnston, and from there they will begin their journey to Government House. They will continue with their tour. They will have a party for the children. They will ride in canoes to see ancient Haida villages. They will hang a plaque at a hospital. They will dedicate a monument. They will sail on a tall ship. They will support student leadership in mental health advocacy work across Canada.

When the SUVs have gone, the music stops playing. Volunteers gather the teacups. Photographers hoist their gear. Parents make plans for groups to ride down the mountain. Adults look at each other a little searchingly, like, Something just happened, but what? One by one the vans head back to Whitehorse. The town is a low pale scatter against the mountains. Clouds have blown in. At twilight the sky is like smoke viewed through blue glass.

But Not Like Your Typical
Love Story

In 1952, the year before she loaded a stack of oil paintings into her run-down Studebaker convertible, sputtered onto the highway, and disappeared, Lydie Marland carried a nickel-plated automatic pistol in her handbag, along with rolls of cash, sometimes fat ones, because she didn't trust bankers, she said. She needed cash more often than usual that year, and in larger sums, because her lover, Louis Cassel, kept asking her to finance his schemes, and she didn't like to disappoint him. Possibly she was afraid to disappoint him. Louis was always dreaming up something. He'd have an idea for a business that would make his fortune. Or else he'd say, let's get us a little booze and round up the boys, hit the road a few days. Louis never had any money and neither did his friends, but Lydie had a little—it was hard to say how much. There were some heirlooms, objects from her past. A few stocks. She didn't have a job and she wasn't rich, in fact she often made do with little, but there were things she could sell. She never expected to see any of the money again. Louis wasn't the sort of man whose plans came to anything, you could tell that right off. But he was young and handsome, and he was fun, and Lydie hadn't had fun in a while.

The relationship had begun two years earlier, when Lydie was fifty and Louis was thirty-one. Lydie lived in a cottage on the grounds of a Felician convent in Ponca City, Oklahoma. The estate had once belonged to a powerful oil tycoon who built an enormous mansion on the prairie near the town. Now nuns walked the grounds in twos and threes and Lydie occupied the former chauffeur's quarters. She couldn't afford to keep the cottage maintained, or else she neglected to maintain it, so it was falling into disrepair, but in any case she had few visitors. She was a well-known figure in Ponca City, but there was something about her that made people stay away. When they saw her in town, they pointed her out to each other—look, there's Lydie—in a tone that meant, See the eccentric.

Partly this had to do with the way she dressed. She was a small woman, just five feet four and 115 pounds, with dark hair and a wide mouth. The thought of aging alarmed her, so she read endless articles about hair and skin care; she knew that scientists were continually making discoveries that could delay or even reverse the effects of time, and she wanted to know what these were. People sometimes said she looked younger than she was, and she liked hearing that. But when it came to her clothing, it was as if she had frozen in time. She wore cloche hats that had been stylish twenty-five years earlier, antiquated flapper dresses cut for a young woman long before the war. Her outfits were carefully chosen and had been beautifully made, long ago. But at her age, in her conservative small town, they made her look like a Jazz Age scarecrow.

In fact she couldn't always be sure how she looked, because her eyesight was failing. Her vision was so bad that she needed a magnifying glass to read, but she thought spectacles would make her look old, so she refused to wear them. When she went out in the green convertible, she drove slowly and commandeered the road, veering from the right lane to the left, following the center line as it revealed itself. She'd never had a driver's license. Patrolmen stopped her more than once, but they always let her off with a warning. She ignored the warnings. Thinking about other drivers— thinking about other people—made her nervous. It would be better if other people could simply keep out of her way.

One summer day she answered the door and there he was, smiling in his uniform. He was with the Water and Light Department, he said. He had come to read her meter. Louis had black hair, which he wore slicked with grease and parted on one side, and he had a big forehead and jug ears and full, drooping cheeks. His eyebrows were low, which gave him a hard look, as if he were peering out at the world from under the brim of a fedora. But he grinned easily, and although he was rough, he had a way of suggesting life was a game, not to be taken too seriously. She found herself inviting him inside. Then she found herself searching for reasons to invite him back. Her books, she remembered, were in grave need of organizing. The window in the bedroom was awfully hard to close. She would pay him, of course. Couldn't he come around one day soon, and help?

He could. Louis had lived in Ponca City his whole life, except when he hadn't. It was his home, but things had a way of coming along. When the war came along, for instance, he shipped out with an artillery company. A job as a brakeman came along, so he spent some time on the rails. He'd been a soda jerker, a night watchman, you name it; he never stuck in any job for long. He liked doing what he wanted and he didn't like being told no. His second wife was a theater cashier. Cops put him in handcuffs three times for beating her, and when she left him, he slashed his wrists open with a pocketknife, but he was married again by the time he met Lydie. This time his wife was a nurse.

Louis quit his job as a meter reader. He started spending most of his time at the cottage, ostensibly as a handyman, though in fact he did little work. Lydie was finding that she could not do without his presence, and she was happy to pay if it meant freeing him from the need to go elsewhere, such as to a job. They started going out together in public, to restaurants and bars, and that opened a new dimension of life for her, reclusive as she'd been. What a thrill it was to drop a coin in a jukebox! Of course she would pick up the check. They went on trips; Lydie bought the tickets. It was a strange sort of love affair, even she could see that. But it had been a long time since anything so exciting had happened to her, and in any case, she had reason to believe that love stories sometimes were strange.

In the summer of 1952, Louis came to her and asked for five thousand dollars. He had a mind to take up wheat farming, he said, and he needed money to buy land. By now, two years after their first meeting, the relationship was troubled. Lydie worried that Louis was bored. He no longer seemed so grateful when she sold some little memento to buy him a present or pay for a vacation. When she talked, his eyes wandered. The force of her jealousy frightened her. Once, on a trip to Phoenix, he'd given her the slip, and she hired private detectives to track him down. They caught up with him near San Francisco. Another time she pulled her pistol on him. There were screaming telephone calls, scenes in public. There were fights that left her gulping for air. Surely, she thought, things between them would settle as soon as he had a place in life, a proper home. Then they could be married, and she would never have to give him up.

She gave him the money, having sold some stocks to get it. He used it to buy the acreage, as he'd promised. But before long, in February 1953, he sold the land for six thousand dollars, paid what he owed in child support, and skipped town with a friend named Lewellen, traveling west. A few weeks later, Lydie herself left town, in her dinged-up Studebaker. A few weeks after that, she vanished.

I'm lifting most of these details from reports that appeared years later, in the late 1950s, when the mystery of Lydie Marland briefly became a subject of interest to newspapers and magazines. The most complete version of the story appeared in *The Saturday Evening Post*, though "complete" is in this case a misnomer; neither the official police investigation nor subsequent investigations by journalists turned up much real information. No one knew the exact date on which she left. No one knew precisely what had caused her sudden flight from town. It seemed reasonable to conclude that Louis Cassel's betrayal had something to do with it, but no one could say for sure. It was even hard to say when, exactly, she'd last been seen by a reliable witness.

Some of her movements after she left Ponca City could be traced. It was certain, for instance, that she had taken some paintings with her, because she had tried to sell them, so there were gallery workers who remembered seeing her, dates on which she could be placed in particular locations. After a while, however, once she'd been away from Ponca City for a few months, the trail went cold.

The *Post*'s article appeared on November 22, 1958. The cover art for the issue was Norman Rockwell's painting *Den into Nursery*. The lead feature was a profile of Yul Brynner, whose Technicolor remake of *The Buccaneer*, costarring Charlton Heston as Andrew Jackson, was about to open in theaters. The story about Lydie, "Where Is Lyde Marland?," began on page 19. It continued, with a couple of jumps deeper into the issue, for six densely set pages. The writer, John Kobler, later produced a well-regarded biography of Al Capone, but in 1958 he was known mostly for lurid, gossipy true-crime stories; he'd published two collections of middle-brow micro-noirs under the titles *Afternoon in the Attic* and *Some Like It Gory*. His tone in discussing Lydie's disappearance keeps to this wink-wink, imitation-Hitchcock vein, playing up a smirking sordidness for a readership of middle-class voyeurs.

> Among the local belles he was noted for his cinematic profile, and generally frisky spirits.

In Kobler's telling, Lydie Marland spent her final months in Ponca City oscillating between hysteria and denial, confronting Louis's friends and their families.

Mrs. Miller, a salty old party, was alone, and to her distraught visitor's questions replied, "I don't know where they're at, but neither of 'em is worth a tinker's damn." Mrs. Marland bridled. "You can't talk about Louis like that to me!"

Her brother and sister-in-law, who lived in Tulsa, warned that Louis was bad for her, but carried away as she was, she refused to listen.

In vain did George and Laverne Marland remonstrate with her.

She drove east out of Ponca City, not west, as Louis had done. There could be no doubt about this, because she turned up, three hundred miles later, at a place called the Moonlight Motel, outside Independence, Missouri, and stayed there for ten weeks. She befriended the family who owned the motel, or at any rate they took pity on her. They told the police that at her request, they'd allowed her to help clean the rooms, a task she performed, Kobler writes, "clad in an Indian squaw's dress designed for younger women." When she burned a bedsheet with a hot iron, she insisted on paying them back.

In particular she was drawn to the family's older daughter, Deloris. As she grew closer to Deloris, who had been married a few months earlier, she plied her with naive questions about the nature of love and sexuality. How did a woman know when she was in love? Could a young man truly love an older woman?

She also tried, during this time, to sell her paintings, but she felt the prices offered by the local dealers were too low. Finally, in early June, she received a letter from a gallery in Manhattan. The next day she checked out of the motel. She told the family she was going to New York. To their surprise, however (as they later told the police), when she drove away, she turned west, not east, on Route 24. She had once mentioned some people she might stay with in Nebraska; perhaps, they thought, she had gone to join them?

The first few pages of the *Saturday Evening Post* story are full of black-and-white portraits: Lydie smiling with a gentle, intelligent expression in about 1950; a younger Lydie in 1933; Louis Cassel in a tweed coat and black tie, glowering past the photographer. Later, after the jump to page 44, the pages are lined with advertisements, and the advertisements are more interesting than the portraits, because they are precisely the sort of atmospheric flotsam that Lydie found compelling and that she often clipped from magazines. "ORA*Fix* holds dentures fast—all day!" "Did you know *Cobalt* Was used by the . . . ANCIENT EGYPTIANS?"

ATOM TRACER TESTS PROVE
INTRACEL PENETRATES THROUGH
AND BELOW THE SKIN
Kills Muscular Pain at Its Very Source

On page 47, a paragraph tracing the peak of her despair during the breakdown of her relationship with Louis is interrupted by a joke. The joke is unconnected to the narrative, and set off from the main text between two horizontal lines.

The best way to teach your wife to drive is in someone else's car.   —ROBERT FITCH

After she left the Moonlight Motel, Lydie faded from
view—not tracelessly, and not all at once, but so quickly that
it was unnerving. She placed a phone call in 1956, to the
Knoedler Gallery in New York, where she had left a painting, Alfred Miller's *Buffalo Hunt*, to be sold on commission;
when Kobler wrote his story in 1958, the painting was still
in the gallery. Because of the phone call, it seemed unlikely
that she had been murdered. If she had died by some other
means after 1956, it seemed likely that her body would have
been found. In 1959, according to the Uniontown, Pennsylvania, *Morning Herald*, a certain A. M. Peck claimed to have
received a letter from her and to have it in his possession.
But if she *was* still alive, what was she running from, and
why had she refused to contact her brother? The police
tracked down Louis Cassel in Germany, where he had reen-
listed in the army, and where he had married, and separated
from, a fourth wife. They gave him a polygraph test. But he
was little help.

If Mrs. Marland would have contacted me in any way
or manner while I was in Washington, I would have
did anything in my power to aid or help her.

A fact that does not appear in the *Saturday Evening Post*
story, nor in any other account from this period, is that
shortly before Lydie left town, she contacted a worker from
a local monument company. She had a statue, she told him,
that she wanted to have destroyed. The statue depicted

her, Lydie, as the young woman she'd been in the mid-1920s, when a famous artist had traveled from Paris to sculpt her. The monument worker's name was Glen Gilchrist. She told him to smash the face first. She watched as he did so. Then she told him to dispose of the rest. Gilchrist hauled the remains to his own land, where he buried them north of his barn. He told no one outside his family. The fragments were buried on Gilchrist's property in 1953, when Lydie fled from Ponca City, and they were still buried there twenty-two years later, when she came back.

2

When I was seven or eight years old, my mother's father, Gene Ellis, my grandfather, bought a large pontoon boat, which he docked at a remote cove on Kaw Lake, a few miles from Ponca City. My grandparents lived in town. Their house was on Monument Road, just down the street from the walls of the old tycoon's estate. The chauffeur's cottage where Lydie had lived was a five-minute walk from their front door, not that they, or anyone, had much reason to make it. Our house was two miles away. For the next year or so, when the weather was warm we were often on the boat, with sunscreen and potato chips.

Northern Oklahoma on a pontoon boat may not be what you picture when you think of a boating idyll—or maybe it is; I'm not here to tell you how to feel about Jet Skis. It's not Newport. At Kaw Lake the vibe was intensely landlocked. Even swampy in places. Ramshackle piers with tall grass growing alongside them. I have mostly good memories.

Once, it's true, I missed the step off the dock and plunged straight down into the water, too startled to close my eyes, but even that was fascinating in its way. The underwater world of Kaw Lake always fascinated me, because I'd heard that when the Corps of Engineers dammed the reservoir many years ago, an entire town, Kaw City, had been submerged and left under the water (this was true). Whenever I swam in the lake, I half expected nixie fingers to seize me by the ankles and pull me down to the lost city, the kingdom of sprites, where I'd remain forever in the empty post office, lost to the sun and air.

I'd never known my grandfather to show any interest in boating, but even at seven or eight I understood that this was how he did things, with an impulsiveness so decisive and so laconic that the whole question of premeditation seemed somehow beside the point. Explanations, generally speaking, ran counter to my grandfather's mode of being. If he had an idea about how to farm pigs more efficiently, he became a pig farmer. If he wanted to fly, he bought an airplane. Saw a boat he liked? Let's hit the water. Why would someone need to know what he was thinking, when anyone could see what he was doing? One day around this time, he showed up at our house with a trailer hauling a small circus carousel. He'd seen it at a barbecue trade show and traded a smoker oven for it. Now it was a gift for my sister and me. It had a blue horse and a flying elephant. It had candy-striped poles. When they finally got it installed, it took up half the back patio. It played tinny music. If he ever told anyone what possessed him to acquire it, the report never reached me.

Gene was born in 1920. He grew up on a farm in the

deep nowhere of Red Rock, Oklahoma, where his family gritted out the Dust Bowl in a house they'd ordered from the Montgomery Ward catalog. Windmill, chickens, faded laundry on a line. The land had belonged to the Otoe-Missouria tribe—that is, the tribe was forcibly resettled there—before the government broke up the reservations in the 1890s; it was still largely surrounded by Otoe-Missouria allotments. During the war Gene trained as a pilot with the navy. The fighting stopped before he was sent overseas. Like many men of his generation, he left the military determined that no one would ever again tell him what to do, a determination that in my grandfather's case cannot have lain too far below the surface to begin with. Having always been both a little too rough and quite a bit too smart for his surroundings, he promptly moved back to them, returning to Red Rock with a new wife—Judy, my grandmother—and beginning a career of this and that. He tinkered with machines. He farmed. He hunted in the woods. He invented a new kind of feed mill and sold it around the country under the name Ellis Feed & Seed. He got elected mayor of Red Rock. He was brilliant, impatient, not infrequently drunk. He'd build beautiful knotty-pine cabinets for my grandmother's kitchen (where had he learned how to work that way with wood? he just knew). Then he'd come home with ugly plastic furniture he hadn't bothered to show her first.

My mother, the second of three children, grew up in a house with a gas pump at the end of the drive. Her pet raccoon out back. Gene's Cessna in the field. From their house it was miles to the nearest paved road. My grandfather's idea of a vacation was to pile the whole family into the car and drive for a week, then turn around and drive home. Roadside diners and motel pools: You got away, saw what was there, kept moving, went back.

My grandmother also came from Oklahoma, but she met my grandfather in California, during the war. He was in flight school and she worked for Lockheed, building aircraft. A mutual friend introduced them. I have a box of letters he wrote to her after he left California for training in Texas. My grandmother saved the letters. There were hundreds, often more than one a day.

> Dearest Brat,
>
> How's that for confidence—three days with no letter and tomorrow (Sunday) will make four days and then I call you "dearest."

They were wildly unalike. Judy had grown up in Oklahoma City. Her father, my great-grandfather, was a blacksmith. He was also an alcoholic, which can't have helped his metalwork much. During the Depression, Judy had to drop out of school and take a job to bring money home. She worked at a soda counter. So the Baileys weren't among Oklahoma City's elite—the opposite—but still, it was a city; you had culture, taste, refinement, even if only of the shop-window variety. You could hear music they didn't play in the country. You could go dancing. You were close enough to civilization for some of it to rub off on you, if you wanted.

All her life, my grandmother had a quality of delicacy that never quite made sense in her surroundings. She was patient. She approached the world with sympathy and a kind of nervous gentleness, qualities whose frequency fell wholly outside my grandfather's range of hearing, except that he loved them in her. She liked floral teacups, English novels, really anything English; I remember, as a small child, playing in her room while she watched *Masterpiece Theater*. She loved *All Creatures Great and Small*. I didn't entirely know what England was, but it seemed to be a calming influence in the house on Monument Road, where there were elk heads on the walls, clumps of uprooted machinery on the breakfast table, and fierce tribal masks that my uncle sent home from New Guinea, where he lived. My grandmother had a turquoise bathtub, which struck me as deeply exotic, and when I was very small, three or four, I was sometimes allowed to take baths in it. She had sweet-smelling bath salts. I remember hearing her say "Crabtree and Evelyn." To me, not understanding the words but catching the hint of what they meant to her, they sounded like portals to some larger, richer world.

You can imagine, then, what a jolt it was for my grandmother to find herself in Red Rock after the war. In California the world had looked full of possibility; now she was living in a cramped house in the middle of nowhere, with a husband who butchered his own deer carcasses, who periodically vanished on three-day benders, who expected her, if the kittens took sick, to put them in a sack and drown them in the creek. In a county where the dirt roads turned impassable whenever it rained. She rolled up her sleeves, but it was hard. My grandfather had a brother. Family lore is unclear on what precisely was wrong with him—something with his brain, he'd had a high fever as a boy—but he'd drift over from the farm when my grandfather was away, and he behaved in ways that frightened my grandmother. Certainly he was threatening, probably sexually so. My mother and her siblings were taught to hide when he appeared. Finally my grandmother had to fight him off with a broom. After that, Gene paid him a visit, and he didn't bother my grandmother again.

They moved to Ponca City in the 1960s, around the time my mother started high school. No doubt my grandmother had dreamed of the day—Ponca, with its twenty-five thousand souls, being the metropolis of legend where Red Rock was concerned—but on my grandfather's end the change seems to have been characteristically impetuous. He was angry over the result of a school board election? Something like that. In any case, it's undeniable that as time went on, particularly after the move, the balance of their marriage shifted toward my grandmother. In Ponca City, she picked out the furniture.

As Gene was getting tired of pig farming, he found that he was now extremely interested in barbecue, so he invented a kind of smoker oven and started a new company to sell it, along with a line of barbecue sauce and tubs of my grandmother's chili spice. Judy kept the books. They opened a factory outside Ponca City. The company made a lot of money, and success or age or their combination mellowed my grandfather. He drank less. No doubt he still terrorized his employees; to my sister and me he was a lamb. The year before, he'd shown us our first VCR tape: He pushed a button and suddenly the runners (it was a race from the Olympics) were wriggling backward toward the starting line. On a trip to Germany, he got inspired by the construction of some little cottages he saw, and when he came back he built an astonishingly ornate playhouse in our backyard, across from the carousel. It had levels. It had insulated walls.

That playhouse became the base for every game of my child-hood, the command center for every neighborhood battle. Years later, when I was in junior high, my friends and I blacked out the windows and played Dungeons & Dragons by flashlight. Gene's unpredictability, often a frightening quality for his own children, manifested for us only as a thrilling capacity for surprise.

One day in the spring of 1985, we spent the evening on the boat with my grandparents. I was nine. It must have been a Saturday, because it was the evening before Mother's Day. The previous afternoon, my grandmother had taken my sister, who was five, shopping, and they had bought a set of wind chimes for my mother, which we hung near the carou-sel, on the back porch. That evening, on the boat, something felt off. Not alarmingly, but noticeably. It had to do with my grandfather. His voice was loud. He was drinking whiskey out of a teacup, and when he teased me about taking karate lessons (actually tae kwon do, I said seriously), he did a mock *hai-ya!* kick from his seat that caught me on the hip; it was hard enough to bring tears to my eyes. I didn't think any-thing of it. We puttered around the lake in the pontoon boat, wearing our life jackets, and then my father rowed my mother and my sister and me around the cove in the green rowboat my grandparents kept at their dock. We sang "Row, Row, Row Your Boat" as a round (not typically a part-singing family, we must have been carried away by the novelty of being on the water). I got to try my hand at rowing.

When it was time for us to go home, my grandfather said he would stay at the lake a little longer, because he wanted to take the rowboat out and run some fishing lines. My grandmother said she would stay with him. This complicated things, because my grandmother had driven us to the dock in her car—my grandfather had gone out earlier, in his truck—but not to worry: We could drive Judy's car back to our house, and the two of them would come by and pick it up later, on the way back to Monument Road. Simple enough. I was excited to ride home in my grandmother's silver Ford, because it had a keypad lock, four numbered buttons in a horizontal row above the door handle, and I had never seen another car with a lock like that, and it was fun to tap in the combination.

That night, my mother woke up and noticed that the silver Ford was still in our driveway. But that wasn't anything to worry over. My grandparents had probably just decided to go straight home after a long day on the water. We'd all been tired. My grandfather had looked especially tired, my mother thought. They would come for the car in the morning.

In the morning the car was still in the driveway.

Well—it was Sunday, Mother's Day, a day to sleep in. Still no reason to worry. Just to be safe, my mother called Monument Road.

No answer.

It would be just like my grandfather, we all agreed, to have lit out on some trip without telling anyone. My parents decided to drive over to Monument to check whether anyone had been home.

We were sure it would come out all right. This was a temporary confusion, one we'd laugh about later—how dire the misunderstanding had felt, how harmless it had turned out to be.

My parents didn't know how long they'd be gone, so they

dropped my sister and me off at our other grandmother's house, on Berkshire, a block away from home. Our other grandmother, Bonnie, my father's mother, was at that time very sick with cancer. She had become, in her illness, deeply religious, religious in a way I, without knowing many details, understood to be intense and ultra-evangelical, and that morning she was being looked after by someone from her church, a woman whose name I can't remember. Diana? I don't remember seeing Bonnie, though we must have, we would have gone back to her room to say hello, but all I remember is sitting at the counter in her kitchen and looking at a copy of *The Ponca City News* while the caretaker stood over the stove. The newspaper was open to the classifieds—I suppose Diana, or whatever her name was, must have been paging through them—and she explained to my sister and me that we were not worried enough about our missing grandparents. God was watching us, she said, and if we really loved Gene and Judy we would be praying for them. If they were dead, she told us, it was because we were not praying hard enough. God heard. She was making oatmeal, I think, as she said this? Stirring a steaming pot. After what seemed like a very long time, my father came, alone, and picked us up.

Back at our house, things were different. Some adults were there, in the living room. As we came through the front door, I had a glimpse of my aunt, my mother's older sister, sitting on the couch with her feet curled under her, her face looking smeared and strange. My mother met us in the entryway and took us back to her bedroom. She knelt down and put her hands on our shoulders and told us that Grandma Judy was dead and that Papa Gene probably was, too. She said that my grandmother had drowned in the lake. They had found her body. They had not found my grandfather, but Robert Hardee, my aunt's boyfriend, the artist, was back on the water with the Lake Patrol, and they were looking for him now.

Much later, my mother gave me a more complete picture of what had happened. My parents had driven to Monument Road and let themselves in at the back door (my grandparents never locked their house). Gene's pickup wasn't in the driveway, so they knew my grandparents weren't home—the question was whether they'd been home at all since we left them the previous night. My mother thought, I'll check Mom's bathroom sink, and if the sink is wet, I'll know they were here this morning and just forgot about the car. The sink was dry. My mother called her sister and said, I think something is wrong. So my parents had driven with my aunt and Robert Hardee back to the cove. My grandfather's truck was parked in the same place, and there was no sign of the rowboat. The four of them took the pontoon boat out to search the lake. My grandfather liked to use cutoff barbecue-sauce jugs as floats for his trotlines, and they saw one of these bobbing in the water, not connected to a line. Then my mother saw a speck of orange floating a long way off.

The speck was the color of a life jacket. It took a long time, my mother told me, to get close enough to see that the life jacket was attached to a body, and then it took a long time to get close enough to see whose body it was. My grandmother was floating facedown. Her hands were flexed as if she were clutching at something. Later, when they found my grandfather, he was not wearing a life jacket. (Of course not; he never did.) The coroner's best guess was that he had fallen out of the rowboat and my grandmother had drowned trying to save him. He had been drinking, obviously, but there were certain signs, a bluishness of the torso, that suggested a heart attack, which might explain why he had fallen out of the boat. No one really knows what happened. Possibly my grandmother drowned with my grandfather, or possibly she died later, of hypothermia, trying to get back to shore.

I don't remember my immediate reaction to the news that my grandparents were dead. I remember that I was calm. I was not as upset as the caretaker, the maybe-Diana, would have wanted. I said to myself, you will never see them again—my grandparents, whom I had seen several times a week since I was born—but I still felt, at the level of unconscious certainty, that this was a brief confusion, that there would be a happy ending. At some point the doorbell rang and my friend Kyle was there with his dad. They had baseball gloves and a ball. They asked if I wanted to go to the field behind the school and throw the ball around. I said okay, thinking this was a little strange, because Kyle and I hadn't really been friends since second grade, and now we were in third grade, so that seemed like a long time ago. Kyle lived down the street. Later I realized that someone must have called his parents and asked them to take me out, to give me something to do, but at the time that didn't occur to me. This just seemed like the next thing that was going to happen.

Kyle's dad drove a tan truck. The old cab smelled like his tire shop, licorice sweet. There was a soft red grease rag on the floor and behind the seat (I knew) a battered tackle box. We drove to the elementary school and parked in the empty teachers' lot. There were eight or ten elementary schools in Ponca City and most of them were named after presidents, but ours was named after a local mortician, E. M. Trout. We were the Trout Tornadoes. E. M. Trout had been president of the school board. It occurs to me now (it didn't then) that E. M. Trout & Sons, the funeral home he had founded, was probably where they were taking my grandmother. Kyle and his dad and I went behind the school and started throwing the ball. They had a bat so we started doing some hitting. It was a little odd, because I didn't usually play baseball, but I seemed to have acquired a temporary ability to decide for myself how things would feel, so I decided it was fun to be there with them. Kyle's dad pitched for us. I got some good hits.

I thought that what might have happened was that my grandparents had gone to London. They had gone to London on vacation a year or so earlier and I remembered how much they liked it. They had brought me back a handful of funny coins. My grandmother had always wanted to see Buckingham Palace. I had never been on an airplane, but I knew that to get to London you had to ride on one. In London my grandparents went shopping for Burberry raincoats. They took pictures of each other in front of a red telephone booth. In her picture, my grandmother was wearing a raincoat and big glasses and smiling under her small cloud of dark gray hair. My grandfather was wearing red suspenders over his short-sleeved button-down shirt, and he was grinning in a private way, as if he were remembering the punchline of a joke. How was it possible to say someone was gone forever? We needed to check their closets. I would tell my mother to do it. We would find that their suitcases were gone.

Forever would mean: No more walks with my grandmother to the gardens at the Pioneer Woman. No more rides with my grandfather on his green John Deere. No more sweet smell of bath salts. No more runners wriggling backward. No more carousels. All this lost somehow, gone somewhere, pulled down by nixie fingers to the city at the bottom of the sea.

Which was not London.

My brain felt light and distant, but it was okay, I thought. The sky was huge and gray over the field. The wind was coming up. The school's flagpole kept up a steady clanking.

That night, I later learned, Robert Hardee, my aunt's boyfriend, the artist, who had brought in my grandmother's body, went back to the cove and performed some kind of Indian blessing for my grandparents. At our house, a storm blew in. Rain turned dark and glittery on the glass. We could hear the wind chimes ringing.

3

What happened was that the prospector struck oil in an Indian graveyard.

What happened was that one sister had money and the other sister had children.

What happened was that in the Republican machine that controlled Philadelphia toward the end of the nineteenth century, there was an operator named Samuel Collins, born 1850, a fixer and glorified ward heeler who bounced around among official posts. His home base was the Fifteenth Ward. He was a state legislator for a while, then a "deputy collector," then later a tipstaff at the Superior Court of Pennsylvania. His real role, as I imagine it, was to be a laugh behind a cigar, the man who knew everyone, a wise-eyed, well-dressed patriarch of the steakhouse who could recite poetry over cognac and then get down to brass tacks. Gentlemen, I know I can count on you to do the right thing. His wife, who was also born in 1850, called herself Eliza; Eliza Collins is the name she appears under in most official records. Her given name, however—the one that appears on her death certificate, and on her gravestone at Mount Moriah Cemetery—was Lydie.

According to the Philadelphia census of 1900, Sam and Eliza Collins had five living children. One of the children who had not lived was a daughter, also named Lydie, who died in infancy in 1882. So it was a family name—one they were interested in passing on to later generations.

Among the children who lived, the oldest were two daughters: Maggie, who was born in 1874, and Mary Virginia, who was born in 1877.

What happened was that Maggie and Mary Virginia grew up to marry very different men. Or at any rate that marriage sent them down very different tracks.

Maggie's husband, a man called George Roberts, sold fruits from a wheelbarrow in Flourtown.

Mary Virginia's husband was an oilman who became, for a time, one of the richest men on earth.

The oilman's name was Ernest Whitworth Marland. He went by E.W. He was three years older than Mary Virginia—in his mid-twenties when he first met the Collins family, somewhere around the turn of the twentieth century. Sam brought him home; they were friends, despite the age gap. E.W. hadn't yet struck it rich, but he carried himself as if he had, with a genteel swagger that made people stop and take notice. He was beautifully dressed, well-mannered, a dreamer with a gift for convincing people his plans were bound to succeed. His father was a Pittsburgh industrialist. Affluent, certainly, but not gaudy rich, not by the standards of the day. His ancestry was English—the Marlands were an old family, with a name that went back six hundred years in the village of Ashton-Under-Lyne, near Manchester— and E.W. had been raised to think of himself as a gentleman. "Of him to whom much is given," his father told him, warmly, at their estate on Mount Washington, where the library was lined with Walter Scott novels, "much is required."

Alfred Marland, the father, had felt what was required of him so keenly that as a young man, in the 1860s, he sailed from England to enlist in the Confederate army, fired with the dream of defending agrarian gentility. (It probably didn't hurt his feeling for the cause that the economy of Ashton-Under-Lyne, a center of textile manufacturing, relied on cotton imports.) He lost his illusions where the South was concerned, but held on to his vision of a society governed by fine manners and chivalry—by old carpets and riding crops. He invented a new kind of hoop for holding cotton bales together, then established himself in a kind of high-toned industrial earldom: Episcopal church, tweed jacket, local politics. His dream was to make E.W., his American son, chief justice.

When the time came for E.W. to be educated, Alfred

sent him to the Rugby Colony, in Tennessee. Rugby: truly one of the strangest pedagogical experiments in this nation's history, one of those rare keyholes through which it's still possible to spy on the late nineteenth century in the act of discovering itself. Rugby was a utopian community founded by Thomas Hughes, the author of *Tom Brown's School Days*, the popular Victorian boarding-school novel. Its aim was to offer an English public-school education—think playing fields of Eton—to a mix of rowdy Americans, working-class boys imported from Britain, and the younger sons of English aristocrats, whom the law of primogeniture prevented from inheriting their father's estates. It's almost totally forgotten now; in its time it was a locus of enthusiasms brilliant people believed could change the world. What if the solution to inequality was to teach young men of all nations and classes the manners of a duke and the morals of a Christian socialist? They played croquet on the Cumberland Plateau, staged fox hunts through Polecat Hollow. The whole thing collapsed after a few years. E.W. loved it.

He held on, all his life, to his father's ardor for nobility, but he also had an American nose for hustle. After law school, at the age of twenty-one, he set up shop for himself, using his father's money, in an office under the stairs. He was irresistibly drawn to backroom deals, ingenious exploits, get-rich-quick schemes. He did a little bit of everything. When he noticed that the advertisements in Pittsburgh streetcars were unappealing and dull, he started a side business selling brightly colored placards. He spent hours at the courthouse, poring over mortgage records for loans he could profitably transfer. He scouted potential coal lands for a pair of promoters with the Dickensian names of Guffey &

Galey. He shook hands. He made friends. He played poker obsessively, and he played well, but it was when he lost that you saw his real character; it was a pleasure, his friends felt, to watch him lose. He waved off setbacks so casually. Just a little money, boys, nothing to get excited about.

He was able to do this not because he was indifferent to money but because it played such an outsized role in his fantasies. He wanted to make money, and not just a respectable amount of money, the way his father had done, but a spectacular amount, so much that he could do anything, carry out any grand gesture he liked. Whatever he lost at poker was insignificant compared with the scale of the fantasy. One of his side businesses during this period was writing fairy stories for a Pittsburgh newspaper: Fantasy was a powerful influence on him. He knew, too, that it was vulgar for a gentleman to think about money. That was why he had to make so much of it—to free himself from the need to have vulgar thoughts.

How could he make that kind of money? His work for Guffey & Galey had quickened his interest in geology. Everyone knew that America, the land itself, was a fathomless source of riches. The ground brimmed with coal, gas, copper, gold; best of all, it brimmed with vast pockets of oil, demand for which was about to shoot sky-high as the country surged into the twentieth century. Figure out how to find the oil reserves and your millions were there for the taking. Oil had been the source of John D. Rockefeller's fortune; Standard Oil was one of the great commercial behemoths of the age. Perhaps a great oil strike could set him on the same path?

His obsessive urge to know where the levers were and

who really pulled them was probably what drew him to Sam Collins. His father had served in the legislature with Sam, but it was E.W. who befriended him, drank whiskey with him, sang Irish songs with him in brass-trimmed rooms. Sam wasn't rich, not the way E.W. planned to be. But he knew how the game was played, and that made him interesting.

E.W. and Mary Virginia were married in 1903, when he was twenty-nine and she was twenty-six. Over the next four years, E.W. made his first million, drilling for oil in Pennsylvania and West Virginia. Then the panic of 1907 hit, the banks failed, and he lost everything.

In 1908, he went to Oklahoma—he was so broke he had to advertise for backers just to pay the train fare—where, in a few years, he would make his spectacular fortune, a fortune so vast, so nearly infinite, he'd be able to do as he pleased for the rest of his life. Or anyway so he thought.

There's no record of whether the Collins family came to see him off at the train station. If they did, he might have said goodbye to his oldest niece and nephew, a ten-year-old boy and eight-year-old girl, the son and daughter of Mary Virginia's sister Maggie and the fruit seller from Flourtown. What we do know is that a few years later, sometime around 1912, the children made the long journey to Oklahoma to visit their newly wealthy uncle and aunt.

They traveled by train, watching the changing country scroll past.

That was how Lydie first came to Ponca City.

———

The best description I have found of Ponca City, Oklahoma, in the early twentieth century comes from a biography of

E. W. Marland. Really it comes from the *only* biography
of E. W. Marland; you can find others, but they tend to have
a local-enthusiast, semi-spell-checked quality, Bible verses
on the copyright page, that sort of thing, and this book, the
one with the description, is the work of a serious scholar. An
artist. The book is called *Life and Death of an Oilman: The
Career of E. W. Marland*. John Joseph Mathews is the writer's name. He published it in 1951. It's one of the strangest
books I've ever read. In part this is because Mathews's vision
is so uncompromising. The subtitle of the book is accurate.
Mathews is intensely interested in Marland's professional
life and cold to, or at least highly reluctant to talk about, his
private life. So unlike most biographies, which say, in effect,
here are the public deeds of this person and the private oc-
currences that explain who he or she really was, Mathews
presents a weirdly romanticized foreground of geological
exploration and the hammering out of contracts, with almost
no background at all. Marland's marriage is mentioned
maybe four times in passing. In the meantime, the angel,
the goddess, the siren Petrolia, the imaginary Spirit of Oil,
appears again and again, guiding Marland's eye as he ponders
the angles of anticlines.

John Joseph Mathews—what a fascinating person. He
was twenty years younger than Marland, and knew him.
Mathews was part Osage, the grandson of a legendary white
mountain man, Old Bill Williams, who'd married into the
tribe in the early nineteenth century. He grew up in Oklahoma during a period when the Osage were making immense
sums of money by leasing drilling rights to the immense
reserves of oil under their land, a period about which he later
wrote a novel, *Sundown* (1934). He flew planes with the

Twenty-Fifth Squadron during World War I, studied at Oxford, traveled in Africa, and later returned to Oklahoma, where he spent a decade living and writing in near seclusion in the Osage Hills. He wrote important histories of the tribe, including one, *Wah'Kon-Tah: The Osage and the White Man's Road*, that was a Book-of-the-Month Club selection and a bestseller in 1932.

The biography of Marland is in some ways a missed opportunity. Mathews wrote at a time when many of the principal figures were still alive, and he knew them, spoke to them, yet he left out so much of the story. Mary Virginia, for instance. We know so little about her, hardly anything beyond local gossip. She was dead in 1951, but living people remembered her. Mathews could have filled in the gaps, and chose not to. "She had the alertness of mind and the type of wit that E.W. liked," he says. Which type was that? One detail in particular gnaws at me: Mathews says that she was working as a stenographer in Philadelphia when she met E.W. That's confirmed in the census of 1900, where "court stenographer" is listed as her occupation. So someone in the Collins family must have told the census taker that. But we also know that Sam Collins was employed at the Superior Court of Pennsylvania in 1900, and Sam was enmeshed in the Republican machine's patronage system. Had Mary Virginia studied shorthand? Did she go to the court every day? Record trials? Or was it some sort of phantom appointment, a way for Sam to collect two salaries? Worlds of possibility unspool around that single line, and the possibilities could be real, or they could be smoke. The Oklahoma Historical Society's encyclopedia describes her instead as "the daughter of a court stenographer," which is almost certainly a misreading; I simply can't be sure. Mathews says nothing more.

Yet the book, despite its shortcomings, is lyrically thrilling and psychologically astute, the more so for being built from such unconventional materials. Built from geological surveys and committee minutes, basically. It may be a more authentic look at the emotional life of this peculiar businessman, at the currents that shaped his lived experience, than a more traditionally complete portrait could have been.

There's a moment—this is the first part of the description of Ponca City—that takes place in the lobby of a hotel. This is 1912, so around the time Lydie and her brother first arrived in town. It's night. E.W. is sitting up late at a table in the Arcade Hotel, where he's living; his oil refinery is under construction down the street, but his house on Grand Avenue, the first and considerably less magnificent of the two magnificent mansions he built for himself, hasn't even been designed yet. He's talking, by candlelight, to Dr. Irving Perrine, a geologist from the University of Oklahoma. E.W. has already struck it pretty big, he has twenty oil wells going, but his interest in geology is swelling along with his fortune, and he's thrilled to have a real scientist in town, someone he can ask questions. The hour advances.

The traveling salesmen would one by one leave for bed. The soundlessness of those days can scarcely be imagined. A horse's hooves thudding the dust, or the creaking of a late wagon, occasionally the shout of a drunken Ponca or cowboy, nothing more. Lights would go out all over the little plains town, except for a few gas street lights, and only the night breeze of the plains would be astir as the two men sat and talked of the wonders of the geological past and the formation of the Red Beds, upon the thin edges of which their hotel stood.

Mathews was a teenager in 1912, living forty-fives miles away, in Pawhuska. He remembered that darkness. How the gas lamps looked against the prairie. Oklahoma had been admitted to statehood just five years before. We're on the threshold—literally, in this conversation—between the Old West and what came after it.

The other part of the description is set four years earlier. It's 1908; E.W. has just gotten off the train. Ponca City is at this point just fifteen years old. In 1893 the Cherokee Outlet was opened for homesteading—that's the famous land run, the scramble to stake claims on the vast territory the government had forced the Cherokee to sell—and the town was founded. So when E.W. arrives, everything is still new, the city has barely been scraped out. (In fact, it isn't even called Ponca City yet; it's still New Ponca.) Downtown is the sketch of a few streets, "which terminated suddenly," Mathews says, "in a limitless plain of close-growing grass." To the south is the Ponca Indian Reservation. West of the reservation, there's an enormous ranch, known as the 101, which covers more than a hundred thousand acres. "101": That's the mark the ranch brands on its cattle.

The ranch is the real center of the region. It's owned by the three Miller brothers, Joe, Zack, and George junior, and it's famous for more than just its size: It's also the home of the 101 Ranch Wild West Show, a traveling extravaganza that in the course of its history will employ a young Tom Mix and an elderly Geronimo. (Geronimo's act involves shooting a bison from the front seat of a car.) Also Bill Pickett, the great black cowboy, who dazzles crowds by leaping from horseback onto the back of a running steer, biting the steer's upper lip to subdue it, and wrestling it to the ground. That year, 1908, the show will tour Europe, where in Germany some of its performers, a group of Oglala Sioux, will be arrested as Serbian spies. Mathews writes,

> Buffalo stood and looked stupidly at the passer-by through a game fence, and out on the tawny swells camels grazed, blending so perfectly in this strange habitat that they could scarcely be seen. Circus wagons stood immobilized among the manure and mud-stained workaday wagons. Along the railroad siding stood the circus cars, less gaudy than the wagons.

What we're watching here, in other words, is not only the end of the West. It's the West memorializing itself, performing itself in the moment of its own ending. There are real cowboys in New Ponca, but one of the ways to make a living as a cowboy now is to become a "cowboy"—to pretend to do, for a crowd, the thing you actually do. There are Indians still living in traditional ways on tribal lands near town, and the region itself is one of the nation's great hubs of Native American heritage—mostly for tragic reasons, but still—yet the Indians who play "Indians" for the 101 are arguing with the Millers about their overtime pay. The citizens of the town are living out an authentic drama of frontier settlement; at the same time, silent film studios are already cranking out Westerns, and the citizens know this, and have seen them.

The point being: This was an exceptionally fertile place and time for anyone interested in trying on roles, making dramatic gestures, and experimenting with various narratives of civilization.

And this was the setting when E.W.—penniless, genteel, ambitious, headstrong, an American, an Anglophile—stepped off the train, looking for a hotel room.

Of course he fell in with the Miller brothers. They were all showmen, just of different centuries. E.W. leased the rights to drill for oil under the ranch. They rode out together, on horseback, to scout the terrain. (There are pictures of this; E.W. wore spats.) For a couple of years, their wells turned up nothing but gas. Then, in 1911, E.W. found a promising spot, a kind of sea swell on the plain, Mathews says, a hill on an allotment belonging to a Ponca Indian named Willie-Cries-for-War. The hill was a sacred burial ground.

> The Ponca, like the Osage, had never buried their
> dead until persuaded to do so by the white man. The
> Ponca had bound them and laid them upon scaffolds,
> or swung them into trees where they could be seen
> by the Great Mysteries.

With help from the Millers, whom the Indians knew and respected, E.W. persuaded White Eagle, the chief of the Ponca, to grant him the lease to the allotment. History says that White Eagle, who was then in his nineties and who agreed to the deal with extreme reluctance, told E.W. the well would be "bad medicine," for the tribe and for E.W. himself.

Equipment came by train. Oxen dragged heavy loads from the depot across the muddy plains. Soon the derrick was rising on the hill. E.W. slept there, ate there; while the drilling was under way, he ran out of money.

He gave Mrs. Rhoades, owner of the Arcade Hotel, promises, and she, a realistic, kindly, profanely compassionate soldier in the ranks of men against the temperamental plains, allowed him credit.

When the well finally struck oil, E.W. was some distance away, in the middle of the Salt Fork of the Arkansas River, where he was helping to lay a gas pipeline. Everyone remembered that he'd taken his pants off to wade into the river and had to shimmy back into them when the news arrived. He raced to the well. A black feather of spray was standing up and over the derrick and trailing away in the wind. He stared, hardly believing it. He was rich! His hands shook.

4

I have in my possession a copy of a diary that Lydie Marland kept in 1921, beginning in July, three months after her twenty-first birthday, and ending in late September. The diary is a travel journal—I mean the book is, physically; each page opens with the printed heading "Places Visited" and includes blank lines for the date and locale. Lydie wrote, with a few exceptions, one entry per page, in small, rounded, sharply angled handwriting. The period of the journal coincides with a vacation to Europe that she took with E.W. and Mary Virginia. They sailed from New York Harbor on RMS *Olympic*, the sister ship of the *Titanic*, on July 16, bound for Southampton via Cherbourg, France.

> July 17—slept late, walked deck & killed time generally.

The day before the ship sailed, a massive electrical storm roared over New York City. Lightning struck buildings. Block after block went dark. The *Times* reported that two oil tanks had been hit in the yards at Bayonne, New Jersey, causing huge fires despite the heavy rain; "pillars of flame," the reporter wrote, "stabbed hundreds of feet toward the sky." In Manhattan, a fourteen-year-old girl named Sadie Stone, who worked in Samuel Kamininsky's kimono factory at 171 Wooster Street, collapsed in hysterics during the storm and had to be treated by a doctor. The lights went out in the Essex Market Police Court, terrifying the hundred or so people in the courtroom; Magistrate Simpson, the *Times* assured its readers, restored calm.

Lydie watched the storm from high up in the Plaza hotel, where the Marlands now kept an apartment. Or else she was out shopping, buying things for her trip, and had to dash into a store to escape the rain. Or else she was lunching with friends and thinking of the gifts she'd bring back from Paris. Lydie and her older brother, George, had gone to live permanently with E.W. and Mary Virginia in Ponca City soon after their first visit. When Lydie was sixteen, the

Marlands legally adopted them. (Lydie's birth parents appear to have embraced their role as poor relations with an almost Victorian relish; their two younger children, born after E.W. made his first millions, were a boy named Marland and a girl named Virginia.) Having been raised as the daughter of a pushcart vendor, Lydie became an heiress. She lived in the mansion on Grand Avenue, with its eight acres of private gardens, its hanging staircase, its indoor swimming pool. E.W. organized English fox hunts on the prairie; Lydie rode in them, wearing a jacket and tie. E.W. organized a polo league; Lydie went to the matches. She had books, gowns, jewels, horses. She went dancing. She drank champagne.

The Marlands' parties were still remembered, were still written about, decades later.

> An orchestra would play on the terrace and Marland's
> blocks of gardens were softly aglow with blue lights.
> They would dance, go on giggly walks down this lane
> and that, and sip bootleg scotch and bourbon.

A few years ago, there was talk in Hollywood about a Lydie Marland movie, which was going to be called *The Ends of the Earth*. Jennifer Lawrence was supposed to play Lydie; Harvey Weinstein and David O. Russell, probably the last people you'd want anywhere near Lydie's story, would produce and direct. Nothing came of it, but if it had, these would be the scenes you can imagine the camera loving, the soft montage of opulence: clods flying from the polo ponies' hooves, the red coats of the fox hunters, the trumpets, the gardens, the glow of the blue lights.

What was she like, this girl whose life seemed lifted from a fairy tale? It is easier to say what she saw. She saw Ponca City transform, fill up with fountains, fine houses, crystal decanters, electric chandeliers. She saw her uncle—that is, her father, though she never called him that—grow astoundingly, impossibly rich: By 1920, when he was in his mid-forties, he controlled 10 percent of the world's known oil reserves. She saw the insides of the private train cars that carried her to eastern boarding schools. She saw the Pacific Ocean from the deck of E.W.'s yacht. She saw Hawaii. In photographs from this period she appears high-spirited, giddy in proportion to the times. She never stops laughing. Here she is in a stylish dress, striking a comical pose on the veranda. Here she is holding a horse by the bridle, grinning hugely, with her riding hat pulled down over her eyes. Yet her friends later remembered her as somehow reserved, shy in a way that was hard to identify, as if some part of her were always hanging back to observe her own experience from the outside. As if she were consciously testing the fabric of the romance to see if it would hold.

This is the voice that comes through in the diary:

The sun didn't rise to flood the entire world in gold as it seemed to on the morning we entered that never to be forgotten harbor at Honolulu; but rather half heartedly, now here & now there, it chose a small Gothic church almost smothered on the hillside, or one of the fairylike sail boats which lazily bobbed on the deep green water bosom of the harbor. On our way across the channel to Southampton we passed the Scarborough Castle where Queen Victoria died.

In 1921, she was sufficiently accustomed to luxury that she could write about the *Olympic*, probably the most glamorous ocean liner in the world, the ship Mary Pickford and Douglas Fairbanks had chosen for the return voyage from their honeymoon, without bothering to mention the orchestra, the Turkish baths, the swimming pool, the lounge patterned after Versailles. What struck her instead was an incident she witnessed among the lower-class passengers.

> July 22nd—We stood on the after deck & looked down into the steerage, while two Jews handed over some candy and nuts. A scene ensued in which babies got mashed while their mothers tore at each other in mad desire to have the good food for their own. Poor children groped & snatched & shed the tears—poor women lost hands full of hair & mighty near blood.

This voice—intelligent, observant, and precise, but not critical, permeable to cliché—belongs to a reader, to someone whose first frame of reference for her own experience is the stories she knows from books.

> Aug. 25—Thursday
> Had dinner alone upstairs & started Evan Harrington which Ed left for me with his letter.

> Aug. 26—Friday
> Unpacked this morning & read a little. Walked around dear London this afternoon & bought some soap & ordered two pink match cases.

Monday—29th Aug.
Read "Evan Harrington" all day.

Aug. 30th
read myself to sleep.

Thurs. Sept. 1st
E.W. wanted me to have some things from Burberry's, namely a hat & plaid coat. As I told him, those things are impracticle. Why arm myself for rain & wind when doing the same thing for a dinner dance is so much more invigorating. I am still reading Evan Harrington.

Sat. Sept 10th
Fitting this morning. Am still reading Ainsworth's Tower—& cannot drag myself away from it.

The sun is meant to flood the world in gold when the princess sails into the harbor. The poor women are meant to be grateful when the Jews give them candy and nuts. These are picturesque features of reality, and she has been taught to expect that reality will be picturesque. She came to the lesson late, however, and has not entirely been able to absorb it. She knows what it is to be poor; she remembers what it is like not to be a princess. And so she cannot help noticing that the magic often wavers, and that even when it does not, its effect on her is not always what convention might have led her to suppose.

I'm in London and it tells me one thing: I've been suffering, unconsciously, nostalgia all my life.

Her days are a whirl, full of luncheons, fittings, cocktails, museums, shows. What fun to walk along the Strand, to order pink match cases, to dine at the Trocadero, to see the crown jewels.

> Lady De Freyne gave a dinner at the Ritz & I felt almost at home with the orchestra. It tried to be American and jazzed Bright Eyes and a few more good old home tunes. Lady De F. says "Topping rooms you have!" I believe they *are* topping—K. & Q. of Belgium occupied this same suite a few weeks ago.

Yet she is sometimes caught out by a sudden gust of melancholy, surprised, even in rooms recently occupied by the king and queen of Belgium, by a sense that something is missing.

> Gen. Kenley took me to Buckingham Palace this morning to see the guards in formation. Their high black bearskin shakos look most hot & top heavy—red coat, black trousers—all in all the veritable tin soldier of the nursery. The Savoy is superb—just the sort of place you expect—especially gay at Luncheon—excellent service, food & music—a Princeton son here & there or an east Indian maharajah or Turkish sultan—and en costume! To the National Portrait Gallery alone this afternoon & to Westminster Library. What I don't know appalls me.

In Paris she dines at Maxim's and visits the Louvre to see the Venus de Milo. In Edinburgh she is interested in the

closes, the dark alleys off the Royal Mile. E.W. tells her that
this is where most of the city's murders happen.

In Ashton-Under-Lyne, the ancient seat of the Marlands,
E.W. takes her to the old church, where she walks "over all
the dead Marlands from 17th cent. on." Perhaps he wants her
to feel that this is her history, now, as well as his. Perhaps
she does feel it. If she has any thoughts about this glimpse
into the Marland past, however, she does not tell her diary
what they are. She notes, instead, that she was driven that
same afternoon to see Shakespeare's birthplace. She writes
that Stratford is "a veritable dream spot."

———

In my parents' house in Oklahoma City, there is a painting
by Robert Hardee of E. W. Marland's second mansion, the
walled manor on Monument Road, which was built between
1925 and 1928. I'm not sure how the painting came into my
family's possession. My aunt and Robert Hardee broke up
not long after my grandparents died. I remember him only
slightly, a thin, dark man in a tight flannel shirt and black
jeans. He had long hair and a heavy black beard and his eyes
were serious and strangely hooded, so that from one angle
they might look wounded and from another angle they might
look cruel. Yet he was gentle, almost painfully so. Once he
brought a horse to my aunt's backyard and led it around in
circles while my sister and I sat on its back. Their whole existence, his and my aunt's, seemed inaccessibly adult, and
therefore intensely mysterious. My aunt had parties to which
children were not invited. Objects you had to be careful not
to break. Strange books. *Skinny Legs and All* on a glass end
table, under an exotic-looking lamp. Not long ago, I learned

from the Internet that he died, Robert Hardee, in 2008, at fifty-five, and that he had been teaching art at a public high school in Tulsa, and that he was an Indian activist, and that years ago he had been adopted into the Ponca nation. He is described in one biographical statement, apparently written by him, as "a human being who happens to be non-Indian." The biographical statement mentions that he raised an Arabian horse named Khalifa and rode him bareback, with no saddle or bridle, on the plains.

I hadn't known any of this, because at a certain point Robert Hardee vanished from our lives. Except that in the late 1980s and early 1990s he painted a series of historic buildings in Ponca City. For years, you'd see these works hanging in local businesses. Over supper-club doors, near the gumballs. My parents somehow acquired signed and numbered prints of each of them. I have no idea how or why; we're not art-buying people. Possibly they were a gift? A few years ago, I helped my parents repaint their kitchen, and when the job was done I rehung the prints in their places over the cabinets. They looked newly strange against the pale green walls, with the light shining on them.

Of all the prints, the painting of the mansion is the one that always draws my eye. It comes back to me like a remnant from a drowned city: the Renaissance palace, with its light brown sandstone walls, its crinkled red-tiled roof. Its porches. Its gargoyles. Its four roofed chimneys that as a child I confused for prison towers. In the painting, there are 1920s sedans parked outside, as if for a party. A family in period clothes holds hands and walks toward the house.

My grandparents lived down the street from that house.

My high school held its prom in that house.

What happened was that the bottom fell out of everything.

E.W. lost control of his company. Officially in 1929, though in fact the process started long before that. Marland Oil was famous by this point. Its logo, an upside-down red triangle, was found on hundreds of filling stations across the middle of the country. Its generosity toward its workers, rare for the period—it provided health insurance, as well as affordable housing, literacy training, tennis courts, a golf course—was much discussed. E.W. embraced the role of enlightened lord, as he'd been trained to do: of him to whom much is given, much is required.

In 1923, J. P. Morgan Jr. invited E.W. to his office in Manhattan, wreathed him in flattery and cigar smoke— what an outfit you've built, sir; what a mind for business, sir—and persuaded him to sell the J. P. Morgan Company twelve million dollars in stock. The investment was a crack that widened over the next several years. The Morgans slowly took over. E.W. had always hated bankers, whom he dismissed as "still-faced boys." He liked gamblers and adventurers, not cautious men who built their fortunes on decimal points. Yet there's a curious blur around E.W. in this period. As the Morgans moved in on his executive committee, he seems to have been preoccupied with increasingly fantastic distractions. He sent experts to Europe to buy art for his collection. He built his palace. He brought artists to Ponca City to decorate it and to paint whimsical portraits of himself and his children: George as a roustabout, Lydie as Georges Bizet's Carmen. He briefly became obsessed with rigid airships. He joined a new company that planned to manufacture both military dirigibles and luxurious passenger craft in the style of German zeppelins (Franklin D. Roosevelt was one of his co-incorporators). Once, on a bear hunt in Mississippi, he bought a plantation on a whim for $750,000.

In 1926, Mary Virginia died. Here the blur grows even deeper. She was forty-eight (maybe forty-nine; her death certificate gives a different birth year from the old Pennsylvania census records). What killed her at such a young age? The official cause of death was listed as pneumonia, and the duration of the illness listed as four days. John Joseph Mathews, however, says she died "after a long illness." Possibly she had an undiagnosed cancer. For years, there'd been rumors that something was wrong. Stories passed around town that she drank too much (probable: cirrhosis of the liver is listed as a contributory factor on her death certificate), that she drank laudanum, that she made scenes in public. She hated living in Oklahoma, people said, had always hated it, hated the plains and the sky, hated the people, hated the muddy saloon town she'd moved to and the grandiose oil town it became. She was sharp-minded and sour-tempered. "I saw him with a girl!" she is said to have screamed, drunkenly, at a church social, when someone asked why she was crying. We do have some strange details. E.W. had central air-conditioning installed in her room, and only her room, at the house on Grand Avenue. The plans for the new mansion, which were drawn up well before her death, apparently did not include a room for her. So had her death already seemed imminent by 1925? Or was she planning to go on living at the Grand Avenue house while E.W. moved on with George and Lydie? Or something else?

One of the passengers on the *Olympic* during the Marlands' voyage to England was a young man named Edward Donahoe, who came from a prominent Ponca City family. He knew George and Lydie well and he saw Lydie several times in Europe: He was the "Ed" who left her the copy of *Evan Harrington*. "He dances well," Lydie wrote in her diary, "& is intelligent also—great combination." Donahoe went to Harvard, then worked at Alfred A. Knopf for a period in the 1920s. He became a peripheral figure in the Harlem Renaissance, closely associated with Nella Larsen. Later he became a tragic drunk. Somewhere on the threshold between those two states, in 1937, he published a novel, *Madness in the Heart*, which told a fictionalized version of the history of Ponca City. His story included characters based on the Marlands. The E.W. character is selfish and cruel. The Mary Virginia character kills herself.

The suicide could have been Donahoe's invention, of course. He was in a position to know what had really happened, which doesn't mean he told it straight; *Madness in the Heart* is a novel, not a biography. Still, this particular story about Mary Virginia's death has persisted across decades. It has, at least, the virtue of completing a coherent picture. A picture whose parts are individually unconfirmed and unconfirmable, true, but one that, taken as a whole, seems charismatically plausible. An unhappy woman, brought to a strange place; she turns to drink; her powerful husband takes up with other women, or with another woman; her depression and anger are euphemistically called "ill health" by her conservative society; her suicide is covered up. Certainly Donahoe's book was radioactive in Ponca City. His father, who was close to the Marlands, tried to buy up every copy, and he burned the ones he bought.

Around the time of Mary Virginia's death, the blur extends to cover Lydie.

More rumors, more uncertainties.

She took several trips with E.W. alone, as the townspeople said, which means something or it doesn't.

She was hospitalized in 1927, as *The Ponca City News* said, or else she wasn't.

She had a baby in secret and gave it up for adoption, as *The Saturday Evening Post* said, or else she didn't.

On January 6, 1928, the following headline ran on the front page of *The New York Times*:

> *E. W. Marland to Marry Adopted Daughter;*
> *Oil Man Plans Wedding Within a Month*

Then four days later, on page 26:

> *Marland's Adoption of Fiancee Annulled,*
> *Clearing Way for Marriage to Wife's Niece*

There was no doubting the accuracy of these reports: E.W. himself announced the engagement. Lydie spoke at the court hearing to have the adoption annulled. E.W. was fifty-three; Lydie was twenty-seven. The story of the tycoon who fell in love with his own daughter caused a national media frenzy.

News of the engagement of her daughter, Miss Lydie Miller Roberts, to Ernest W. Marland, oil millionaire, came as a shock to Mrs. George F. Roberts, who refused to discuss the coming marriage, at her home on Old Mill Road, in Flourtown, late today. She broke down and wept when she learned of the engagement, regretting particularly Mr. Marland's reference to the adoption of the girl. She refused to discuss her daughter's reasons for leaving her parents.

In February it was reported that the wedding had been delayed because Lydie was hospitalized with anemia. In July it was reported that the wedding had been further delayed because Lydie was suffering from what the press called a "nervous ailment."

Having recently opened his $2,000,000 mansion in Ponca City, Okla., E. W. Marland, oil financier, was reported yesterday to be on his way to New York on a mission which he refused to discuss when leaving his home town. . . . Mr. Marland's friends believe he is coming to visit his fiancee, who is said to be in a sanitarium near New York.

On July 14, 1928, E.W. and Lydie were married at the Roberts house in Flourtown. Her parents had opposed the marriage, or at any rate reporters said they did. But her father gave her away, and her younger brother, the son they had named Marland, was one of the attendants.

There were five guests at the wedding.

After the honeymoon, the new couple returned to Ponca City and moved into their new mansion, which, the *Times* reported, "is said to rival in splendor the sumptuous manor houses of old England."

In October 1928, three months after the wedding and a year before the stock market crash, the bankers succeeded in forcing E.W. out of Marland Oil.

The fortune was gone before 1930.

Lydie's old life ended, then ended again and kept ending.

5

The fairy tale. The palace. The drowned city.

The entrance to the Marland Mansion lies through a pair of arched wooden doors. The doors are studded with iron. Across from the doors stands the entrance to the hedge maze. The hedge maze is in fact not a maze but only a formal garden whose ornate pattern of paths creates a maze-like effect. The hedges (though this is visible only from the upper windows) form the shape of a gigantic, stylized *M*. The hedges are cut low, so it is possible from outside the garden to see the statue of George Marland at its center. George Marland, who was at various times Lydie's brother, nephew, and stepson. Rendered in white stone as a young scion, a sporting Yale man of the 1920s, in riding boots and an open-collared shirt. White stone hand slipped into a white stone pocket.

In the mansion's early days, the garden around the statue of George Marland was larger and more open, less labyrinthine. In those first years, the estate was itself larger, was in fact immense, a barony with three lakes, an Olympic swimming pool, woods, fields. A secret tunnel led from the mansion to the boathouse. Only later, after the crash, when the mansion passed into the hands first of an order of monks and then of an order of nuns, did the margins begin to collapse, the woods to disappear. Two of the lakes and the swimming pool were filled in. Outlying lands were sold to developers. Houses went up just outside the walls, on Monument Road.

From the shade of the porte cochere, you pass through the heavy doors into the deeper shade of the vestibule and then, through an elaborate archway, into the gloom of the grand foyer. The purpose of the foyer is perhaps less to embody any particular beauty than to tell you in unmistakable terms what kind of house this is. This is the kind of house where footsteps echo. This is the kind of house where the quantity of stone, the depth of shadow, the massive height of the ceiling, create an effect calculated less to please than to overwhelm. This is the kind of house where wall sconces take the shapes of satyrs. This is the kind of house where the stair rails terminate in wrought-iron dragon heads. This is the kind of house where the ceiling of the loggia is muraled in hand-painted chinoiserie canvas and where the ceiling of the ballroom is coffered in gold leaf. This is the kind of house in which one repeats the familiar real-estate terms—forty-eight thousand square feet, fifty-five rooms—as if they retained any meaning in the presence of a dining room whose pollard oak paneling was cut "by special permission from the royal forests of England." There is a secret room, concealed within the mansion's third kitchen, where

a secret door designed to look like a safe leads to a cavern-
ous cellar in which whiskey was once kept hidden from Pro-
hibition agents: That is the kind of house this is.

It is the kind of house that requires vast sums not only
to build but also to inhabit. E.W. and Lydie managed to live
here for a little over two years. In 1931, they found they could
no longer afford to heat the ballroom, to light the satyr-head
sconces, to pay the large domestic staff necessary to man
the three kitchens and keep the royal oak paneling free from
dust. They moved, first into the artist's studio E.W. had built
on the estate and then into the chauffeur's cottage. They
opened the mansion for special occasions. Political events,
for instance. Broke but still famous in Oklahoma, E.W. ran
for Congress in 1932 and won. He ran for governor in 1934,
on a platform of bringing the New Deal to Oklahoma. He
won again. He turned the mansion into a political headquarters. He strode through the halls, signing papers. He threw
an inaugural ball in the ballroom, under the gold leaf.

Lydie became First Lady of Oklahoma. She filled the role
for four years, though in fact she seems to have taken little
part in E.W.'s administration in Oklahoma City. In fact by
this time—after the mysterious hospitalization, the rumored
pregnancy, the newspaper frenzy, the wedding, the change,
the crash—she seems to have started down the path toward
the anxious reclusiveness of her later years. She still smiles,
in photos from this period, but her smile is different.

Less steady somehow.

Uncertain somehow.

She was too shy to speak at political rallies. She stayed
in Ponca City. Read her magazines. Read her books.

E.W. lost two bids for a Senate seat. He tried to start a new oil company, but the world had changed, and he failed.

In 1941, a few months before he died, E.W. sold the mansion to the Discalced Carmelite Fathers for sixty-six thousand dollars.

In 1948, a few years before Lydie disappeared, the monks sold it to the Felician Sisters for fifty thousand dollars.

The nuns occupied the estate for twenty-seven years. They were there in 1950, when Louis Cassel first knocked on the door of the chauffeur's cottage. They were there in 1953, when Lydie drove away in the green convertible.

They were there for twenty-two years after that.

In 1975, three things happened.

The first is that Ponca City bought the mansion from the Felician Sisters for $1.4 million. The city's aim was to restore it, open it to the public, turn it into a tourist attraction. Half the money was raised through a special one-cent sales tax. The other half was put up by the company that had once been Marland Oil. In 1929, shortly after E.W. was forced out, Marland Oil acquired a smaller outfit, Continental Oil, and because the bankers, the still-faced boys, wanted E.W. entirely out of the picture, they used the latter name for the newly combined operation. Continental Oil later became Conoco, which in 2002 would merge with Phillips Petroleum to form ConocoPhillips, which eventually split into separate companies whose combined revenue in 2016 was more than $111 billion. But even by the mid-1970s, Conoco's prosperity had sufficiently softened its attitude toward its own founding drama for it to agree to match the proceeds of the sales tax.

The second thing that happened in 1975 is that the gates were opened at Kaw Dam and Kaw City was submerged under the lake.

The third thing that happened in 1975 is that Lydie Marland came back.

———

She was now an old woman. She had been gone for more than twenty years and the years had been hard ones. Her teeth had fallen out. She wore a scarf wrapped around the lower part of her face to hide her mouth. She wore a long black dress and sometimes a long raincoat and a plastic hood and she wore bulky tennis shoes, and in warm weather she walked around town dressed like that. In press reports from the period, she is compared to a scarecrow, a witch, a ghost. She wanders the grounds of the mansion, in accounts of varying believability, at one and two in the morning. Her letters, the few that survive, from the time of her return to Ponca City stress the shock, the strain, the exhausting struggle of nerving herself to see the old places again.

> The nightmare of my life since I left there—I'm a humiliating physical wreck—and dread seeing you, and the impulse is to put it off.

The neat handwriting of 1921 is now a wobbly scrawl, and she nearly always writes in red ink, possibly because it is easier for her to see.

> I'll try to be brief, to keep my mind on the *facts* (altho facts are surface things, and never tell the story).

She is haunted by suffocating guilt (over what isn't clear) and by a sense that the insurmountable complexity of every situation makes decisions tormentingly difficult.

> Some days I long to let it all go and let others unravel a tangled-up mess. It would be just one more way I failed E.W. and everyone who ever liked me (my brother).
>
>   Perhaps what appears to be right and wrong is just cause and effect.

She does not reveal where she has been since 1953, although there have been sightings through the years. More rumors. She was spotted at an antiwar rally in Washington, D.C., in the 1960s; she showed up in California; once, in Arkansas City, Kansas, two reporters staked out her post-office box. When they approached her she fled and hid in a supermarket. She is obsessed, in the letters, with the idea that she has been followed by journalists and spies ever since she left town. Perhaps she is paranoid, or perhaps she is still traumatized by the newspaper furor over her engagement. Perhaps she is right; I simply do not know.

> The invasion of and exploitation of one's private life is being called "The New Cannibalism"—and it *is that—psychological* cannibalism. I was *never* a "missing person," I have spent years trying to evade the relentless surveillance, and *never succeeding.*

The cottage was falling apart; her money was gone. Her return to Ponca City had been facilitated by community lead-ers, there were bank presidents and lawyers and oil executives interested in her welfare, but when they tried to help her, she either stalled or refused outright. She would not let them sign her up for Social Security, because she would not take money from the government. She would not let them sell her things, because the strain of deciding to sell them was too great. Their letters to each other grow increasingly bewildered.

> Howard, Mrs. Marland never makes a decision today that she can put off until tomorrow. She continues to live a deprived existence but is almost impossible to help. If you have any ideas, I would appreciate your sharing them with me.

Somehow she managed to acquire a house on South Fourth Street that was within walking distance of the grocery store and the drugstore, and in the winter, when the cottage became uninhabitable, she lived there, keeping KFC buckets in the refrigerator, hanging blankets over the windows.

Why arm myself for rain & wind when doing the same thing for a dinner dance is so much more invigorating.

I cannot remember a time when I did not know this story.

I grew up knowing this story.

I was born in 1976, the year after Lydie returned to Ponca City. That was the year the mansion opened to the public. The year water began to pour through the last-completed gates at Kaw Dam. As a child I would sometimes see her, in her long coat, in her long scarf, shuffling on the sides of roads. We would drive past her. Look, there's

Lydie, out for a walk. Most often near my grandparents' house, because she stayed in the old cottage during the warm months. My grandmother might point her out. Lydie, who had lived in the mansion. Lydie, who had disappeared and no one knew where she had gone.

Perhaps what appears to be right and wrong is just cause and effect.

We did not know what to make of her. No one did. It was not merely her eccentricity that baffled us; it was also the dark unintelligible fact she lodged in the heart of our founding narrative. Our town existed because of the oil industry. E. W. Marland had built the oil industry. E. W. Marland was revered. Maintaining the status of E. W. Marland as a great man was a matter of civic importance. A statue of E. W. Marland seated, almost throned, stood outside city hall. The story of E. W. Marland was a story of frontier conquest, of civilization building. This was our history, or we said it was. This was our story, or we wanted it to be. Yet E. W. Marland had done this one viscerally shocking and unaccountable thing: He had married his own daughter. Now, fifty years later, the daughter-wife wandered the streets in a long black dress with a scarf wrapped around her mouth. She couldn't be written out of the narrative. She was right here. Yet she offered no explanations, either of the distant past or of her own mysteriously shattered present. From the car window, she eluded all interpretation. How could we make the pieces fit?

Part of the mystery was the nature of her marriage to E.W. Had it been a real love story? Some people tried to say it had, but there was something in the basic character of the relationship—the age difference; the family connection, which was intimate even if not precisely incestuous: there are photos of the two of them together when Lydie was twelve years old—that made the claim feel inadequate. Was it a story of coercion, of abuse? That might have been convincing in a different way, but Lydie herself never presented it as one, and there were other indications, memories from the 1920s and before, that seemed to suggest a less awful version of events. Many people had noticed a change in their relationship, noticed for instance that she glowed in E.W.'s presence, noticed that they were spending much more time together, in the mid-1920s, when Lydie was already an adult. When he came back from business trips, she insisted on meeting his train at the station. When he took up with other women after Mary Virginia's death, she was furious and fled to California. These were not definitive details, certainly, particularly given her obvious mental distress in later years. But wasn't there also a danger in simply assuming that she had no agency—in simply assuming the worst?

She had been a radically displaced girl, whisked away to a strange sort of Edwardian frontier-kingdom ruled by a man whose whims had the power (briefly, but during most of her childhood) to reshape reality. Are we not already, here, a good deal beyond simple questions of love and propriety and consent?

We didn't know. We couldn't say.

Had the affair begun before Mary Virginia died?

Same answer.

In any case, no one asked these questions directly. But you felt them, even children felt them, below the surface.

One way to describe such questions is to say that they were the implicit cause of an unstated anxiety about frontier conquest, about civilization building, about who and what we were.

Another way to describe such questions is to say they were nixie fingers.

When I think, now, about what happened, I return to the fact that Lydie was a reader. She had been taught she was living in a romance. E.W. was the center of the romance. E.W. was the organizing principle, the closest thing her story had to a writer. Is it strange to imagine that the emotional logic that led her to marry him was essentially the logic of searching for an ending to a story? Of joining herself to the strongest trunk of a narrative whose essential fragility she must have long since begun to perceive?

All I have of her are fragments. A copy of a century-old diary. A painting by the artist my aunt did not marry. A worn magazine. If you turn left in the grand foyer of the Marland Mansion, away from the gift shop, and then pass through the formal dining room, you come to the service kitchen. In the kitchen there is a safe. Once it held the family silver. Today, it's full of boxes. Some of the boxes contain photographs or mementos, relics from the mansion's past; most are full of papers. The papers are a patchwork, covering everything from Marland Oil committee minutes to the death certificates of family members, and covering them unevenly, because so much has been destroyed or lost. (I have never seen a personal letter written by E. W. Marland, for instance.) One of the boxes contains the contents of Lydie Marland's desk at the moment of her death in 1987. It is perhaps only because of this box and the overstuffed folders and envelopes contained inside it that I sometimes have a sense of her as a mind literally exploding into text, fracturing into thousands of newspaper clippings. She read constantly, peering through her magnifying glass, and she cut out whatever interested her, and she underlined the key passages in red pen.

So, for instance, she saved articles on the Founding Fathers, on appreciating wine, on scotch, on an "amazing new arthritis treatment" whose rate of cure, according to a Dr. Toshio Yamauchi, "is 100 percent." She saved a map of the planets, an advertisement for the smallest alarm clock in the world, a story about the Mother Jones collective being framed on drug charges in Baltimore.

> The complexity of a single human brain is comparable to all the telephone switchboards, exchanges and wiring patterns of computers, radio, TV and other electronic equipment in the world.

She had discovered radical politics (I am thinking here of the antiwar rally where she was supposedly spotted in Washington), but her politics lacked focus. She saved many articles about the environment, in which she seems to have taken a passionate interest, along with granola, the youth serum of Dr. Ana Aslan, the prices of real estate in Big Sur and Puget Sound, water filters, Vitamin E Complexion Soap, and scientific inquiries into human hair: Would lanolin make it grow? Rocking back and forth in a swing could perhaps improve one's vision, and solar power could possibly solve the energy crisis, and here is a Japanese prayer book and here a bookmark with the text of the Magnificat. She made notes on the backs of envelopes:

> Some places to migrate to—or visit, or—see—go—live—Iceland—no police, no crime—

What I don't know appalls me, she had written in 1921.

She spent her life trying to find things out.

Only I think that somehow she could never get the picture to make sense, could never quite locate the key that would resolve the fragments of her reading and experience into a comprehensible whole. The shocks were too great. The surveillance was too terrifying. The changes were too immense.

Later people said her decline had begun with E.W.'s death, that she had loved him so much and relied on him so entirely that she was lost without him.

"The light just went out of her life," the executive director of the Marland Estate told a reporter for the *Tulsa World*.

I don't believe this, which doesn't mean it isn't true.

Cause and effect.

6

Once, when I was eleven or twelve years old, a therapist asked me if I had cried when my grandparents drowned. My parents had taken me to see this therapist, a child psychologist whose name I no longer remember, after I told them I felt nervous all the time, a true statement if not, clinically, a particularly interesting one. The therapist I recall as a sagging man in his late thirties with large clear aviator glasses and shaggy straw-colored hair. He wore baggy suits. His office was in a sort of prefab office park just outside town. I liked going to see him because at the end of one fluorescent hallway in the medical suite there was a small refrigerator, and at the start of every session I was allowed to take out a Coke. After that we sat in his office and talked, or else he gave me little tasks to perform and watched me do them. I had to arrange blocks in a certain way, or he'd show me how to draw triangles in a pattern that would create an infinite series of triangles, then tell me to "stop when it's finished." I didn't see how any of this was supposed to help me feel less nervous. I didn't see how questions about my grandparents were supposed to help me feel less nervous, either. They had died a long time ago, two years, and what did that have to do with anything? But I was used to being given quizzes and tasks, and I liked the Cokes, so mostly I went along and made things up only if I thought he wouldn't understand the real answers.

I told him that I had cried when my grandparents drowned, but only alone, in the bathtub, where no one could see me.

This was one of the times when I made something up in order to seem understandable.

In fact I had not cried when my grandparents drowned. In fact I had not even felt sad when my grandparents drowned, at least not in the way I understood the word. What I felt was something else, a big, loose, empty feeling, and the right words for it didn't seem to come from the language of emotions at all. I didn't think I was wrong to feel this way, exactly. But I sensed that in some way it was a wrong answer, an answer that lay outside the interpretive paradigm we were meant to be working within, so without really thinking about it I told the therapist a story I thought he would know how to explain.

Note that I never imagined *I* might not understand what he was looking for. Only that it would be impossible for him—for other people, possibly for anyone—to understand me.

Where on earth, at eleven years old, had I gotten the idea that it was my job to be easily understood?

I spent a lot of time dreaming about leaving Ponca City.

This, too, was something I had to be careful about expressing, because it could so easily be taken the wrong way.

The problem wasn't that I didn't *like* Ponca City; it was simply that I did not belong there. Liking Ponca City, even loving it, as I sometimes thought I did, was a trap, because I could only relate to Ponca City from a kind of sideways angle, and if I loved it too much, I might end up never finding the place where I was supposed to be. I was not supposed to be in Ponca City. I was not supposed to be surrounded by churches. I was not supposed to have science teachers who believed in the gospel of creation, was not supposed to hear commercial country music on every radio, was not supposed to spend my life cruising down Fourteenth Street with its strip malls and chain restaurants, was not supposed to see distant searchlights from the Ford dealership at night. I was not supposed to feel obscurely haunted by the half-ruined and mostly abandoned downtown, full of crumbling relics of the oil boom, or by the residential streets that bordered it, where what had once been the grand houses of Marland Oil lieutenants were now going to seed among old cars and trampolines. I could see that these things suited other people, somehow fit the DNA of other people, often people I loved. But when I imagined spending my life among them, I felt a wild desire to escape to the ends of the earth.

When I was a little older, the place where I went to escape was the Marland Mansion. I would drive there, past my grandparents' house, which had long since been sold, and park in the little parking lot beside the hedge garden. Then I would go in through the heavy wooden door under the porte cochere. I opened and closed the door as quietly as I could, because I had to sneak past the admissions desk in the gift shop. I had to sneak past the admissions desk in the gift shop because I could not afford the entrance fee. Also because I liked imagining I had the freedom of the place, that I could come and go as I pleased. I would walk straight across the grand foyer, stepping softly on the hard floor. I would climb the vaulted stone stair. The stair was dark, like something in a castle, and on the landing a pair of stone owls stood on pale columns. They looked down on you as you climbed. There were tiny red lights in the eyes of the owls. The owls' eyes, in the dim stair, were four bright red points.

For me, climbing the stair was like passing into another world. What my grandmother had found in the idea of England, I, having hardly ever left Oklahoma, found here. A place where things felt old. Where things were beautiful. The mansion made me feel a bit of what I'd felt when I discovered the 1960s book-club copy of *Poems of Byron, Keats, and Shelley* in my parents' bookcase, a book I'd read so often it was now almost in tatters. I hadn't known anything like that existed before. I wanted more things like it.

The mansion was a link to the larger, richer world—the place where books like that came from.

Upstairs, I didn't have to be so quiet. I walked among the bedrooms, trying all the doors. Especially the ones with NO ENTRY signs stuck to them. Sometimes I'd get lucky and find one unlocked. Mostly that just meant I'd see a closet full of folding chairs or boxes, but once I found a narrow stair to an attic I hadn't known existed, where there was a cart that held several antique hats.

Always, when I went upstairs, I visited Lydie's room, which was my favorite in the mansion. Not because it was the grandest—it was modest compared with the spectacular public rooms downstairs—but because the quality of its loveliness was the hardest to define. The delicately carved lime-wood paneling around the walls had been contrived in such a way that there were no sharp corners anywhere in the room, only curves. The effect was serene, yet somehow also unnerving, as if the very fineness of the design blurred out something that might otherwise have been apparent. I thought about the young woman who had slept here, some of whose clothes were on display in the hall outside, and I thought about the old woman in the raincoat I remembered from when I was small, and I shivered a little.

Lydie, who had lived in the mansion.

Lydie, who had almost escaped.

At around this time they brought her statue back to the foyer. The one she'd ordered the monument worker, Glen Gilchrist, to destroy. The one he'd buried in pieces behind his barn, telling no one the secret. *Smash the face first,* she'd said. As it turned out Glen Gilchrist did tell someone the secret, but only on his deathbed. On September 11, 1987, D. J. Van Nostrand, the husband of a niece of Gilchrist's, mailed a letter to an executive at Conoco, disclosing the probable whereabouts of the fragments:

> You may not be interested in doing anything about this, but possibly you know who would be. Perhaps nothing can be done now since a total stranger owns the property.

When the curator of the Marland Mansion, a man named Paul Prather, went to the site to dig, he took special sensing equipment donated by Conoco. The first piece he found was Lydie's hat, where it lay among a maze of oil pipelines. He got down on his knees and began to dig with his hands. When he found the first piece of Lydie's face, he later claimed, he experienced "an unexplained two-and-a-half-hour blackout." This stretch of missing time, so similar to what the victim of an alien abduction might report, was, he thought, "an omen," a sign that Lydie, if she could know that this final shred of her privacy had been violated, "would be displeased." Possibly he was joking when he said this. He dug up the rest of the fragments. He hired art restorers from Washington University in St. Louis to plan a reconstruction. Monument workers pieced the statue back together over two years. The reconstruction was unveiled in 1993.

The artist, the American sculptor Jo Davidson, has depicted Lydie at the age of twenty-seven, in a thin dress through which the outlines of her nipples are visible. She has one hand on her hip and the other hand, which holds her hat, behind her back. She is standing with her left leg slightly in front of her right, and the dress's skirt clings to her left thigh. The first time I encountered the statue, in the mansion's foyer, I came close enough to see the pale lines crisscrossing Lydie's white stone face where the sledgehammer struck it. I tried not to notice them. The hopes I had invested in the mansion, which I saw, impossibly, both as a means of escape and as a power capable of bringing lost things back, made it seem unwise, almost rude, to notice them. You see I was still so young that I thought I should be looking at the statue. I should have been looking at the cracks.

Acknowledgments

This book would be immeasurably different, and worse, and probably nonexistent, and I would certainly have run into the woods and starved to death, without the kind assistance of the following:

Sandy Baldwin, Theodore Baskaran, Alex Bates, Sarah Bolling, Alyssa DeBlasio, Priyvrat Gadhvi, Alfie Goodrich, Spencer Hall, Noriko Hayashi, Eva Holland, Jackson Howard, Jane Hu, Jerry Jaleel, Raza Kazmi, Evan Kindley, John Knight, Emily Ryan Lerner, Janaki Lenin, the Marland Estate Foundation, Joshua Mathew, Paul Murphy, Supriya Nair, the Oklahoma State Archives, Steve and Sheila Peiffer, Dan and Janie Phillips, Mahesh Rangarajan, Leah Reich, and Emily Sovich;

Everyone at *Grantland* and MTV News, especially Monica Schroeder, Dan Fierman, Sarah Larimer, Rafe Bartholomew, Holly Anderson, Megan Creydt, Jay Caspian Kang, Sean Fennessey, Patricia Martorana, Danny Chau, Alex Pappademas, Molly Lambert, Emily Yoshida, Taylor Trudon, Caitlin Wolper, and Bill Simmons;

Everyone at FSG, especially my wonderful editor, Emily Bell;

Chris Parris-Lamb;

Siobhan Phillips, most of all.

———

I am grateful to Yuri Norstein and his assistants for opening their studio to me in the spring of 2016. "The Little Gray Wolf Will Come," the essay I wrote based on that experience, is further indebted to the work of Clare Kitson, whose book *Yuri Norstein and Tale of Tales: An Animator's Journey* is an invaluable source of information on Norstein in English.

———

My friend Jay Baldwin, who taught me to fly in Alaska, was killed in the summer of 2015 while leading a training expedition in the Alaskan wilderness. "Out in the Great Alone" is included here in his memory.